Thank
God
I'm
Crazy

Thank God I'm Crazy

My Journey to Sanity

Grace Avalon

All of the picture-symbols are images of the original subject, with the following discrete exceptions: To avoid invasion of privacy, the driveway with evergreen trees image is a similar likeness; the Volvo is shown but the license plate could not be to comply with California DMV regulations; the hot tub by the ocean has been demolished and a similar likeness was used; the scissors with the rose is a mock up of the actual slide.

Thank God I'm Crazy: My Journey to Sanity
Copyright c 2017 by Grace Avalon

Published by

Waterside Productions, Inc.
2055 Oxford Avenue
Cardiff, CA 92007
www.waterside.com
Distributed by Waterfront Press
To place orders through Waterfront Press
Tel: 760-632-9190
Fax 760-632-9295
Email: admin@waterside.com
Significant discounts for bulk sales are available. Please contact
admin@waterside.com

Cover Design and Book Layout by Neight Adamson, FIND Art Media
Copyediting by Kenneth Kales
Author Photography by Angenieta Van Lyndt Wuerth
Pictures Prepared by Chris Taylor

Library of Congress Cataloging-in-Publication Data
—Avalon, Grace
Thank God I'm Crazy: A Journey to Sanity
ISBN 978-1-945390-76-0 pod
ISBN 978-1-945390-77-7 ebook

RELIGION / Spirituality / Personal Memoir
SELF HELP / General / Abuse / Happiness
NON-FICTION / New Age / Inspirational
COURSE IN MIRACLES / New Thought / Healing

Praise for
Thank God I'm Crazy

"Grace Avalon has written an amazing story. Her trust in her own inner voice—using love to guide her during situations more painful than most of us can even imagine—inspires all of us to trust the wisdom of our hearts. Here is spirituality in practice. I found her journey a clarion call for renewed courage to live an illumined life."
—Marianne Williamson, New York Times bestselling author of Return to Love, teacher, and internationally renowned speaker.

"Thank God I'm Crazy is a wonderful read and has a dramatic style that takes you from the depths into an exotic life. Through Grace's heartbreaking story we feel our own vulnerability. Through her unwavering trust we find our own greatness."
—Lynn Andrews, New York Times and internationally bestselling author of the Medicine Woman series

"I recommend Thank God I'm Crazy to anyone with a desire to listen to their heart and learn to love their life right now. Grace has one of the greatest hearts I've ever met...and I've been to Canada. Whatever she says, I always know is true. Her desire to evolve, expand and impact the world is truly inspiring. Grace will empower you to do the same."
—Kyle Cease, Comedian and Transformational Speaker

"Grace Avalon's courage to share her secret visions that led her out of deep abuse to heal through forgiveness brings a whole new level of understanding to the principles of love found in A Course in Miracles. In Thank God I'm Crazy, she writes of deep self realizations that acutely mirror aspects of every person's existence."
—Gary Renard, International bestselling author of Disappearance of the Universe

"A Course in Miracles defines a miracle as a shift in perception from the insanity of fear to the healing answer of love. Grace's journey is a lesson in miracles for all of us. From the depths of despair she emerged to teach us all that only love is real and only love can heal. Her profound story will move you to make the choice for miracles now."
—Beverly Hutchinson McNeff, Founder/President,
Miracle Distribution Center

"As we spoke, I saw a golden glow in Grace's aura. Imagine my surprise as I read her book, to learn of the painful learning experiences she's had in this lifetime. Like all who read her book, I am inspired by her continued evolution, an extraordinary example of 'triumph of the spirit.' Her accounts of how sound and music helped awaken long dormant past-life memories, parallel some of my own experiences. Her insights on emotional release, endorphin release, and beyond, may well stimulate insights of your own. Thank you for sharing the miracle of your life with us, Grace."
—Steven Halpern, Grammy-nominated composer,
sound healer, producer

"How wonderful to find a book that demonstrates we are so much more than the world we see with our physical eyes. Grace Ävalon, an inspiring teacher and leader, in her courageous confessions has materialized for us love's potent force against all odds. By trusting her inner voice, she sheds new light on the meaning of miracles. Her book enlightens us all to love more of ourselves."
—Rev. Sandy Moore, InSpirit Center, Mission Viejo, CA,
and author of The Green Intention

"Whoa, I get the picture. Good job...this might become a bestseller."
—Stephen Blake Mettee, President,
Quill Driver Books/Word Dancer Press, Inc.

This book is dedicated in everlasting love to

my daughter and my son

And

In love and devoted sisterhood to

my niece and my two sisters

And to all of my sisters and brothers around the world

Contents

Foreword—by Gary Renard

I was intrigued by Grace Avalon's ability to capture the experience of dreaming. As the modern metaphysical masterpiece, A Course in Miracles says, "Awareness of dreaming is a function of the miracle worker." For the uninitiated, the miracle in the Course is a certain kind of radical forgiveness, which is the heart of its discipline. I like the way that Grace, whom I've known for years, describes the different phases of dreaming and the many twists and turns one goes through while awakening.

The idea that the universe of time and space is an illusion goes back thousands of years in this cycle of history alone. The ancient Text of Hinduism, the Advaita Vedanta, goes so far as to be non-dualistic, teaching that our illusory world has no inherent reality whatsoever, and that the truth of Brahman, which is our Source, is all that truly exists.

The teaching that this world is an illusion is of limited value because our experience is always convincing us that the world we appear to live in is real, and that we have real problems, real bills to pay, real relationships to be in and a solid world that's always in our faces. Add to that the fact that knowing the world is an illusion doesn't give a way out of the illusion. It's simply an unconventional description of a problem, not a solution.

A Course in Miracles does an amazing job of taking the idea that the world is an illusion and refining it into the idea that this world is a dream, and if it's a dream then it's possible to awaken from it. And it's that awakening that is enlightenment. It gives you a solution, a way out, a way home to your Source. It's what Buddha was talking about when he said, "I am awake." But Buddha didn't mean he was more awake in the dream, which is what passes for enlightenment among many. He meant that he had awakened from the dream. That's not a minor distinction. It's everything.

What happens when you wake up from a dream? It disappears, which is why my first book was called The Disappearance of the Universe. What replaces the dream is reality, a reality that was always there but was out of your awareness. Jesus said," The Kingdom of the Father is spread out upon the earth, and people do not see it."

Thank God I'm Crazy is not a text book. It's a wonderful, experiential work that illuminates the path Grace has taken from the madness all the separated ones feel to the sanity of her Source. Like me, I'm sure you'll be richer for taking the trip along with her.

—Gary Renard, international speaker, and bestselling
author, including *The Disappearance of the Universe*

"Our mind is always processing information and energy. We are living in what has been called the information era. The reality is that what we call information is really contained within the soul. Every entity in the universe has information. This information is carried by matter and energy, and the ultimate information is contained in every being, both animate and inanimate. At first it may seem paradoxical to say that the soul is primary to the other components of existence, and as I show in my scientific papers, the origin of all matter, information, and energy actually comes from what can best be described as the divine soul of creation. The theory of grand unification that Einstein and other physicists have contemplated is going to be revealed once we understand the true nature and properties of the divine soul."

—Rulin Xiu, Ph.D, theoretical physics, University of California, Berkley and one of the world's leading authorities on string theory and grand unification theory.

"The most important decision we make is whether we believe we live in a friendly or hostile universe."

—Albert Einstein

CHAPTER 1

The Waking Dream

I sat surrounded by a sea of pale, expressionless faces, their staring eyes abandoned by their owners. Old men shuffled up and down the hall. Overweight women sprawled like crabs on two-decades-old, 1940's furniture. Suddenly, men's voices bellowed profanity. Frozen in fear, my back braced so tightly against a wooden, slatted chair that welts started to rise. The ruckus ended in one man's sorrowful moan. Heavy steel doors slammed shut, echoing down the hallway and into the dismal waiting area where I had been ordered to sit.

The scuffle continued. Now they were right next to me. I stiffened. Jerking up my legs, I hugged them to avoid contact, wrapping myself in the navy blue gabardine skirt I'd worn for a week.

"Y' all better lemme go, God dammit," a red-faced, middle-aged man with greasy hair and dirty cowboy boots rasped in desperation. "Y' all gotta get outta here. Gimme my gun. Satan's a comin'! Ain't nothin' we can do about it... gotta keep a runnin'."

"Yeah, Jesse, we know. That's what you told us last time," a pot-bellied attendant roared through his shaggy beard as he and three huge orderlies in white coats wrestled him to his knees.

Pinning him to the floor, they wrapped him in a straight-jacket, binding his arms tightly to his sides. I watched as they dragged him across the hall and into a freight elevator.

As the doors closed, he shouted, struggling to be heard. "The world's a comin' to an end! Run! Save yerselves!" I caught a glimpse of his terror-filled eyes and distorted facial expressions as he continued to implore them. They stared right through him, ignoring his desperation.

No one noticed me.

How am I going to save myself? I wondered. Have I stopped existing? Not one nurse had asked me how I felt. Instead, they ordered me around like a child. I'm twenty-two, for God's sake. I'm an adult.

Oh, dear God, please, please, get me out of here!

I don't belong here. Why had Jack—my own husband-brought me here? Things with him had been unbearably hard. He could be cold and arrogant, but didn't he care about me at all? How could he deliver his own wife—the mother of his children—into this hell on earth?

Days, I felt certain, had passed since I'd been "dropped off." My mind raced. I'd lost track of time. I searched frantically for some means by which to make sense out of this nightmare.

I needed to clear my head. How could this be happening to me? After all the brutality and abuse I'd endured while growing up, I'd counted on my marriage, my new life. I believed that it would be better. What had happened? How had I come to this place?

Only a few nights ago my husband had led me out of our home for a "little ride."

I could hardly comprehend his words. My mind had found a new world—a safe world—a world filled with superb and kaleidoscopic rainbows.

As he drove, a weathered sign near the side of the road blurred its way into my vision. The dim, incandescent beam of headlights exposed black letters that read:

WESTON, West Virginia State Mental Hospital

I laughed out loud as pink, fluffy, clouds hastily swept me up into to a land of exquisite brilliance. Part of me had already escaped, liberating me from the hellish prison that was my life.

A few nights previous, without warning, I had been drawn into a powerful and magnetic presence of profound inner peace. I'd been sucked into a grand enfoldment of love. My mind cracked wide open. Somewhere deep inside of me, my worn spirit spied an avenue of escape. For the first time in my life I had felt safe. In the window of my mind, I spied an open portal smack in the center of a whirling, spinning, all-consuming nexus. It drew me nearer. It fully embraced me. Grateful, I offered no resistance.

As the hours passed, my mind had played within this welcome refuge. I became aware that way deep inside of me, there existed a longing. I had been hungrily seeking sanctuary, a safe harbor, a place of retreat. I gladly surrendered to this mysteriously nurturing crack in my reality.

As a baby chick pecks through the embryonic shell to a wondrous new dimension—I had escaped. I was free. This magnificent presence catapulted me into clear skies of azure blue and baby pink aurora borealis.

Something snapped as my mind left my twenty-two-year-old body. Like a limp puppet, my head had slumped onto the back of the grey and white striped denim sofa in the tiny living room of our college campus barracks-style apartment.

The room spun. I floated within a giant, radiant kaleidoscope. Then, as though watching a movie, I witnessed various unrelated images. Miscellaneous scenes drifted across my interior screen. I had laughed with joy as I was transported on a magic carpet over a winding driveway lined with evergreen trees, a road sign bearing a state highway number, a bubbling hot tub near the ocean, a flat-top mountain where below it lay the ribbons of a five-lane highway with a giant blank sign stretched over several lanes…on and on it went. I felt like a stowaway on a flight to ecstasy. Incredibly light. Joyful. Free. Just like that—brand new! Born again! I was a creature of nirvana! A child in a garden of glee. I felt as though I had come home.

Only six weeks earlier I had given birth to my own baby girl. But now, suddenly, it was me who was an innocent babe, safe in a world of peace. Weightless, carefree, and engulfed in innocent delight, all I'd wanted to do was laugh. And I did. I burst into gales of laughter.

All the next day, I laughed and languished in the euphoria of this new world as light and images roamed in and out of my mind— aware, yet oblivious to my responsibilities as a mother of two babies. The bliss was irresistible, indescribable.

I had glimpsed ecstasy. I could taste a profound simplicity in all of life. I had slipped outside of time and space. During that period, nothing could have interrupted my peace.

But now, as I sat there in that wretched place—everything I previously knew to be true made less sense to me than ever. Not only my life as a young mother who'd finally escaped an abusive childhood only to find myself trapped in an unhappy and abusive marriage, but everything I'd taken for granted—everything I assumed was real—my perception of a black and white, right and wrong, good and bad world—had all had been turned upside down.

"You're new here, aren't you?" A weathered but gentle face leaned into mine. "Your paperwork was mixed up with someone else's. I'll try to find out what's goin' on for you. They've assigned me to your case. I'm Peggy, your social worker."

I waited what seemed like an eternity. I wondered if she would even return. A few hours later she came back, but what she told me was horrifying.

"No one can be released from here unless they appear before a board of doctors. You seem to me like you might be able to talk to them. I'll get that arranged for you. Then, they'll decide if you're ready to be discharged."

Oh, my God! My heart leapt into my throat. What if I say the wrong thing? What if they don't like me? What if they don't believe me? Does that mean I could be here forever?

A door bearing a big red sign warning Caution-Electric Voltage burst open and two orderlies rolled a stretcher by my chair bearing a middle-aged woman. Her eyes bloodshot, she lay motionless, glaring at the ceiling in semi-consciousness.

I began to pace up and down the hall. Then, realizing I was only adding to my fear, I scanned the sitting room with the big skylighted rotunda ceiling for a place to calm myself. I settled for a faded, overstuffed, barrel chair with an ottoman held together by patches of silver duct tape. Taking a deep breath, I succumbed to a gush of memories from my past.

During the three years since my marriage to Jack, I had constructed a suffocating, emotional box around myself. Why? To protect myself from his insidious aggression. I constantly restrained myself in order not to aggravate him. Except for the parenting of our two-year-old son, David, and our new baby, Jennifer, we shared almost nothing. It broke my heart that we had come to this.

Jack demeaned me at every turn, and he expected sex upon demand. I learned that to refuse him created tension, provoked berating, sinister innuendos, or name calling or physical violence. Sometimes though, he pushed and punched me without warning.

I don't know which was worse—his physical assaults or the constant tension. His outbursts brought back my past. Unlike the blatant violent temper of my father, where I recognized his anger and my danger, Jack's demeaning and unpredictable ire ate away at my very spirit and was far worse than the open violence. Although we had known each other for four years prior to our marriage, very shortly after the ceremony I could no longer deny that the six foot, five inch, handsome, seemingly gentle man I thought I'd married wore a mask of so-called humor that cloaked a seething, underlying rage.

Due to his devious nature, I never found a way to approach him for honest communication. I hungered for even the subtlest genuine exchange. More and more each day, I grew estranged from myself. I focused solely only on whatever I could do to appease him. I'd tried to leave my childhood prison of abuse, but again, the doors were closing around me. By the time I was six months pregnant with our son, when Jack shoved me across the room into the floor of the closet, I knew I did not want to be married to him any longer. But we had moved from my home in California to his home in Morgantown, West Virginia. I knew no one. I had no place to go.

I clearly recalled the day, two years earlier, when I'd stood on the edge of a steep cliff, just off the turnpike, above the Monongahela River. I wanted the peace that I thought death would bring...but I was carrying another life. I could not take that life too. I didn't know what to do. Divorce was a disgrace in the late fifties, and I knew my family wouldn't help me. Daddy was glad I was gone.

And then the situation had gotten worse. I remembered the devastation I felt when Jack deliberately sabotaged my relationship with his mother at the time of the birth of my son, our first child.

I longed to reject that memory, my entire being recoiling in emotional pain as I withdrew my feet into the big barrel chair under the rotunda, and endured waiting away the time in the mental hospital. I had needed Jack's mother's love, anyone's love.

In the beginning Jack's mother had been extremely fond of me. She had immersed herself in plans for her son's child, her grandchild. The relationship I initially shared with her brought me the first real comfort I'd ever known. She bought baby layettes and furniture, and never ceased to come up with new ideas. Even though I felt I had lost control of the preparations for my own child, at least I was the recipient of love and attention. She doted on me. I was delighted that she was making elaborate arrangements to attend me when I was in the hospital. In the late fifties, in the depressed Appalachian region of West Virginia, mothers were placed under full anesthesia for birth, and then moved to a recovery room for five to seven days afterward. She planned to visit me every day.

Jack, however, had begun to make snide, mocking remarks in our presence regarding her efforts, and didn't seem to be very appreciative. Although I did not really understand it, I sensed that he was jealous of my relationship with his mother. He had always been the apple of her eye, and he could do no wrong.

One hot summer night in August, three weeks before our baby was due, he coaxed me into the car for a little drive to cool off. We drove for an hour before he admitted he was headed to his parent's cabin in the mountains. We never went there without his family, and certainly not without telling them. I started to feel uneasy. It was late evening, and the return drive would take over two hours.

Once inside the cabin, he held me against him while pushing me into a wall. The force he employed made it clear he wouldn't stop. He intended to rape me. Refusing him was not an option. Even so, I pleaded with him to think of the baby. The doctor had warned us several weeks earlier to stop having intercourse.

Blood dripped down my legs and spattered on the floor, and the center of my back was burning. I knew something was very wrong, and I became hysterical. "The baby is coming," I shouted. "Please stop!"

When he saw the blood, he realized the birth was about to take place. He stopped. With all the energy that was left in me, I struggled to climb up the steep incline from the cabin that led to the narrow country road where our car was parked as Jack followed.

I don't remember much of the ride to the hospital. I only remember that I was sobbing as I pleaded with him to drive faster.

When we arrived, the crown of the baby's head was visible, and I was taken straight to the delivery room. When I became conscious much later the next day, I saw my beautiful blond, blue-eyed little boy for the first time.

"Where is everyone?" I asked Jack.

"Oh. Well, they don't know yet. This was somethin' just between us. We can tell 'em later."

Oh dear God! I couldn't believe my ears.

This made no sense to me. His mother would be so angry. She'd been living for this day. Why hadn't he told her? I wanted her to be there...I needed her to be there.

In the few weeks that followed, some of the pieces gradually came together. When he finally called his mom at my insistence, she had been furious. She never came to see me. Not once. Nor did his sister. When I came home from the hospital it was blatantly evident that he'd allowed his mother to think it was my idea not to let her know about the baby's birth. I tried to explain to her that I had nothing to do with what happened, but my words fell on deaf ears. She believed her only son.

From that day on, she spoke to me only with an air of bitterness and resentment. For the longest time I'd painfully resisted to allow myself to see the real purpose of his actions. I couldn't face the truth, but, my heart knew that he had taken away the first and only loving family relationship I'd ever known. And he had done it deliberately.

I recognized his dark side, his callous disregard for my feelings, but I'd never really suspected the true depth of his cruelty. This felt like an attack on my very soul, and I fell into a deep state of depression. A vacuum of abandonment enshrouded me in emotional darkness for many weeks after David's birth.

During the time following David's arrival, probably to help me hold onto my sanity, I made up a haunting little melody. I found myself humming a tune that came from somewhere in my head reminiscent of an old country music song. I sang softly, as if chanting to center myself, "When I had my baby, I almost lost my mind." I had wondered some months later, as I attempted to restore my balance, what that could have been all about. I had tried to shake off the memory and all association with that time.

Faint beams from the setting sun streaked through the windows in the rotunda of the mental hospital. My body had grown rigid, stiff. I realized I had curled myself into a fetal position. Unwinding my legs from the walling arms of the musty chair, I allowed my feet to drop back down to the floor. My breathing was restricted and shallow. I sighed deeply, suddenly aware of my fatigue.

I realized it had been only six weeks since Jennifer's birth. She was born under more ordinary circumstances, unlike the trauma of David's birth. We had planned for her and her birth was routine. Again, however, I went through the event and the hospital stay without any attention or assistance from Jack's mother. She had remained distant and cold.

I loved my children, but I was exhausted—my hours spent alternating between corralling my active little two-year-old son and settling down in a rocking chair to nurse my lovely baby daughter. I felt lonely and alienated. My heart longed to be comforted. How welcome a kind word or a small compliment would have been during the aftermath of her birth. I also struggled against a sense of hopelessness. I tried to remind myself of even the tiniest blessings. I made an effort to assemble the pieces of the previous few days … what I could remember of it. Some of it was coming back to me. Oh, yes. The darkness. That loathsome sadness.

I shrunk deep into the chair for protection as I remembered one particular night about a week ago after Jenny was born. For no apparent reason, a strange feeling overtook me. I felt removed, as if I was being pulled out of myself. I understood that I'd been depressed, but this experience seemed very different. It was late in the evening, and the children were finally asleep. I wearily dragged myself to the bathroom sink to begin my nightly routine.

From the next room, Jack groaned, "Come to bed. Do you always have to be so dammed perfect? Do ya' have to do everything just right!" Why did he constantly criticize my efforts? Why didn't he appreciate that I wanted to take good care of myself?

I mumbled a few words and then closed the door between us. I glanced into the medicine cabinet mirror.

But it wasn't my image that I saw!

A mysterious, huge energy was welling up inside me. I saw the giant face of a tiger, flashing agate-yellow eyes as it roared at me.

With the reflex of a cat, I watched myself pounce toward the mirror, growling back with a vengeance. As I projected my face into the mirror, the tiger image suddenly transposed itself into the regal head of a lion. It roared, projecting itself towards me. Again and again, I seized control from it, baring my teeth and roaring back to the creature in the mirror. The images faded in and out, tiger to lion, lion to tiger, and tiger to lion. I lost all sense of time. I felt drunk with power until, with a sudden jolt, I became aware of what I was doing.

I stood there frozen, too terrified to even think about what had just happened. I brushed my teeth, hurried to bed, and pulled the covers tightly under my chin. I tried as hard as I could to convince myself that it never happened.

My routine of that next day had been harder than ever. I couldn't focus or make the simplest decisions. In the wee hours of the following morning, around 4:00 after nursing Jennifer, I went to the living room and sank down into the sofa. I began to cry. It had happened a lot. For years. No reason, just the need to cry. This time, though, I heard something.

Something important inside of my head snapped!

Although still aware, I could no longer hold up my head. It drooped like dead weight to my right shoulder, slumping onto the couch. Then, a releasing sensation. I was leaving my body. Floating upward. I was losing control. I was terrified.

With every ounce of energy left in me I managed to jump up. I raced to the bedroom. I shook Jack awake.

"Something is wrong. Talk to me, say something." I pleaded.

I needed his help. I needed to get back in touch with myself—to get grounded somehow. I really wanted him to hold me and tell me everything would be all right.

He was angry that I had awakened him in the middle of the night. He rolled away from me. Mocking me in a singsong voice, he muttered, "Mary had a little lamb its fleece was white as snow. Now, get back in bed."

That's all he would offer me?

Suddenly, I no longer cared. Somewhere inside of me the final threads of hope had snapped. I stopped trying to hang on. I stumbled back to the living room. Jack mumbled something about my being dramatic as usual. The bed creaked. I knew he was turning over to go back to sleep. I collapsed back down into the sofa. I wept in heaving sobs for the emptiness, and hopelessness, of my life.

A moment later, I was overcome by an engulfing, magnetic-like force. It drew my focus upward. My gaze became fixed on a corner of the ceiling; that place where the ceiling meets two side-walls. Like an intersection where two roads become one. It invited me, tempted me, begged me to escape via the crossroads. The last of my will slipped away. I succumbed.

My very spirit felt consumed—vacuumed into an expanding hole in the apex of that corner. The hole transformed into the open-ing of a shutter lens image, similar to that in a camera. Head first, I was pulled in. The lens curled, closing around me.

I escaped all boundaries. There was no time. No barriers. No longer did I occupy my body. My mind enlarged, encompassing some-thing else. This something else merged with me and I with it. I was whole. I was without fear. The love that replaced my fear extended to that which had freed me, as I surrendered to it, certain of my pur-est innocence. I was not a body. I was one with something beyond. I could reach to heaven.

Relief. Lightness. Freedom. I was gently embraced within a nexus of revolving, rainbow crystal lights; revolving, evolving, con-tinually transposing themselves into thousands of brilliant, unique geometric circular shapes. A warm, loving energy emitted from this spectacular light. I had been plugged into the master current. Life was charging through me. With it came an all-consuming comfort that I had never known. It flowed around me, through me, in me. I welcomed it. I embraced the love. It poured forth, asking nothing in return. The prisms of light were studded in every color of the rain-bow. Palettes of a radiant spectrum created patterns that sparkled like rubies, emeralds, diamonds, amethyst, and colors I'd never seen before.

The beauty was hypnotic. I watched the rainbow radiances blend. The shapes shifted and shimmered into new shapes. It was like looking through a kaleidoscope, yet I was swirling on the inside of it. In its very center, I was lovingly stroked by each micro movement. A pleasant sound, a strong, vibrating hum was building in my ears. I grew giddy and lightheaded. I floated freely. This experience was so beautiful I wanted to stay there forever.

What a relief. I felt the joy of a child—suspended only in love in a mysterious, heavenly toy, a cosmic kaleidoscope. A toy the size of the universe. I laughed. The more I laughed, the more I wanted to laugh. I loved this place. I had never ever known such joy. I laughed and laughed.

It was hard to say how much time had passed. I must have been laughing loudly, because Jack abruptly entered the room. He showed obvious dismay at what he saw. Unwilling to get involved, he gruffly barked, "Do you know what time it is? What the heck is wrong with you? What's so damned funny?"

I could see he didn't know what to make of my atypically jovial mood. By then, I didn't care what he thought. "Get to bed. It's late," he ordered in a nervous tone.

With robotic obedience I followed him to bed, but the visions continued. The divine celestial visions playing through my inner landscape now were joined by images of places; a row of evergreen trees along a curved driveway, a dark highway identified by a state road sign with the number 144, a small, sphinx-like mountain with a highway below, straddled by a giant white, blank road sign. On they went. They carried me into a hypnotic deep slumber. At times I awakened with a fearful start, but a loud hum in my head lulled me back under its euphoric spell.

The beautiful carousel of colors continued to come in and out of my mind all the next day. Like a glorious movie, they danced, twirled, and teased through my consciousness. I was enthralled by them. I laughed as though I had never laughed before. Great big belly laughs! How wonderful it felt to laugh! I laughed, and I ate ice cream. I ate all the ice cream I wanted.

It grew harder and harder to focus and to care for the children. I struggled to resist the tempting force that beckoned me towards escape. I tried to shake it off. In desperation, I groped deep inside myself for the will to resist. Again and again, I forced myself to return to the pain that defined my life.

Obsessively, I darted through our three little rooms. I straightened pictures. I dusted the spotless furniture. I cleaned already empty ash trays. I fluffed pillows. I changed David's clothes for the third time, and I brushed his golden locks again and again. The more I frenetically tried to fix everything, the more David cried and slammed doors. He ran from the kitchen to the bedroom, and back again, his actions a reflection of my inner storm.

That evening when Jack came home, his parents followed him through the door. They said they had come to babysit. I was confused. It was unusual for them to visit at all, especially in the middle of the week. But any resistance I might have had was disarmed as I gratefully succumbed, enfolded again and again by that euphoric, kaleidoscopically-colored womb.

My mind wandered unrestrained in and out of two worlds. I tried to reason, finally, they must understand! They were sorry for the times they'd judged me, rejected me. Now, they had come to help me. I was so happy. I began to laugh. And laugh. And laugh.

It was almost dusk. Rather stiffly, Jack commanded, "Come on, we're going to get you some fresh air. It'll do you good. We're going for a little ride." I relented. But when I got into the car, our neighbor, Jerry, was seated in the back seat. Why? I wondered.

As the car pulled away from our apartment, I felt liberated of my responsibilities. I sighed with relief at the panoramic view, the colorful fall foliage along the country road, the only part of poverty-stricken Appalachia I liked. The mélange of bright colors and lights still lowing effortlessly across my mental screen melded with the glare of the headlights on the road. The exotic waves of brilliance and the hypnotic sounds in my ears elevated my spirits. Colors merged in my head as one, romancing me again into a state of ecstasy.

A flashback from the past floated by as the motion of the car gently rocked me.

Captured in a time warp, I was back in California, a teenager again, riding in the homecoming parade. It was my first and only semester in college. I wasn't the queen. My best girlfriend had been crowned queen. I was a member of her court. As one of her attendants, I perched atop the back seat of a brand new, fiery red, 1956, Corvette convertible. It should have been a happy time in my life, but it wasn't. Even then, my whole world had toppled like a house of cards.

Jack briskly turned the car onto the state highway. The homecoming memory faded. I giggled to myself; I guess that was the *crowning* blow!

"Hey, that's a good one, *crowning blow*," I playfully blurted out loud.

Jack gave me a stern, anxious glance. Can't anyone be funny but him? I used to think he was really funny. That was one of the reasons, when everything meaningful in my young life had fallen apart that I'd decided to marry the easy-going sailor I had known for four years. Or I thought I knew.

It didn't really matter anymore. I was in a happy place. Those were worldly concerns. My liberation was exhilarating. I started to sing. Softly at first—and then louder. Why not! I bellowed out, "I'm The Sweetheart of Sigma Chi." My own sound intoxicated me. I'd never had a sip of alcohol in my entire twenty-two years. Was this what it was like to be drunk?

Our eight-year-old, 1952 green Chevrolet turned into the entrance of a long driveway. Headlights flashed on a sign WESTON West Virginia State Mental Hospital. For an instant, I was seized by an overwhelming, incapacitating chill. Icy waves engulfed my body.

But then—out came the biggest belly laugh I'd ever had. This was all a joke! Behind that big, old, ugly red brick building ahead laid a football field. I was sure of it. They were just taking me inside to get me ready for the prom. That's why Jerry is here. He's going to drive me in the red Corvette in the parade. It's a surprise. I'm going to be the queen!

I was led to a tiny, dreary room illuminated by one lamp. It sat on the edge of a cluttered old oak desk. A crippled figure, smoking a cigarette and carrying a briefcase exactly like my father's, limped towards me. Puzzled, I struggled to focus. I wondered what this had to do with the homecoming ceremony. This person put a pen in my hand. I couldn't tell if I was looking at a male or a female.

"You need to sign here, dear. It's the best way," the shadowy figure counseled. I looked up to Jack. He nodded. More waves of cold chills. I rationalized that this was part of the surprise—and, of course, Jack was in on it, too! As I signed the papers, the pen took control and nearly flew out of my hand.

Three women clad in blue cotton smocks led me down a long hall to a giant shower room. They began to undress me. Removing the soiled navy blue, gabardine skirt and sleeveless white cotton blouse I'd worn for nearly a week, they instructed me to step into a large square bathtub. They poured shampoo and warm water onto my hair.

"Well, I declare, Ruthie, look how purty she is," one of them said.

"She shore is."

"You got the butteriest blond hair I ever did see, honey."

This is it! I thought. This is when I get all dressed up for the parade. They're here to help me, but they'd taken off all of my makeup. Why? It will take forever to get it right again. I hope there is enough time.

Before I knew it, I wore a blue smock. Just like them. But theirs had badges with their names on them. And they had different kinds of pants on underneath. Mine had blue cotton pants to match. Then, I was led to a folding chair outside a dormitory-like room.

"Are you hungry?" one of them asked. It had been a long while since I had eaten the last of the ice cream. I was ready for a hot meal. They brought me a cold grilled cheese sandwich before they disappeared down the hallway. I'd always hated cheese. I'd rather eat wax. But by then, I was convinced there had to be a reason for everything. I obligingly bit into it. My mouth was bone dry. I tried to swallow, and I choked.

Panicky, I left the paper plate and the rest of the sandwich on the chair and wandered down the hall. I came to a large, poorly lit room with a high ceiling. The center of the ceiling lifted into a bulging high rotunda. The room dwarfed the shabby furnishings. Curtain rods sagged with maroon velvet drapes.

People, old and young, were spread out around the room, some listlessly positioned in the chairs, all clad in blue smocks with blue bottoms, just like mine. These people weren't dressed. They weren't dressed for a football game. There was something different about them. They didn't seem able to focus on anything. No one spoke, and most just stared off into space. Some of the men had straggly beards or whiskered faces and the women had unkempt hair. One little girl had a large bandage around her head.

As I sat down, I noticed the middle-aged woman next to me stared fixedly at her hands, turning them over and over and over. I heard a moan, and I looked to my left. A frail looking, blue-smocked black woman sat on the floor, legs crossed as she rocked back and forth and chanted unintelligible sounds. Her arms and legs were bandaged.

"She throws her own self in a fire while she's performin' some kind'a ceremonial ritual!" a woman seated on my other side whispered like an old gossip. Seeing my disbelief, she said, "This is the third time she's landed in this place."

This place. What place? I felt instant panic. It suddenly hit me that Jack and Jerry were gone.

This was not prom night, it wasn't homecoming, and I wouldn't be the queen!

I shot out of the chair, darting forward into the middle of the room. Imploringly, I lifted my face upward, and threw my arms straight up above my head to the skylight in the ceiling of the rotunda.

Like an endless bellow of rolling thunder, a shrill, primal scream permeated its way through every cell of my being. I didn't think it would ever stop. Then, seemingly out of nowhere, four nurses with needles grabbed me and a shroud of darkness fell.

Once again, I glided into that dimension of light and color and jeweled kaleidoscopic images. Spinning, floating, and turning while humming vibrations washed in to fill up my head. But this time, I could guide and propel myself with only the slightest thought. Like a feather, empowered by my own will, I levitated through the gleaming geometric figures. I had super powers. The least little hint of a thought whisked me like a Sabrejet to whatever location I projected.

As I played with this awesome freedom, I became aware that I now watched those same images as before, the ones I'd seen in the tiny living room of our college campus barracks apartment. There were several, but some dominated. They were scenes—or were they pictures?—floating past the window of my mind. I was content to watch.

As if viewing a travel video, again I saw a row of tall evergreen trees. They lined a long, curved, driveway with the setting sun streaming through the limbs. Again, came the vision of a long, dark highway identified by a state road sign bearing the number 144.

Like a wingless bird I floated past the small, sphinx-like mountain with a flat top. There was a highway at the foot of it. Over the highway was a giant road sign, which extended across five lanes of traffic and was held in place by a post on each end. But, there were no words on this giant sign. It was long, and white, and blank.

Embraced by a deep, pleasurable peace, I watched as the guideless tour continued. Letters floated by; a word, a name, perhaps a last name...Lawson or Lawless. On it went...a mystical hot tub somewhere on the West Coast and near the ocean. The hot tub bathed me in serenity. The bubbling water lapped me up, and I disappeared into an ethereal abyss.

It seemed it was only a few hours when I opened my eyes. With great effort, I struggled to awaken. My husband's face was suspended over me, flushed with confusion.

Did I just say what I think I said? "Thank God, I'm going to get my divorce." I didn't at all understand why I said those words. They came out of nowhere...from wherever I was. Jack and the nurses were glaring at me.

I laughed nervously. "I guess I must have been dreaming." I lied. This was not like any dream I ever had. Instead, it was a knowing, unlike anything I'd ever experienced. It was other-worldly. Beyond myself. From another dimension? I was sure they thought I was hallucinating. I felt a stinging prick in my buttock. Once again I surrendered, this time to a deep, engulfing slumber.

When I opened my eyes sometime later, I became aware of my body positioned on a hard and flat surface. It was a narrow cot with a thin, gray and white ticking mattress. Wetness trickled into my arms. My breasts were swollen, hard and throbbing painfully. A biting ache spread down my arms to my elbows. It hurt to breathe. Beneath my blue smock, which was untied and gaping open, I saw wide strips of white cheese cloth wrapped tightly around my breasts.

"My milk. My baby's milk! What is this? Why are my breasts all wrapped up?" I shouted as loudly as I could. I struggled to remain focused. The light coming in from the window faded in and out. Where was I? How long had I been here?

It seemed like hours before someone finally came. "You are here to rest for a little while and get your strength back," said a woman clad in a blue smock. A stethoscope hung from around her neck.

"Why am I bound this way?"

"To stop your milk."

"Why? Why? You can't do this! My baby needs my milk. I want her to have it."

Even though most every mother in America bottle-fed their babies then, I strongly believed in nature's way. Even the nurses in the maternity ward in Morgantown, where Jenny was born, had resisted my wishes to breastfeed her. "Are you sure you know what you are doing, dear?" each one asked.

Yes, I was very sure, and I was determined not to let them step in—but now it was happening anyway. I had lost control of everything.

I needed to get back home. I sobbed, desperate for my little blue-eyed Jennifer with her fluffy blond hair. What will she do now? Who will feed her if I'm not there? Would my mother-in-law take my children? Would I ever see them again?

"I have to get back to my children," I told the stranger with the stethoscope. "They need me. My mother-in-law gives David M&M's and Kool-Aid. It makes him irritable. He gets all wound up, out of control. He won't be able to sleep!" I struggled to turn onto my side to roll out of bed. Someone else in a blue smock sat down on the edge of the cot holding out two pink pills and some water.

"This is what you need right now. This will help you sleep. Now drink," she ordered.

Oh, dear God, how had I come to this? How would I ever get out of this place? Would I ever be able to leave? Oh God! Once again, darkness overtook me and nothing seemed to matter.

I could barely comprehend that it had been only three days since I'd entered the institution. My fourth day unfolded with all of its gruesome reality. The beautiful images stopped. No escape. My laughter disappeared. Just sober stares at a grim world that now resembled a three-ring circus. Minutes seemed like hours. Mostly I just sat in one after another of the tattered and worn chairs positioned up and down the hallway outside of closed doors.

On the ninth day, Peggy came to tell me that the time had come. The small board of directors wanted to talk with me. I desperately wanted to be released from this mental and physical prison. This was it. I needed to be home with my children for Thanksgiving, which was only a few days away. As we walked down the long hall, I sent up a silent prayer for help—to whom or to what entity or higher power I wasn't at all sure. All I knew then was there was more to this life than I'd ever known or had ever been taught. Nothing from my Baptist upbringing had prepared me for the extraordinary world I had seen.

The room was small and not as barren as the part of the hospital floor I was on. I didn't recognize any of the people. Five of them sat in a semicircle facing me. I was told that three were medical doctors, and the other two were a psychiatrist and an administrator. Instead of generally questioning me, as I might expect, the psychiatrist asked one question. "Why do you think you are here, Grace?"

His informality was warming, and he actually called me by my name. I felt myself becoming a little less tense. It was the first time any one of the staff had spoken to me as though I could understand English. I had not received any information or counseling from anyone. No one had even asked what I was experiencing.

"Why do I think I'm here?" I echoed. I released a big sigh and speculated aloud, "I suppose I am overworked and tired and especially run down. Having my last baby has made it harder." I realized that I hadn't really seen it that way until that moment.

"You have had a nervous breakdown, Grace," he said.

What does that mean? This was an age-old term I had heard many times. As nearly as I could tell, it was a catch-all phrase used to describe a myriad of personal problems, without identifying anything specific. I said nothing, avoiding the combative feelings I was experiencing.

"How do you feel now?" he continued.

"I feel okay, now," I said, resisting the temptation to be super-Grace and overdramatize. "I've had a chance to rest and I am very, very anxious to go back to my children. I miss them so much. I know they must miss me." I didn't ask any questions for fear that I might give the wrong impression or say the wrong thing. They responded warmly to my comments about my children.

They also inquired about my home life. For the first time, I didn't try to hide anything. I knew they understood I wished my marriage was better.

"What do you think you will tell people about all of this, Grace?" the psychiatrist asked.

I paused for a long moment. "I guess I won't tell anyone any-thing," I responded. "I don't think anyone could possibly understand. They will just think I'm crazy."

A faint smile formed on his face. I could tell I'd given the right answer. "You know, most people think we in the world of psychiatry are crazy. Our profession is so new, the public knows very little about us. We have yet to be respected as a legitimate scientific field."

That was certainly true. If anyone consulted a psychiatrist in 1960 his sanity was automatically suspect and even his livelihood could be in jeopardy. No one could predict how people would react to news that someone had spent time in a mental institution.

"Well," said the first doctor on the left. "We are pleased to tell you that, according to the observations from your social worker, you seem to be doing quite well. I think I can speak for all of us when I say that we agree with that opinion. You may go home today."

"Today? Today!" I responded joyfully. "Oh, thank you so very much." They seemed to share in my enthusiasm.

"In fact, let's call your husband right now," the doctor said.

Dressed in my navy blue gabardine skirt and sleeveless white blouse, I sat in an old leather chair in the admissions office by the window as I waited for Jack. A few toiletries he'd brought me were in a brown grocery bag near my feet. I had hastily applied my makeup. I needed "my face on" to go home.

Looking out the window at the long driveway below where I had arrived, I saw Jack's car. Out of the blue that little tune I'd sung to myself after David's birth floated back into my head. The one that went, "When I had my baby, I almost lost my mind."

Well, I really had lost it this time. A cold shudder ran down the inside of my arms and legs as the reality hit me. I was going home again...to a life of misery. It was better than the last few days I had spent in the institution. But not by much.

The memory of the warm world of kaleidoscopic light burned within me. Like a home. A real home. How ironic. Now that I was considered well, I couldn't return to that sublime place—to that peace. I wanted where I had been in my mind to be my home. That escape now seemed like a faded dream.

I would reenter a different dream. A nightmare world where young people die in insane wars, where prejudice treats some as privileged while denying others basic human rights, where corporate greed and politicians betray the very people they are supposed to serve, where hungry, homeless people are abandoned to the streets.

And there were men like Jack, who abused women—just because they could. This life was a circus. A bizarre, three-ring circus, replete with crazed crowds and people acting like idiots. This was sanity? Finding the strength to make my life work resembled summoning the courage to race through a house of horrors at a county fair. For the first time, I saw the world as through a dark passageway leading into a house of mirrors while distorted faces leered back at me. Panic, a deep longing to return to the calm and safe haven of the kaleidoscopic illusions, rushed over me.

No! No! No! I can't afford to think about it. I must not! I pushed it back to a secret place in my mind.

Jack stepped into the room. He nervously gave me a ceremonial squeeze and then complained loudly to the outpatient clerk about the inconvenience. Why hadn't I been released yesterday when he was there visiting?

Finally. We drove out of the parking lot, down the long driveway and onto the highway. The car was filled with awkward silence. We hardly spoke. I glanced at Jack. His hands were white-knuckled as he gripped the steering wheel, his jaw muscles tensed. He glared out over the steering wheel.

How had this happened? I was leaving the institution with no idea of why I had been taken there in the first place. I had no understanding of what had happened to me.

Nine days I had been locked up. Nine days of nurses telling me what to do, when to do it. Nine days of patients groaning, complaining, and screaming. Yet, during my nine days in the psychiatric ward, no one had told me what was wrong. No one had told me how to get better. No one had told me how to cope if I didn't. I don't think they really knew.

How could I ever be sane again? How could I trust myself? How could I be a good mother? Nine days in a psychiatric ward had destroyed my confidence. Was I really crazy? I wondered.

All I knew was I needed to fight my way back to some semblance of normalcy. Whatever it took, that's what I would do. The problem was mine. I had to solve it.

I will not let this happen again, I vowed, feeling helpless and determined at the same time. I would stay focused. I would control my thoughts. Remember the children. They loved me. I must think of every good thing I can, I told myself. I'm young, I'm strong, and I've survived hard times before. I can do it again.

We drove northward towards Fairmont and the campus of Fairmont State Teacher's College in West Virginia where we lived. That's it, I thought. Just forget that you were ever there, Grace. I would tell no one. Be strong—wipe it out of your mind.

With a heavy sigh of resolve, I stared out the car window. The trees were barren of their colorful fall leaves. The white, dilapidated fruit stands were closed. The cornfields were bleached by a heavy frost. A grey sky stretched out overhead. It was late November in West Virginia.

On that dreary fall evening, I didn't realize that what had happened to me in those last few days would change the course of my life forever. Something wonderful within me had come alive. I secretly embraced the joy, the peace, and the innocence that had awakened within me. I knew that I would never be the same. That inner place that was the fledgling *me* determined that I had to reclaim those feelings...in order to reclaim *me*. But how? I wondered.

Thus, my long journey began. Over a span of thirty miracle-filled years, and with the support of many others, in a now dreamlike world of absurdity, I learned to trust a silent communication from unordinary sources. As the walls confining my reality and beliefs crumbled, I knew I had met a loving voice within that insisted there was more of me. To some even now I might sound crazy, but I grew to trust in my own sane perceptions. I savored that sanity. However, nothing could have prepared me for the grandeur of the final revelation given to me in the kaleidoscopic light.

Together, you and I will share this journey of the heart as I undertake to fully reclaim the part of myself that I first discovered during my darkest days—those days before and while confined in a mental hospital. I invite you to suspend the boundaries of ordinary perception, and allow for the possibility of pure wonder. It is my deepest desire that somehow my story will lead you to the discovery and celebration of the love and peace to be found within your own pure innocence.

CHAPTER 2

Entering the Dream

H ome never was a place I wanted to be. Growing up, as the oldest of three girls, I always had to be strong. In fact, much of the time it was as though I mothered my own mother, a weak and fear-filled woman. Daddy terrified her, too.

I have few memories of being a child—except for a strange flashback of the first few moments of my life. I don't know if there are other people who can recall the moment of their birth, but I've carried with me throughout my life a fleeting vision of being an infant—and even before. I can remember the moment during which I became aware of life and, later, of being placed in a bed beside my mother. I also recall feeling a rush of relief at being there. Something I could not understand had happened in between those moments. Eventually though, my childhood became too painful to remember.

Even though I had been raised in California since I was four, both Mama and Daddy were from the hills in the Blue Ridge Mountains of East Tennessee where I was born. Daddy told us once, in a rare moment of vulnerability as if we were suddenly worth his attention, that he was the eleventh of twelve children. He complained that when he'd left home in the fifth grade, no one had even missed him. Among his many pursuits, he had become a real estate broker and a layman Southern Baptist preacher. Daddy was fanatical and demanding with a violent temper. His raging outbursts were sometimes followed by remorseful periods of shame and regret.

He periodically sat in his worn, wingback chair and held his head, sobbing. He was two people and the two sides fought against each other; the self righteous, religious side, and the dark, raging, angry, demanding side. By his early fifties, he'd read the Bible completely through five times. He spent an hour every morning on his knees in prayer, but some torment inside of him would eat its way through his control before day's end. Then, even if he didn't have a real reason, he would create a situation or find someone upon which he could unleash his inner rage. I always feared him when I saw his sharp stare. His face would redden and his brown eyes would bulge.

Sometimes he would remove a just-washed glass from the kitchen cupboard and hold it up to the light. If he found a speck on it, which he always did, he would beat us with a belt.

Mama, twelve years younger, called him Daddy, too. She'd witnessed at the age of twelve her mother's painful death from tuberculosis at home alone deep in the Blue Ridge Mountains. Abandoned by her own father, she'd watched her twin brother die of the same devastating disease at sixteen. She had known very little love or security.

She fell to pieces whenever Daddy took the belt to us. She would wring her hands, cry and beg him to stop. Depressed much of the time, she became a stern, cold woman over the years. I always thought it was her way of showing her own hurt and anger. Although often critical of us, my two sisters and I knew she loved us in her own way.

My mother was an epileptic, which terrified me. I lived with a dread that she would experience one of her "spells," as she called them. I found it strange that my sisters were not nearly as disturbed as I was about the possibility she could collapse at any time. The very thought of her condition made *me* feel helpless. I would feel terrified and vulnerable for weeks after one of her attacks. I think I feared I would inherit the disease. I felt a sense of relief when Jack and I left California, breathing easier at not being exposed to the possibility of witnessing anymore of her "spells."

My father remained angry and disappointed throughout his life that he had fathered three daughters. He thought girls were worthless, although he made us dig deep holes in the garden and plant vegetables and scrub floors.

Much of the time, as I grew up, we lived on chicken ranches. My little sister, Sue, was thirteen years younger. During my adolescence and early teens, Mickey, my other sister, and I often took care of her. Our chores were endless. We gathered the eggs from the hens and carried the fully-loaded three-gallon buckets to the shed where we sanded off the chicken droppings and weighed and sorted eggs into graded cartons. That was before we did our homework. Daddy got mad if we used too much water to wash our hair or spent more than a few minutes in the bathroom. His rare attention to us was usually confined to warnings to keep our dresses down and to be good girls.

My father often complained that I was a strong-willed child. It was true. I stood up for myself, even though I knew it would end in a beating. Something deep inside me refused to give up. I needed to feel that I mattered.

My father even beat me for singing, which confused me. What was wrong with singing? For as long as I could remember, singing had sparked joy inside of me. It took my mind off of my life and made me happy, at least for those few moments. Although it was incomprehensible to me that my being happy made him angry, it did.

Most of my childhood remained a blur. I feared going to bed at night, but I didn't know why. I felt anxious that I would draw the attention of whatever lurked in my bedroom. Some mornings I felt profoundly sad. I was a hard sleeper. Sometimes, I would sleepwalk and awaken in another room of the house. Often I was rousted out of bed for school by my father, who beat me because I had not gotten up the first time I was called. This continued into my high school years.

The defining moment that forged my resolve to escape our home happened when I was fifteen. At a time when money was tight, Daddy could be even more angry and mean. I arrived home a few minutes later than I was told to from my girlfriend's house because her dad, who was my ride, was delayed at work, and my father would never take me anywhere. My father waited behind the door with his belt.

My girlfriend's dad was still in his car parked at the curb. He heard my screams and called the police. When the police arrived, they saw the red welts on my back and asked me if I wanted to press charges. Oh, yes. I wanted to.

But who would support us if he went to jail? Besides, he would be released at some point and then he would beat me to within an inch of my life. Given his temper, he might even kill me. That had become my greatest fear. In that moment I came face to face with my complete powerlessness. I declined to press charges.

There were no shelters, halfway houses, or counselors for victims of domestic abuse in the 1950's. The term "domestic violence" had not yet been coined. People didn't even talk about such things. The laws and the courts assumed the sovereignty of parental authority unless blatant evidence of abuse was revealed. In those rare instances a temporary removal of the victim from the home was ordered by the authorities. I had nowhere to go.

We girls often begged Mama to leave him. We didn't care how poor we would have to live. She might have considered it, but only briefly. She lacked faith in herself and feared being on her own. In her defense, there were few opportunities for single women to earn a decent income in those days.

A few weeks after the police were summoned to the house, I came home from a high school play rehearsal, at around 9:30 p.m. I walked through the darkened living room towards the hall to go to my sister's and my room. Suddenly, someone grabbed me and pulled me down onto a chair. Yes, it was Daddy—and he was kissing me—and it was awful. It was long. I thought he would never stop. I went limp and just waited. When I could, I said, "I want to go to bed now, Daddy." To my surprise, he released me. Over and over, I scrubbed my face and washed my mouth out. That night, at the age of fifteen, I resolved to leave home. I *would* figure a way out. A way to escape. But I knew it would take awhile.

In high school the only money I had was from a part-time job as a clerk at Marvin's Young Set, a teenage dress shop. Since I was earning money, my father demanded forty dollars a month in rent if I was going to continue to remain in his house after graduation—that took most of my income. I enrolled in tuition-free Mount San Antonio Junior College and then Daddy also made me buy my own clothes and books. I hated it at home more than ever but I was determined to get an education or some type of training so that when I finally left I could live sufficiently and be respected.

Anxious and determined to prove myself, I enrolled in an eighteen credit, full-time college curriculum, kept my twenty-hour per week job, joined several clubs on campus and was elected as a student body representative delegate-at-large for the freshman class. I lived in two worlds; at school where I appeared to be normal, pretending to laugh with my friends at their petty problems, and at home, where I did my level best to be invisible.

I was baffled by the life that most of my popular girlfriends led. A song from a play in which I was cast during high school lingered in my mind. The song touched upon my inability to really grasp the stark contrast of my friends' lives with my own:

Brisk, lively, merry and bright, allegro.
Same tempo, morning and night, allegro.
Don't stop, whatever you do,
Do something different and new,
Keep up the hullabaloo,
Allegro, allegro, allegro!

Away from home, I appeared to be outgoing and lighthearted. I always smiled even if I had to force it. The closer I got to home, the fear and dread started to build. With all I had piled upon myself at college, the strain became intense. I rarely slept.

Then, I was invited to run for homecoming queen, which should have been a happy time in my life. It wasn't. I was asked by five campus clubs, including the Vet's Club, whose candidate won most of the time. Because of fundamental convictions beaten into me by my father, I thought the only way to do something so vain would be to represent the Christian Club. I think I expected God would be on my side because I had made a faithful choice. But I lost by seven votes—to my best girlfriend.

The stress mounted. Losing by such a small margin to my best girlfriend, who had become the candidate for the Vet's Club, became the last straw in my very precariously balanced and abuse-filled life. It seemed that no matter how good I was or how hard I tried, I just couldn't win. It really wasn't losing the election so much as it was the fact that it had created one more hurt that I had to hold inside of me. There was no more room. I felt my *self* crumbling.

One day, out of the blue, everything in my world began to bleed together. As I rode the city bus home from work, I became completely disoriented. I could not remember where I was or what street I lived on. I panicked. I pulled the overhead bell chord and fled off the bus. I started to wander, walking for over an hour trying to find my home. When I finally stumbled upon the house, it was then that I realized that somehow I had to let go of something. I couldn't keep on … pretending … driving myself so desperately. I just couldn't live in a double world any longer.

I had been secretly dating Jack since my junior year in high school. I lived in fear that Daddy would find out. Mama lied for me, telling him I was at a school function or at work. He would have beaten me within an inch of my life if he ever caught me with a "nasty boy." Even worse, Jack was a sailor.

Soon after, Daddy discovered that I was dating Jack, but by then he wanted me out of the house. I finally found the courage to invite Jack to dinner desperately hoping to get Daddy's approval so I could live without so much stress. All of us were nervous, even Mama. Of course, my father created an ugly scene.

When Jack came in the door Daddy hardly spoke to him. We tried to create small talk and Daddy left the room. Jack followed in an effort to make some connection with him. Then I heard Daddy and Jack's raised voices in the kitchen. As I moved closer, I caught a glimpse of Daddy, who was about five feet, eight inches tall, waving a butcher knife in the air at my six-foot, five-inch boyfriend. "I know what you want. You've found free pussy … you just wanna keep on taking the honey, doncha?"

My heart sank to the floor. I turned away, only to see that Jack had left the house and was pacing outside to avoid further confrontation with Daddy. Mama wrung her hands wailing, "Now, Daddy, please don't do that. You know that isn't nice." With that final incident, I lost all hope that my life might ever be anything close to normal while I remained at home.

So, I quit college and the struggle. Jack and I slipped away one weekend to Las Vegas, and we were married. By then, we had known each other for four years, including the seven months he'd been stationed in Japan. I expected the freedom of a normal life; a life lived far from the secret hell that had been my existence.

It was not to be. Within the first month of our marriage, I discovered that I had never really known Jack. One night only weeks after we were married, I began to get a sense of the real Jack. That moment is seared in my memory.

While we were dating, we had actually "gone all the way" as we girls called it. It was something most of us did but no "good girl" would admit. I felt tremendous guilt over it. When I settled into married life, I began to relax emotionally. I was ready to let go of the guilt and embrace the physical part of our marital bond. The first time I allowed myself to relax a little turned into a night of stark terror. I was thrown into a state of emotional shock.

With eyes flaring in anger that I had never seen in him, Jack stopped dead in the middle of our missionary position. He stood up. "What the hell do you think you are doing, you over-sexed female!" In that moment a stranger had entered our bedroom. I was terrified. What had I done wrong? All I did was move a little more. My ears started to ring, and my head spun. Everything seemed to be coming apart, in slow motion. I burst into tears. He mumbled a few more obscenities and then grabbed his robe, slamming the bedroom door behind him as he left.

I felt helpless. I felt trapped. I felt dirty. Was I a bad girl? Why was he so furious? I wondered. Maybe I was doing it wrong. Maybe I wasn't feminine enough. I knew nothing about sex or adult intimacy.

I had just met Jack's other side. His dark side. The sadistic stranger who continued to reveal his true ugliness in countless ways as time unfolded.

I tried to be a good wife. I endeavored to make up for my shortcomings.

A few weeks later, I spent an afternoon making little custard cups from scratch to fill with lemon custard, Jack's favorite. I wanted to be a good cook. Jack entered the kitchen with his tennis racket, bouncing a ball. He sliced the ball onto the cutting board and dead center into one of the shells, custard splattering the wall and running down the side of the sink. He said without emotion, "Oh, I'm sorry." Then he bounced another ball back up and destroyed two more, whooping with laughter. Both skidded across the kitchen floor, the crusts now in crumbles. He didn't quit until they were all broken and ruined. His cruelty made me cry.

"Oh, don't be such a baby. I was just having a little fun. Can't you take a joke?"

Can't you take a joke! Dear God, how many times over the years did I hear that mocking question? It was Jack's way of legitimizing any hurtful thing he chose to do or say.

Over time, his dark side grew; the pain becoming almost unbearable when it progressed into public degradation. He was particularly clever at hurting me in oblique ways that no one else understood, such as shortly after the custard cup incident, we were having dinner with his friend's family and Jack announced, "Oh, she's a good little wifey, even if she doesn't know how to cook." They all thought he adored me. I was devastated by his heartlessness.

I didn't know how to fight his cruelty. It was even worse than the violent past I had known because of its subtlety. At least I had clearly known what to be afraid of in the past—Daddy's irrational, violent temper. But Jack could be funny and charming and attentive. Then, he would suddenly turn and become sarcastic and mean-spirited.

His callous disregard and habitual denigration ate away at my very spirit. Confused by his unpredictable moods, I often blamed myself. His behavior brought back a flood of helpless feelings from my past. Dear God, I thought. I had consciously tried to choose a new life, a different life. One that was normal. Instead, I was back in a darkness that was somehow even blacker than before.

The gentle, tall man I thought I had married was two people. Part of him was funny, intelligent, and charming. The other was sinister and cruel, just like my father.

But then, I had developed two sides as well. I had grown up defensive, insecure, and scared. Away from home, though I projected an air of confidence and composure, inside I searched for the real me. So there we were. Jack and I, with our four faces. Somehow, fate had brought us together.

CHAPTER 3

Spirit Emerges in the Dream

B y the time Jack graduated with a teaching degree I had reluctantly suppressed the memory of my days prior to and in the mental hospital. They were locked in a secret chamber. I longed to find the key to that part of me.

Upon Jack's graduation, we moved from our barrack-housing apartment on the campus of Fairmont State College to a rural area in a Maryland county just outside of Washington, D.C. Jack took a job as an industrial arts and history teacher in a senior high school. Before David's fifth birthday, we bought a little one-story home in the historical community of Frederick. I had begged him to move away. I wanted a chance to start out on our own, away from the hostility and domination of his mother and from the darkness of my days in the mental hospital. Much to my surprise, he gave in. I think the shock of my collapse after Jennifer's birth might have mellowed him. At least, for a little while.

I loved my children. I felt satisfaction and pride in them, and was happy to be their mother. But Jack's dark side dominated his relationship with our son. Jack had been overbearing and rough with David ever since his toddler days. Before David turned three, I watched as Jack held him pinned to the floor during a supposedly playful time of wrestling. David screamed and fought to be let go. "You might as well get used to it now, Slugger, that's the way the world is. You'll find out," Jack said, holding David's arms with one hand, and his feet with the other. Jack ignored my pleas to stop. Each time I stood by helplessly, a coil of fear for my son tightened around my heart as I watched his spirit being taken from him.

During our first years in Maryland, we had lived in a remote area of the county with no neighbors so David did not have any playmates. At four years of age, he often played games with an imaginary friend named Linda. I sensed it was harmless, perhaps an expression of some developing creativity. Jack was outraged. First, that David was imagining things, and then that his son's imaginary friend was a girl. "The kid is weird. He's a goddamned sissy," he blurted, within earshot of David.

Jennifer, our little girl, was a docile, easy-going child. Her placid personality worked well with Jack's domination. There was very little conflict between them. Perhaps it was because she was a girl, and he didn't feel any competition.

On Jennifer's fifth Easter, I was completely overwhelmed by an experience which revealed to me the core nature of my child. She had accidentally overheard in school that there really was no Easter Bunny. On Easter morning, she lightly tapped me on my leg, as I stood at the kitchen sink. "Mama, are you and daddy really the Easter Bunny?" she asked. Although shocked that she should become aware so early, I felt I had to tell her the truth. When I did, she quickly followed up with, "Does that mean you're the tooth fairy and Santa Claus, too?" My pause was extra long, trying to think of a way to get around confirming her startling and wise conclusion. When I opted to tell all, I was prepared for tears or even anger. Instead, my precious little girl wrapped her arms around me and uttered two words. I shall never forget them. She said, "Thank you." I hugged her with teary-filled eyes and deep gratitude for my wondrous child.

I became employed as an aide in Jennifer's kindergarten class. For my children's birthdays I liked to design and bake cut-up cakes in the form of various shapes and symbols. On Jennifer's fifth birthday, the local newspaper wrote a feature article about us, the cake I baked shaped like a Raggedy Ann doll, and a mother and daughter together in school. The published story covered most of two pages, including pictures of us in the baking process and after the cake's completion. Jennifer had always been a little on the somber side. When the camera flashed though, she opened up with her first really big smile. I was filled with pride and joy, every time I looked at those pictures.

I insisted we take the children to Sunday school and church at Calvary Methodist, where both of them had gone to kindergarten. There were no pre-school programs in that county's school system in the 1960's, and instead private programs were offered by local churches. It seemed a logical choice. Jack agreed to go, as they were big on social events and not too rigid about doctrine. He tended to avoid church services, while I didn't know *what* I believed about God or the meaning of life. My father's ugly fanatical version of religion had been lorded over me, and he certainly didn't live what he preached. Even so, I felt drawn to provide some spiritual guidance for the children. To me, it was part of good parenting.

Life, in those earlier years had actually begun to feel almost sweet, thanks to the children. The dark days of all of my past, and particularly those of the time leading up to, and in, the mental hospital, were beginning to fade. Certainly life was better for me than it had ever been.

We even took a road trip back to California to see my family and allow our children, and Mickey's children, to get to know each other as cousins. By then Mickey had married and also had a boy and a girl, both just a little younger than David and Jennifer. Ironically, almost comically, I learned from Mickey that Mama and Daddy had never been married! I found out that Daddy had another family, now all grown, that he'd abandoned in Tennessee. Mama and Daddy finally went to Las Vegas the year after Jack and I were married. At that point it didn't matter to any of us. We just laughed. Nothing surprised me about Daddy.

But, as the years went on, the dark and strangely sadistic side of Jack continued to overshadow our relationship. Jack usually made dutiful attempts to say all the right things to others about my efforts, but he inevitably managed to slip in a slightly veiled insult. He balked over the littlest things, especially when he didn't think he looked good. He always needed to be right and the center of attention. Sometimes, I actually felt sorry for him. Most of the time I didn't know what to think. I monitored myself and hid those parts of me that might make him look bad. And I said little of my own achievements.

Yet, as he pointed out my shortcomings in back-handed ways, a growing new sense of strength was building up inside of me and wanted to be heard. I had begun to taste a modicum of harmony and it was empowering. Sometimes, even though I tried, as with Daddy, I couldn't hold back from defending myself which led to more fights and more violence between Jack and me. Things usually erupted when we were downstairs in our bedroom. I prayed the children could not hear us from their bedrooms upstairs.

He drank more every year, even lacing his coffee with Jack Daniel's at night and keeping it by his side as he graded papers. When he drank heavily, he hurled profanity at me—bitch, ball breaker, and his favorite, hussy. Violence often followed. Later, he might apologize, but then he would turn it around, putting the blame on me, adamant that I had been the one who'd caused him to hit me.

Nothing had really changed between us in twelve years of marriage, although we'd been able to create a respectable public image. I became close friends with Penny, whose daughter was in Jennifer's kindergarten class. Penny and her husband Bill, the latter a scientist in cancer research, had a boy and girl similar in age to our children. We did a lot of things together: camping, dinners, crafts like knitting and ceramics and cooking. We had some festive times, and Jack seemed to like getting together, especially as our time with them always involved drinking.

We were relatively active in the community. In addition to Jack's involvement in the PTA, he sang bass in a community chorale group and eventually became the director of a female chorus. I, too, sang in the chorale and the church choir. I also served as a secretary of the PTA and as a Girl Scout leader.

After my time as an aide in Jennifer's private Methodist Church kindergarten class, I was invited to train as a teacher under a certified kindergarten teacher. I accepted and took it very seriously. I enjoyed five years of dedicated teaching with five-year olds, the happiest years of my life. Those little ones with their innocent faces gave me new life each day.

Then, I was asked to become full-time director for the preschool of nearly one hundred and fifty children. I had worked long, hard hours developing significant respect and rapport within the school, among the parents and with the community. For the first time, I felt genuine self esteem and trust in my own ability. I made friends easily and began to entertain a lot. Jack cooperated, partly because it proved to be another opportunity for him to look good and to drink.

So there I was again. Living the same double life as during my growing-up years. A secret, unsafe and unpredictable home life. And a public image of a capable, hard-working professional.

Our kindergarten had been one of the two most prominent schools in the county. But by the time the children started high school, the county public school system had incorporated a kindergarten program into their curriculum. The public school program dramatically decreased the demand for private kindergartens. Having experienced genuine success and self respect, I needed to continue. I decided to return to college in order to become a state-certified teacher. It was like starting over. But going to college and becoming all that I could be was what I had wanted to do ever since the day I graduated high school.

My first classes were at the community college. My goal was to transfer to Hood College, a very prestigious women's college located in our town. Though the demands of the class work and my home life proved to be quite intense, I maintained excellent grades. I was always on the dean's list as an honor role student. A whole new aspect of me was emerging, that spark of powerful determination I possessed now was paying off. I really was more than I knew.

Yet, I felt responsible for holding the family together. Sometimes I was consumed with guilt for spending so much time on myself. I struggled to manage so my studies did not interfere with my household and motherly responsibilities. The children supported my return to school, and they voiced their pride in me.

It was in my second year of college that, just as nearly fifteen years earlier after Jennifer's birth, something astounding and other-worldly happened to me. Something I could not explain. It changed forever the way I looked at life.

As part of my curriculum, I enrolled in an art class. The last assignment we were given was to paint a monochromatic abstract in multiple images of one single object. My first two artistic compositions in the class had taken weeks to complete. Art was pleasurable, but not one of my talents. Without much thought, out of the basement, I dragged a small table lamp Jack had made. It was a sample for a project he had given to his industrial arts students. The entire base of the lamp was made from a car piston, with a socket for a light bulb built into the top. I lifted off the metal cone-shaped shade, exposing the bare bulb. I liked the starkness of it and I decided this would be the subject for my third composition.

I sat down at my easel, which I had set up in our family room in front of the sliding glass doors for good lighting. The lamp sat by itself on a small table to my right. I drew in a deep breath, soaking up the warmth of the morning sunshine beyond the window. I tried to clear my mind of the perpetual stress I lived in. I glanced over at the lamp and then back to my canvas. Since this was to be an abstract, free-form composition, I relaxed my hand and allowed my brush to flow freely.

With a sudden, strange burst of energy, my brush began to travel over the canvas—on its own! Involuntarily I created; each stroke moving faster and faster—and faster. A monochromatic image formed on the canvas. It was exhilarating. My back stiffened, and my breathing became shallow and intense. I felt overwhelmed by a consuming focus. But, *I* wasn't really doing it.

Something had taken control of my brush. In less than forty-five minutes, I was finished. Exhausted, I stumbled out of the room and flopped down on my bed.

As I awoke, those bizarre moments at the easel rushed back into my awareness. I wondered if I'd dreamt the experience. I returned to my easel. There it was. I had no idea how to explain what had just happened. What had come over me? How had I done this painting which was beyond my ability? And, how had I done it so quickly?

Standing there, I was completely mesmerized; the image was pulling me into my own painting. My consciousness was being lured into a world of its own.

It felt like a door had been opened inside me. The painting *came alive. The* multiple green and yellow images of an iron lamp with a bare light bulb…pulsed, reflecting *messages* back to me.

I understood them.

I was in awe. These abstract, linear images were communicating symbolically. I don't know how I knew this. The painting radiated a deeper level of understanding than what I knew as the reality of my everyday life. Yet, I did not fear it. I realized these were more than just images. This was an omen of some kind!

My knees weakened. I dropped down onto the stool. I stared in amazement upon this collection of shadows and shapes. I shut my eyes and shook my head several times. But I could not deny what I was seeing. The painting was speaking to me. With precise subtlety, I felt the presence of a deep knowing. I could see in the abstractness of the figures...my own future. And I knew that it was tumultuous.

I saw that my family and everything I had would be taken from me. We would all be torn apart. My mind rejected the very idea. But what I saw was more authentic, more real, than the stool upon which I sat. The images made me understand that my marriage, my family and everything I knew then as my life would be completely and permanently changed. I tried to resist. I didn't want to believe it. And I certainly didn't understand it. I had spent almost two decades since the children were born, struggling to make our marriage and family work. But, this was a profound portent that I could not push away. A transmission of weighty truth, whether I wanted to believe it or not.

Rather than becoming fearful, I felt oddly comforted; as though I had discovered a friend who'd always been there. As though discovering gravity for the first time, and then realizing it had always existed. This was like having a personal guardian. A guide. I had been given a momentary glimpse of some secret order of things, or perhaps a master plan within my span of life. For some reason, I was being shown a message.

But this time, unlike my response to the mysterious images that had come to me in the mental hospital, I didn't feel a need to suppress this message. In spite of its upheaval, I sensed the message's purpose was not to frighten, but to prepare me.

In the midst of my confusion, familiar warmth hovered around me, permeating the room. I briefly fought it. I knew its magnificence. I had first felt it during my visions after Jennifer's birth. But now I no longer feared losing control. I was keenly aware of myself. In a heightened state of sobriety, I'd been joined to an elusive presence. This presence was like being cradled by the perfect parent I'd always longed for. It was simply present, comforting me.

My instructor was amazed at the sudden improvement in my artistic ability. I framed it and hung my work on the wall near my side of our bed. It was the first thing I saw as I awoke each day. I would just wait and see, I decided. No one else knew about this experience. It was my special secret.

But now I had another secret to hide, on top of my visionary experiences in the mental hospital. I certainly wouldn't tell anyone of this creative evolution—nor of the meaningful message it delivered to me. How could I explain it to others within the framework of reality? After all, I didn't actually *know* how it had come about or from where. I only knew that I knew.

The next semester, to my sheer delight, I was not only accepted into Hood College, but received a partial Women's Seminary Scholarship. The tuition was considerable and the scholarship helped. Academic life was both challenging and exhilarating.

One of my required courses as a special education major with psychology minor was a class in abnormal psychology. One day the instructor announced at the end of class that our next topic would be about epilepsy. I was struck with such a surge of fear! I immediately went to the bathroom before I had an accident. Why did any mention of the illness still bother me so much? Fifteen years had passed since I had seen my mother in one of her spells. I had returned home only a few times since leaving California.

How could I sit through a class about epilepsy? Yet, it wasn't like me to run away from something. I left a note on my professor's bulletin board, requesting an appointment. Dr. Powell listened attentively to my story as I told him about my mother's epilepsy and my suffocating fear of it. He suggested that listening rationally to all the facts and learning more about others in the same situation might assist me in adjusting. I left his office feeling pressured to attend the class. How would I bear it?

I sat through the class. I felt danger all around me. Throughout the lecture, it took all of my willpower not to bolt for the door. As soon as the class ended, I placed all those thoughts where they had been...completely out of my mind. Otherwise, my time at Hood College was spent welcoming all the knowledge I could soak up. Everything put before me I absorbed with gusto. After two semesters of student-teaching placements, which were required of special education teachers, I graduated in the spring of 1976. I graduated with honors, ranking thirteenth in my class of nearly three hundred and fifty students. I'd achieved my goal, exceeding my own expectations.

On the day of my graduation I was electric with joy. A good friend, Jane, also graduated that spring, receiving her master's degree in psychology. In fact, she had persistently encouraged me and had become my inspiration to go back to school. She had made arrangements to open her own counseling center in town.

When I saw Jack walking across the grass to meet me for the outdoor reception which followed, I anticipated at least some show of support or enthusiasm from him. He passed within inches of me to greet Jane. He gave her a big hug and showered her with congratulations. The only thing he said to me later was, "Well, I'm ready to go when you are."

I was glad I had continued to listen to that little voice inside of me that was so determined. The voice that said—you are more. I landed a choice position with the county as an itinerant special education instructor serving two rural elementary schools. Again, Jack made dutiful, half-hearted homage to my new status as a teacher, but with undertones of resentment growing stronger.

Now employed in the same school system as Jack, we were actually growing farther apart. I had stepped into his territory. He was even more threatened and unpredictable.

During this time, I found comfort by getting involved in singing groups like the community chorus and various church choirs. Even after some knee-shaking auditions, I was chosen for a co-starring lead as the countess in a very successful community theater production, with orchestra, of *The Sound of Music* that ran for eight performances. It turned out so well that, although it proved infeasible to work out, our cast was invited to perform at a Washington D.C. dinner theater.

One evening upon returning home from work, I passed through the kitchen and saw a sheet of music on the table. I asked Jack about it, and he said, "Oh, yeah, I got that for you. I thought it was something you'd sing. You like to sing that blues stuff." I looked at the title: *Face It Girl, It's Over.* I had never heard of it and upon opening it, it didn't look at all like anything I would sing. Besides, Jack had never encouraged me to sing, much less purchase music for me. Every time I'd tried to sing with his accompaniment at the piano, he would claim he'd forgotten the rest of the song. He didn't want me in front of his piano. I couldn't make sense of his attitude.

On another occasion, Jack gave me a book: "Here, I bought a present for you. You might be interested in reading about her." I read the title, *The Biography of Gene Tierney*. I'd never heard of her. "Why would I be interested in her?"

"Oh, you know, she's that screwed-up actress who got into a bunch of trouble and lost it. She went crazy."

What was he talking about? What did that have to do with me? That part of my past was so far tucked back into my memory, I hardly considered it a part of me anymore. And I certainly didn't need to bring it back. Why was he stirring it up now?

The same month I graduated from college, David managed to graduate from high school. Even though he'd tested as exceedingly intelligent, he had lost interest in education. He met me out on the steps of his school where I waited for him after his graduation ceremonies. Still wearing his cap and gown, he handed me his diploma. "Here, Mom," he said. "I did this for you." I was disappointed that he felt no pride in his accomplishment, but I knew he'd lost so much self esteem and confidence over the years through his father's demeaning influence.

Jennifer had elected to take early graduation from high school, through an alternative program offered by the county, and would graduate the next year. She too had lost interest in her academic life and even in herself. Ever since puberty, around eleven years old, she had begun to change drastically. I remember vividly when her father brought her home from her first real trip away from us. She had spent a week at her grandmother's in Ohio. When she returned, she had gained fifteen pounds, had deep, dark bags under her eyes, and had become serious and sullen. She had lost all of her innocence, her child-like exuberance. When I tried to get her to talk about it, her dad sharply interrupted, saying, "Leave her alone. There's nothing wrong with her."

I was astounded and confounded by this severe shift in her personality. She became closed and uncommunicative. No matter how I approached her, she would not open up to me. She spent much of her time in her room from then on. I never knew why she changed, and why Jack had so suddenly made light of it all and told me I was imagining things. He never missed a chance to contradict my judgment as her mother, and to make me look as though I was overreacting to any disciplinary situation. If I said black—he said white.

Though I did not fully realize it until years later, he was deliberately trying to put a wall between my daughter and me. The same way he'd put a wall between his mother and me. It worked. Jennifer grew distant. I hardly knew her. She rarely, if ever, confided in me despite my endless attempts to reach her. I felt as if something was slowly dying inside each of us.

In the last years the children were home, we all seemed to be at undefined turning points. My anxiety and discontent spiked. Jack grew more secretive, more elusive. He refused to account for his time. We were all like ships passing in the night.

CHAPTER 4

Spirit Markers Appear in the Dream

O ne evening, while I kept Jack's dinner warm in the oven as he was late again, the phone rang. The operator asked me to approve a long distance call made by Jack and charged to our number. I approved the call and then asked for the number Jack had called. My heart raced as I wrote it down. I sat staring at the paper for at least five minutes. I got up, checked his dinner, and looked out the window for the hundredth time to see if he'd arrived yet. I went to my kitchen desk and sat down. I swallowed hard, picked up the receiver, and numbly dialed the number.

A woman's soft voice answered. Her voice sounded just like mine. "Is Jack there?" I blurted out.

"No," she said. "He just left. Would you like to leave a message?"

"No, I wouldn't." I dropped the receiver into the cradle. My heart sank. My body went limp.

When Jack finally came home, I was downstairs in the bedroom. I sat motionless at my dressing table. "What's wrong with you?" he asked, tossing his briefcase onto the bed.

"Who is the girl?" I asked.

"What girl?"

"The one you just left." His face dropped, and he turned away from me. For a few minutes he tried to deny it by talking around the issue. I pressed on, demanding an explanation. I didn't care what he did to me. I had always allowed myself to trust that at least we were faithful to each other. This felt more devastating than a beating from him.

Then he admitted that he was involved with a student teacher from his school. I flew into a red rage.

I sobbed and paced and even screamed at him. At one point, I grabbed the hand mirror from my dresser and smashed it into a thousand pieces on the floor. He was uncharacteristically calm, just watching my tirade. I finally collapsed into a heap on the bed. I never undressed. I awakened late the next morning and reached for the phone to call in sick. Jack had already left for work. I had no idea where he slept.

As I lay there, I stared at the watery, yellow and green forms on the painting I'd done, now almost four years ago. The painting of the lamp with the bare light bulb. The one telegraphing my future as completely shattered. I couldn't think. I didn't want to think. I was drained, beyond devastation.

Later that day, I called Jane, my friend from college who now had her own counseling center in town. She heard my hysteria, stopped everything and came over to spend the day with me. I was shocked by her unconditional availability for me. No one had ever shown me such loving consideration.

"I never thought this would happen to me," I said. "It's like a soap opera."

"Honey, life is a soap opera, I see it every day," she whispered as she gently rocked me. I felt self-conscious with her arms around me, an experience foreign to me with someone other than Jack, but I welcomed her comfort.

Just like in the movies, she made me chicken soup. She listened to every pent-up sorrow I had kept hidden for so long. Throughout the day, we became closer than I ever knew two people could be. Her loving friendship empowered me. She helped me to feel I would survive this debacle called my life.

Jack eventually came up with an apology for his affair, and admitted he didn't know what he wanted to do about it. I didn't either. I lived in a state of confusion. I cried every day on the twenty minute drive to and from work. I went through my scheduled routine like a robot. Only occasionally could my little elementary students spark any semblance of life within me.

One Friday after work, looking for distraction, I accepted an invitation to visit my longtime friend, Penny, to paint pottery. I hoped the time with her would lift my spirits. I turned my car up their long curved driveway lined with the once tiny evergreen seedlings we'd planted together many years earlier. Now, they towered straight and slender at the edge of the drive. I allowed myself to soak up the peaceful sight of the setting sun as the evening mist glistened on the pine needles.

I drew in a long, deep breath. As I wearily exhaled, I felt light headed for a second. All at once, the entire scene before me glowed in animation. I sensed that my car was levitating off the ground. I was no longer in control. A velvet space of silence encompassed me. This all felt so familiar. I had seen this row of trees and this lane before! Déjà vu? No! It was not! It was a vivid memory! It was a memory from my visions in the mental hospital sixteen years earlier.

I was so frightened to let these thoughts come into my mind. Was I losing it again? Had Jack's infidelity just been too much to bear? But the image gently faded. I was left with the clear memory of the vision I'd experienced in that hospital sixteen years ago—and that peace. That sweet peace. Now—it was actually happening!

The row of evergreen trees represented the *exact same scene that I'd seen in my vision at the hospital.* How? Why? Had what I'd seen so many years ago been a warning? Like my painting? Or was my life like a movie and now I was seeing a rerun—a part of my life I had already seen? How could this be? Never before had I experienced a dimension to life like this.

Once again, I wasn't afraid, in spite of the disturbing implications. To the contrary, I felt comforted. Something was happening here that was beyond my understanding, yet I sensed a calming message. Some law of truth—another dimension—was being shown to me. Even though my life had come crashing down around me, I felt assured at that moment that there was a greater plan. And, that everything was as it was intended to be...and somehow, I *was* going to be all right.

And so, with growing assurance, I began a gradual surrender and a guarded, watchful acceptance of an unknown phenomenon working around me—within me. I'd been given another glimpse of the sweet innocence and flowing serenity I had experienced in my visions that night on the couch in our barracks apartment. That night when my mind had slipped through a nexus and into rainbow-colored, kaleidoscopic wonder. I had tasted it again. I wanted more of it. I would continue to allow myself to secretly watch. I would be patient. I would wait and see.

I didn't feel much of anything for the year that followed my discovery of Jack's infidelity. I buried myself in my teaching. Special education was a new program in the mid-1970's, and it had been mandated into the schools by the federal government. Added to an already burdened curriculum, there was a great deal of resistance and misunderstanding among both the parents and faculty. I had real success with my students and soon my alma mater, Hood

College, decided to send student teachers to work with me in what they called their Master Teacher Program. With the time flexibility their help allowed, I was able to write and construct a workshop based on promoting understanding and empathy with the special education program and with a student's learning *differences,* rather than disabilities.

I created fun, hands-on activities designed for group participation to offer the experience of an actual learning situation and the students' challenges. I minimized the use of new terms and labels which had been thrust upon the public and concerned parents, such as learning modalities, auditory or visual learner, kinesthetic integration, and aphasia or dyslexia. It was an immediate success and I was asked to present the workshop for other faculties and PTA organizations, as well as for the county board of education.

At home, I felt like a failure. I tried to forget about Jack's affair, but I thought about it all of the time. Even though he insisted that he'd ended it, our fights increased and intensified. He called me shrewish and bitchy, implying that I was the one who caused him to betray our vows.

I was asked to teach my workshop at the college where I had graduated, my alma mater. I taught in one of the very same rooms in which I had been a student. For a brief period, I was exhilarated to receive such an honor. But at the end of the day, when I shed my professional identity, all I thought about was how and why my life had gone so wrong.

By the fall, I was often sick. My body seemed to be succumbing to the stress. I underwent an ordinary female surgery, and a routine procedure turned into a ten-day hospital stay.

Once I recovered I worked more intensely than ever. The following summer, two other teachers and I were selected for special assignments. I was glad to be involved and grateful for the recognition of my hard work by the administration. We rewrote the entire county curriculum for the special education program. We brought dedication, clarity, and creative innovations to the new curriculum. Our work did not go unnoticed.

In the fall of 1978, a new Title One government program provided funds to our county for a liaison position between the school and underprivileged families of children about to enter school. A central administrative position, the board of administration offered the position to me after only two years of teaching. I was astounded and gratified. Still, in my personal life I felt like a failure. The stress of my home life was tearing me apart. Jack was intimidated by my swift rise to administrative level opportunities. During his teaching career, he had applied several times for higher level positions and always been passed over.

I turned down the job. I was unwilling to make the situation at home any more stressful. The next semester my county supervisor offered me another administrative position, suggesting I might like this one better. This time, not only did I not take the job, I made the decision to retire from teaching altogether. I was desperate to relieve the tension, to somehow make the way for more calmness and peace of mind. I hoped that by stepping away from the same career as Jack it would lessen the competition between us and make things better at home.

Not long after, I decided to go into a completely different area of work. I needed to have my own world outside the home. My father had been a real estate broker during my final years at home, and I knew a little about what to expect in that profession. So, I decided to become a real estate agent.

"Isn't she cute? She'll probably make five hundred a year in real estate. But that's okay, I make enough to keep this family afloat," I overheard Jack say to my friend, Donna, at a surprise party I gave for her when she'd earned her master's degree. But I didn't make five hundred per year. I sold a million dollars worth of property in my first year, in a market where an average townhome was appraised for around sixty thousand dollars. I was even nominated as "Rookie of the Year" by the local board of realtors. My new career turned out to be exciting and stimulating. The people in the Long & Foster office where I worked became like family to me.

At the end of 1979, David made the decision not to return to the community college he'd half-heartedly attended for a semester. Instead, he joined the Air Force. "It'll make a man out of him," Jack snickered. He'd been pushing military service to David since his high school years. I didn't protest. I yearned for David to find himself, and I hoped that being away from the negativity of his father would help him to discover his strengths.

That December Jennifer graduated mid-year from high school. She, too, had lost interest in education. After a brief attempt at community college, Jennifer decided to leave home. She had gotten a job with a newspaper and had found an apartment in Baltimore. She was only eighteen. She wasn't ready. I wasn't ready. I hadn't known her. I hungered to know my daughter.

I redecorated her bedroom and called to invite her to return home, if only for a short visit. I often went into her vacant room, sat at her desk, and talked aloud to her. I always ended up in tears as I gave in to my sorrow that we had not been closer. Did she even know me? Could I have done more? Had she ever really felt the depth of my love?

So, there was just Jack, and me, and the marriage. The more effort I put into having small dinner parties, creating intimate occasions for the two of us or with friends, the more tension grew between us. Counseling was out—Jack wouldn't even consider it.

Jack made friends with two men who hung around the school where he taught and from which they had graduated. Bailey, a retired doctor, was a known alcoholic, and Eugene, a local man from the railroad town in which the school was located, collected Hitler memorabilia. Jack regularly went out drinking with them. I didn't like it, or them, and he knew it. He dared me to challenge him about it. I overheard him tell them I was a bitch and didn't want him to have any fun.

Jack eventually began to spend evenings in the downstairs family room, sipping Jack Daniels and watching documentaries about the Holocaust. He was obsessed by the way Hitler had gained massive, absolute control. It was not unusual for him to indulge in elaborate, animated descriptions of Eugene's memorabilia collection. He was depressing. My marriage was depressing.

My friend, Jane, her husband, and another couple invited us to spend a weekend at Deep Creek Lake in a cabin they'd rented. Relentless in my efforts to make our marriage work, I saw this as an opportunity to bring us a little closer. Maybe getting away from it all might help us to communicate better. I urged Jack to go, and he finally agreed.

The last night of the mountain weekend was filled with good food, laughter and lots of fresh peach margaritas. Jack mixed his with double shots of tequila. Our time together with the other couples had been fun, but Jack and I hardly talked to each other. Around midnight everyone dispersed, and Jack and I climbed up the steps to a lovely loft bedroom.

As he sat on the couch, glass in hand, I made the decision to swallow my pride and give all I had in an effort to connect with him. He was barely listening to me so eventually, I found myself on my knees, sitting back on my heels, in front of him. We had both been angry and depressed for so long. As I began to talk, my words developed into a plea for him to open up to me...to tell me what he was really feeling. Couldn't we talk instead of argue? What had I done to make him so angry?

He said little, and I became quite emotional. As always, I spoke with my hands as I talked. I accidentally swung my right hand into his glass, which he held balanced on his left knee. It flew across the room, ice and tequila splattering everywhere. I opened my mouth to apologize, but he grabbed my throat with both hands, pushing me down. He was on top of me, straddling my torso, with both of his thumbs digging into my windpipe.

"What are you doing?" I tried to ask, but the words wouldn't form. I couldn't make a sound. I couldn't draw a breath. I began to lose focus, everything going dim. One thought flashed through my mind—is this it? Is this the way my life ends? Just before the last light faded, he shook my head violently and threw me away from him. As he got up, he shot a swift, hard kick into my side. "Now leave me alone, woman," I heard him command from somewhere off in the distance.

I couldn't cry. I labored to breathe. Sometime in the night, I crawled over to the bed and climbed in, my clothes still on. My head throbbed. It didn't want to move. I'd reached the depths of despair as he snored loudly beside me. Most of the night I drifted in and out of a tormented sleep. What was wrong with him? I was the mother of his children! Didn't that matter? I found no answers.

In the morning, I awakened still weeping. "How could you?" I asked.

"How could I what?" he snapped.

Shocked by his denial, I described what he had done.

"I don't know what the hell you're talking about. I think you've been having nightmares, girl. You're crazy."

Who was this man? Cold and indifferent, he insisted that he didn't remember a thing! Either he was crazy, or I was. By the next morning, the bruises on my throat and hip declared the truth. Jack scolded me for being clumsy. "You musta run inta something."

Something inside of me shut down. Never again would I risk reaching out to him. At that moment, I built an invisible shield around my heart, vowing not to step outside of it. I would never again provoke him—nor would I allow him to get close to me!

I could not consider divorce. Divorce was a sign of failure in the 1970's. A disgrace. Our vows were sacred, and I was in it for better, or for the worst.

Our lives became isolated events of small talk, avoidance, bickering and pressured sex, which I endured. His sexual appetite seemed to be heightening. It was almost scary. Our physical intimacy was more a silent act of anger than of love.

A few months later, on a sunny afternoon, Jane and I visited a friend for lunch on her jasmine-draped Victorian patio. We laughed and shared the latest news. After the main course, when Mona began to pour the coffee, I sensed a mood change.

"Let's just get it out in the open, okay?" Mona said to Jane. "We're her friends. We have to tell her."

My stomach tightened, and I sat upright at the table.

"Tell me what?"

"It's Jack," Mona dived in. "You know that Jane and I are aware of his affair with the student teacher, but there is more."

"More? More affairs?"

"Yes, and one of the women was Penny."

Penny! My best friend? We had been friends since the children had been in kindergarten. Our children played together, we camped together, gave parties together, cooked, made crafts, and were Girl Scout leaders together. Strangely enough, I had not told Penny of Jack's affair, the one that I knew about with the student teacher. It hadn't felt safe to tell her. Perhaps a part of me had known the truth all along.

Jane took my hand. "Are you sorry we told you?"

No, I wasn't sorry. Upon hearing their words, I felt a shift, as though I'd suddenly become an observer of my own life. A vague intuition came into focus. Over the years, I'd felt edgy and uncomfortable when Penny and Jack were together. I had overlooked their subtle glances and puzzling innuendos. I simply succumbed to Jack's accusations that I was insecure.

"It's not your fault!" Jane assured me, as if she was reading my mind. "I hope you don't think this is your fault. Don't blame yourself. Look at you, Grace. You're beautiful. You're smart and successful! And you have gone to the nth degree to be a good wife and mother. It's him! Don't you get it? It's Jack!" An angry voice shouted in my head, "You don't know the half of it!" I hadn't told Mona about Jack's abuse, and Jane knew nothing about that night in the cabin when he'd nearly strangled me. I was ashamed.

Penny! My longtime friend. I was devastated to hear of yet more betrayal. There was nothing Jack wouldn't do! And Penny—she'd betrayed me! A friendship I'd cherished…someone I believed in and trusted.

Over the following weeks a new page was turning in the story of my world. The evidence continued to mount, forcing me to face the harsh truth about my marriage and my life. I felt immobilized. Overwhelmed. I didn't know what I wanted. Did I want to live alone? What would Jack do to me if I left him? Would he leave me alone? Would he become more violent? I was afraid to do anything.

One Friday evening an office party was to be held out in the county at the rustic country home of one of my co-workers. Suddenly, I was desperate to attend, by myself, and to be where I felt wanted and valued. I didn't just want to go, I *needed* to go. I was scaring myself. An unfulfilled longing seemed to be overtaking me. Jack resented my social life at the office. I'd never attended a party without him before, and I was nervous about it. It didn't deter me. I told him I was going to a girlfriend's home for a visit.

I indulged in a couple of glasses of wine with two friends at the office before driving to the party. Very unlike me. As my car climbed the steep hill towards the home of the party, I drove as if my life depended on it, consumed by the need to be with people who appreciated me. I knew I was out of control—I no longer cared.

The car screeched, laying rubber as I negotiated the sharp, hairpin curves. Then I heard a loud explosion as the right front tire blew. I hung onto the wheel with all my strength to keep the car on the road, but the ninety-degree turn in the road was more than my big Mercury, now flopping on one rim, could handle. I crashed into a tree.

In the aftermath, I shook my head, trying to focus. The car lights illuminated the bigger than life sycamore at the front of the hood. I wasn't really hurt. The accelerator roared, still stuck at full throttle. I ripped the gear shift into reverse, screeching my mangled car away from the tree. Somehow I steered it, bumping over the dirt shoulder and back onto the highway. Chugging and sputtering, flopping on a bare rim, I gunned it up the hill the rest of the way to the party. Nothing was going to stop me from being where I was wanted to go. A voice in my head was loudly warning, "You're not making any sense. This is foolish... not acceptable." Unlike the Grace who had always been so careful and cautious, I made it to the party. I didn't care. I stayed there until everyone went home. I had left the car sitting by the curb near the house, thinking it could be towed later, and I asked my friend Jill to drive me home. We had become quite close, and I knew she sensed my heartache. She didn't ask any questions.

Jack was furious about the car and suspicious of me. My emerald green Mercury had been operating on two bald tires, and I hadn't squeezed the time out of my packed schedule to buy new ones. I couldn't really explain why I had continued to drive it after the tire exploded, or why it ended up far from my girlfriend's house. I didn't bother with explanations.

He demanded, "Whatsamatter, was your boyfriend there? You just couldn't wait?"

He didn't harangue me for long. My behavior was so unusual; he seemed more shocked than anything.

I was adrift. My perspective had become fragmented. Desperation was overtaking me. Perpetually agitated, I became mired in self doubt. I constantly questioned myself. Was I too rigid? Now that the children were gone, should I loosen up a little? Jack had always accused me of being a prude. Maybe if I drank with him we would get along better. I might even be able to forget about the painful events of the past.

A few weeks after the car crash, I invited our neighbors over for dinner and to share our hot tub. I drank more wine than usual at dinner. I tried to be jovial and dismiss Jack's routine backhanded remarks. With every verbal attack, I took a few sips of wine.

Something inside of me was breaking. I wanted to scream, "Don't you see how this hurts me? Don't you even care? Stop it, you son of a bitch!" I grabbed a fresh bottle of Jack's Charles Krug chardonnay and slid down into the hot tub, pouring wine into my glass on the way.

Jack told his version of my damaged car story to our neighbors, Pat and Bob. "Poor little thing, when the tire blew out, she just thought it was going to grow another one. She thought all she had to do was press on the gas and one would pop right out from under the fender, brand shiny new. So she floored it—right into a sycamore, big as a house. Good God, woman! Oh well, it's a good thing she knows how to cook. Guess I'll have to keep her."

My throat ached with decades of resentment, and my head swirled with alcohol and anger. The condescending son of a bitch! Pat had been a teacher whom I had hired during my directorship at the school. We had been friends a long time, but she didn't know about the fights and the violence. I looked squarely at her and asked, "Do you really believe that bull crap?"

Pat stood, waded over to me, and put her arm around me. She jokingly said in her South Carolina accent, "Now, honey, he was jus' kiddin'. We all know you're smarta' than that."

I stunned her with my reaction. "Yeah, he was kidding. He's always kidding…and it's always about me! Jack's hobby is ridicule!" I said in a louder than necessary voice.

Bob stood, too. "I'd better go check on the kids. Sheryl was supposed to be home by now. I better make sure she's mindin' her curfew."

"Yeah, honey, wouldya' look at that. I didn't know it was so late, I betta' go 'long too," Pat said, reaching for her towel.

I barely noticed their departure. The dam in my head was breaking, and the flood gates were wide open. Nothing would stop me now. I drained the glass of wine and poured another.

"I am goddam sick and tired of being the butt of your fuckin' jokes! I've had it, mister! Fuck off! Just fuck off!"

The power of my own words rang in my ears and shot a giant surge of adrenaline through my entire being. My mind hurtled back through the years to the big room in the mental hospital, when I'd stood under the rotunda with both hands thrust upward. Just as I had done then, I let out a primal scream, but this time I released a screaming stream of profanity. It seemed to last forever. Without taking a breath, all of the pent-up bitterness I'd held inside for so many years spewed out.

"Hoow could yoou?" I snarled, "hoow dare yoou?" I literally growled. "You're never proud of me...you, you fucker! Nothing I ever do is good enough for you!"

Jack pulled his body up out of the water with one swish. "You damned son of a bitch," I continued. "You hit me...you undermine my authority with our children...you cheat on me!" I went on. I couldn't stop. I was completely out of control and riding on it. I didn't know whether he was preparing to strike me, or worse. I didn't care if he beat me. I didn't even care if he killed me. I *would* be heard. He wrapped his towel around himself and sat on the edge of the tub, expressionless. My mind traveled back through a hallway of time. As horrific images of painful memories stormed by, I kept shouting accusations, peppered with profanity.

All at once, Jack stood up and went into the house. "I don't have to take this, you fuckin' bitch!" An image flashed in my mind— he might be going for the gun he'd gotten from his Hitler friend. It didn't matter. I kept on screaming my guts out.

With my arms stretched wide as I gripped the edge of the tub, I lifted my face to the starry night sky and, from some primal place in the pit of my stomach, I screamed again, allowing all the rancor of the past to spew forth. As the inky-black bitterness spewed from my mouth, like swarming bees evacuating a poisoned hive, I surrendered to my fury.

Part of me was suspended above my body, looking down. It was the same experience I always had when Daddy beat me. I escaped by watching myself as I lay sobbing on my bed, sometimes for hours. Again, from my retreat, I watched the collapse within myself of the dam that had held back the repressed, emotional dung from years gone by.

Out of nowhere a blurry flashback of Penny's driveway swirled onto the screen of my mind. That long row of evergreen trees we'd planted together when they were only seedlings faded in and out of focus. Penny, my goddamn so-called friend!

The evergreen trees! *The evergreen trees...* the same vision I'd seen in the mental hospital! They were the *same trees* that lined *her* curved driveway!

Within a millisecond, another vision flashed back. The name! I had seen the name "Lawless." It had been part of my visions in the mental hospital! Penny's last name! *Lawless.*

With an abrupt flatness, the fury, the rage, the loud screeching that gave bitter voice to the past lost its fuel and died. In the dim light of the candles, I saw Jack's shadowy figure as he came through the French doors. He stopped and stared at me. I lost focus. My head wobbled to the side then violently heaved forward as I vomited. Then, everything went dark.

Daylight pierced through the window as I struggled to open my eyes. Like lightning bolts, the bright rays zapped through my head. I was in our bed. Jack sat on the edge of the mattress, watching me. His head was framed by my painting on the wall just behind him—the prophetic green and yellow painting of the steel lamp with the bare light bulb I had done in art class more than six years earlier. The one that told me everything and everyone in my life would be torn asunder.

Jack said that I had vomited throughout the night and he'd kept me on my side to prevent me from drowning myself. He had carried me to bed from the hot tub. I was surprised. I hadn't seen the humane side of Jack for years. Not since the brief time following my discharge from the mental hospital. As I groggily recalled the events of the previous evening, it seemed surreal that I had lived to remember them. If I had actually planned to say and do what I did, I would have also surely planned to run for my life.

During the grueling days that followed, I lived with the aftermath of alcohol poisoning. A sobering realization hit me: I was in trouble. I simply couldn't go on as I was. I needed help. Even if Jack wouldn't go to counseling—I needed to. The following Monday, with Jane's help, I found a family therapist and began the first of weekly sessions.

Meanwhile, a new perspective of my visions in the mental hospital occupied my thoughts. I was beginning to regard those visions—and even my own painting, as *symbols*. *They* were like *symbolic omens or signs*. Then, when the time came for them to be lived, along with their presence was a loving assurance—even guidance. They seemed to mark important turning points in my life.

Jack's adultery had rendered me helpless and hopeless. Then with the connection—the memory of Penny's driveway with the evergreen trees and her name—my thoughts turned to wonder.

Having seen those mysterious symbolic forewarnings from almost twenty years earlier, I found the inner strength to manage. The strength to hold onto hope. More than ever, I grew respectful of my secret. Perhaps there *might* even be a divine order.

Was I special? Was I being watched over? Was there a specific destiny for me?

This emerging language of symbology permeated my reality; a reality that had taken on the characteristics of a dream. The *reality* that I knew before my visions was nothing like this. The little glimpse I had been given of what lay ahead had caused me to wonder: could the betrayal of my husband and my best friend, Penny Lawless, have been—planned? Was it pre-ordained?

In any case, symbology provided me with a sort of mystical sense of comfort. A part of me really wanted to believe in the power of these *signs*. Were they from God? And even more important, would they lead me back to that joy? That childlike innocence shown to me in those rare moments of my visions—could I even hope to understand it? Would I ever again experience that profound feeling—that bliss? No, it was more than bliss. I realized that precious time felt like coming home.

Certainly, the God of fear and guilt, hell and damnation taught to me by my father would have condemned my visions as wicked...witchcraft...satanic work of the devil. But I had largely rejected this self-righteous, religious dogma after my mind-altering experience in the mental hospital. This phenomenal journey now becoming my vivid reality would never have fit into my father's world.

Whenever I could summon it back, I bathed in the memory of the radiant beauty I'd seen through the kaleidoscopic light, and the deep peace I had known. I knew in the deepest part of myself that it was good, it was real. But this was new, different. I knew I wasn't a mystic. I'd worked for, and attended, the Methodist Church in an effort to be a good parent. I'd raised my children in that church.

Still, I didn't know what I believed.

CHAPTER 5

A New Dimension in the Dream

Jane continued to be a loyal, supportive friend. Being a therapist, it came naturally to her. I introduced her to Yvonne, my office manager at Long & Foster Realty, and the three of us became buddies. In fact, Yvonne began sessions with Jane regarding her husband's excessive drinking.

"Grace, I know you are aware of how much Philip has been drinking. Yvonne is thinking about going to an Al-Anon meeting," Jane shared with me one day.

"I feel it could be very helpful if Yvonne were to get into a group like that. She is hesitant to go though. Grace, do you think you could help her? She might attend meetings if you went with her?" I'd never heard of Al-Anon, a recently formed support group for the families of alcoholics.

After the third tactful request from Jane, I felt she must be pretty convinced I could help, and I certainly owed her this favor.

When Yvonne and I walked into the basement of a local church, the meeting was already in session. It was a warm summer evening and there was no air conditioning. I was weary from a long day of showing homes to clients. The middle-aged woman who led the group stopped the process and turned her attention to us. Yvonne answered her inquiries regarding her intentions and expectations for the group, while I withdrew to observe, saying I had only come as a friend of Yvonne's.

Each of the ten people assembled began to share their personal situations. They were either spouses or children of alcoholics. A very thin woman with long chestnut-colored hair, who introduced herself as Sunshine, shyly admitted her shame when her husband was rude to her and embarrassed her in public. She had made excuses for him, because she let herself believe that the things he said about her were true. She thanked the group for helping her to realize that she had taken on her husband's blame and guilt.

A gentle middle-aged man named Ken, dressed in khaki work clothes, lamented his efforts to believe in his alcoholic wife. During the good times, he convinced himself their problems had gone away. "But," he confessed, "deep down inside, I knew there was something wrong. It's Celia's thinkin' as well as her drinkin'. But, I still wanna ignore what I know is true…especially about myself."

I began to feel uncomfortable. It must be the lack of air conditioning. I hoped this wouldn't go on too long. I felt anxious to plan my next work day and then get some sleep.

Mary, who kept her arm around her teenage daughter, had been coming to meetings for six months. She sat directly across from me. She was well dressed and quite attractive.

"I always had the nagging belief that I was the one that was wrong." Her daughter leaned her head into her mother's arm. "I just thought I wasn't up to it all, not attractive enough, not clever enough to help Jim solve our problems. I always thought it was something I did, or shoulda' done. Now I know I've always bought into his irrational, defensive, angry way of seeing things."

My throat began to close up, and it ached all the way to my ears.

"I didn't know!" She went on, "I let Jim and his problems dominate me and it has affected the whole family…our children. That has been the most difficult, because it…"

Mary stopped mid-sentence when I crumbled into a heap in my chair. I was sobbing, my head in my hands. I had been straining to hold it back—but I couldn't. In front of all those people, I broke down. I was crying in a way I'd never cried before. Yvonne wrapped her arms around me, lifting me to my feet and placing my head on her shoulder.

I heard the voice of the group leader, as she said, "Oh, my dear, you know what we are talking about, don't you?"

Everyone abandoned their chairs. They encircled me with their arms. That was the first time I'd ever experienced a group hug. An eternity passed. They held me until I could not make another sound. Then my words tumbled out in broken sentences.

Pent-up feelings of rage, helplessness, and insecurity, deeper than I ever imagined. They all listened. They offered genuine, simple love. They devoted the rest of the session to me.

I could taste a sweet newness growing inside of me. Maybe, just maybe, there was hope for something better in my life. Through their own stories, those dear people had reflected—my life—my thinking—my problems. I poured out my own pain. I thirstily drank in the love and consolation from each one of them.

Driving home, my head felt light. My chest lifted more easily as I breathed. I thought I could sleep for a year. I wished I didn't have to go into the office the next day. Then, it came to me. It had never been Yvonne with the problem. Jane and Yvonne had tricked me into going to Al-Anon! *I* was the one with the problem, and my friends had wanted to help *me*. Oh, God above, whoever you are, I thank you.

The Al-Anon meetings became the highlight of my week. Of my life. I looked forward to the new empowerment I was gaining by being able to put my heartaches into words. I looked forward to being heard, to sharing myself in a way I never realized I could. These people understood, and they accepted me without criticism. They were caring, empathy-filled, human beings. I never knew people could treat each other in this manner, no matter how many mistakes someone has made.

"You do know now, dear, don't you, that he is an alcoholic? You understand that now, don't you?" Jane asked gently. I was cuddled on the sofa in her office, surrounded by big, soft pillows. I had come to meet her for lunch. "And the alcohol is how he covers up what's inside. There is more to this situation with Jack than just substance abuse. He abuses others because of problems he himself hasn't dealt with."

There was no denying it. He had a mean side; that dark side I'd seen only weeks after we'd been married. After all, he had almost strangled me. I finally told Jane about that night, and how he denied it the next day.

"He probably had a blackout, Grace. That's what can happen when the brain has had too much alcohol for too long. Alcoholics do things they don't remember."

It was early summer. School was out. This was the best time for families who needed to relocate to do so. I had begun to spend most days and evenings at Long & Foster Realty, or out to dinner with clients or fellow realtors. I went home as seldom as possible, which threw Jack off balance. He demanded explanations—and I wanted to believe it was because he cared about me. But, if he did, it never showed. He still maintained his separate friendships and late hours. Whenever we crossed each other's paths our anger was apparent.

The Al-Anon group gave me hope, which meant that, more than ever, I lived for the counseling sessions I had begun after that dreadful night in the hot tub. For nearly three months, I met weekly with Denise, my counselor. The focus of my sessions with her was my marriage and Jack. The sessions became the highlight of my life. At the same time, it was the hardest thing I'd ever done. Even in a closed, confidential situation, I didn't feel safe enough to completely trust her. I had never before been in counseling, and I didn't know what she might put in my records. It took me four sessions of recounting the painful years of my marriage before I finally risked telling her about my experience in the mental hospital and the visions. She received my story with warm acceptance.

"Don't you see, dear, he offers a rose with a barb?"

"I'm sorry," I said. "What do you mean, 'a rose with a barb'?"

"I mean that Jack hurtfully exaggerates your weaknesses and then in the same breath mentions something menial that you know how to do, in order to portray himself as your only supporter. The unspoken message is…it's a wonder anyone could love you. You're lucky to have me."

"But why?" I asked.

"It's hard for me to know, dear, since he isn't coming to sessions with you. Let's just concentrate on helping you."

When I walked into the kitchen one evening after a session with Denise, Jack was seated at the counter with a double scotch in one hand and a bottle of Dewar's in the other.

"Well, tell me, wifey, what did you learn today?" Jack asked in a sing-songy voice. "Are you any smarter now that you've seen a shrink?"

I walked past him down the stairs and into the bedroom. I closed the door.

Life was changing right before my eyes. I was learning to appreciate my own worth, to focus on myself without allowing Jack to intimidate me. I was developing trust and confidence in myself and in the world. In a way, I was being reborn. As I looked at me, perhaps for the first time, I discovered that I had disregarded myself to save my marriage. I had given up a promising teaching career so that my success wouldn't conflict with his ego. I was a victim of an abusive childhood, and I'd subsequently married an abusive man.

I sensed I was crossing a bridge. Strength was building inside of me. But that strength threatened life as I knew it.

I couldn't be myself in our marriage. Jack continued to refuse any type of counseling. "Why should I? You're the one who thinks there's a problem. You're the one who needs to get your shit together!" I began to feel that he wanted the marriage to end—but he wanted me to end it—to take the blame, to be the bad guy. I remembered the book he had given me about the actress who'd had a mental breakdown. An inappropriate gift, unless he thought he could make me feel helpless again, or worse. And then I recalled the sheet music he gave me entitled, *Face it Girl, It's Over.*

Another month went by. Then one day Mona called to ask if I would house-sit for six weeks while she, and her husband, went to Europe. Both Mona and Jane insisted it would be good for me. So, I accepted. I never spent another night in our home.

Those six weeks convinced me that I could not be married to Jack any longer. Even if it meant the shame of divorce. As soon as the six weeks ended, with one hundred and fifty dollars in my checking account and a modest commission in escrow on the sale of a farm, I rented an apartment in town. It took several weeks for me to convince Jack that I just needed some time to think things over. In truth, I wanted to leave without any more violence. My hunch had been right. Jack barely protested my actions.

My friends from my real estate office came with pick-up truck and boxes to help me pack. I was out in one afternoon. It frightened me to think about the future without a double income. Even worse, it was 1981 and the bottom was falling out of the real estate market. The country was in a recession and interest rates had soared to eighteen percent on home mortgages. Despite all that, everything felt fresh and new.

A few months after my move, I convinced Jack over coffee in a restaurant that divorce was our best solution. I volunteered to get the papers drawn up, and I managed to pay the sixty dollars to start the process. There was a one-year separation period required in Maryland before a divorce could become final. It was hard to believe everything was going so smoothly.

About three weeks later, I received a copy in the mail of a filing by Jack for *involuntary* separation. It contained a laundry list of trumped-up charges, including adultery and abandonment! He denied our agreement of *voluntary* separation. Adultery? He was the adulterer!

But the most devastating part was the paragraph that declared grounds for divorce could not be heard until after a *three year separation* due to the fact that we had an *involuntary* separation. I realized Jack refused to agree to the separation because he knew I would not receive a penny of our property settlement until then. He also knew I dreamed of returning to California, and his delaying tactics could keep me in Maryland for three years. Pure revenge. He wanted me to be miserable.

In the 1980's Maryland's divorce laws were not based on "no-fault," and I was forced to hire a lawyer to defend myself. I would be forced to stay in Maryland. I couldn't possibly afford to live in California's economy until I received my part of the proceeds from our property settlement.

Jack had formally accused *me* of adultery. As I struggled to wrap my mind around the situation, I collapsed on the sectional sofa in the living room of my apartment. How had my life come to this? My son was in the military and rarely communicated, and Jennifer had no desire to establish any kind of meaningful bond with me. And I was about to start over as a single woman, at the age of forty-three.

Just then, I looked at the painting that had come to me—and from me—so mysteriously. It hung on the wall by the dining room doorway. My *light bulb* painting. It was simply there, larger than life. It had told me that I would be separated from all I'd ever known.

A dynamic was going on between me and these signs. Like a red light at an intersection conveys a message to stop, or a female silhouette on a public door identifies a woman's bathroom, the images in my light bulb painting spoke to me.

My future would unfold as it was meant. Once again, all-knowing wisdom within me was at work. I was learning to trust in something—something that felt so familiar, yet so unknown.

Coming back to the present, I pushed myself up from the sofa, put on my leather gloves, reached for my shoulder bag and focused my attention on the concerns and appointments of the day ahead.

One day at a time. I reminded myself. I would re-invent myself; one day at a time…I would create a new life.

CHAPTER 6

Signposts in the Dream

O ne Friday evening, months after I had moved into my apartment and after a long work day, I felt quite weary. I treated myself to a salad and a glass of wine at The Plantation, our town's only real country club. I couldn't afford an entire dinner there, but I craved the comfort of the serene beauty and the luxurious surroundings. I was pleasantly surprised by the company of Jason, the piano player, who came over to my table during his break. I had met him when Jack and I had been there for dinner. He and his wife owned the most successful florist business in town. His wife had filed for divorce but he was trying hard to save his marriage, if only for his little twelve-year-old girl.

He sang many of the ageless romantic jazz songs I liked, and I shared with him my love for singing. At the end of the evening he took a chance on me and he asked me to sing *Blue Moon* with him. We were quite good for not having rehearsed. I loved it! I sang modestly; I knew we harmonized well and the guests liked us. He invited me back for the next weekend. What an unprecedented high this was for me. I finally had the chance to experience openly the pleasure that singing gave me.

These were the first really happy moments I'd had for longer than I could remember, possibly ever—and it was the dream I'd held when I married Jack...to sing with him at the piano. Jason suggested that I come to his house where he had a grand piano and drawers and drawers of music so we could practice together. It never occurred to me what my presence at Jason's house would look like to others.

Having attended a liberal women's college, I thought that in the 1980's the emerging women's movement had ended the old double standard in the minds of most people. Or, so I thought. I could not have been more wrong.

Jason made it very plain that he was committed to reconciling his marriage, and I wasn't attracted to him in a romantic way. Besides, I was still in the painful fog of ending my own marriage. I felt safe with him. We enjoyed a lighthearted friendship and I was actually laughing again. It was so good in my otherwise deadly serious life to have a friend with whom I could play and sing.

Friday nights became our regular practice nights. I looked forward to them like a child waiting for Santa Claus. I could release my problems and anxieties in song for those few hours. Jason never drank; he said he had given up alcohol years ago. "Singin' and drinkin' don't mix with the old vocal chords." So we drank Diet Coke and coffee, and we laughed and sang into the night.

A few weeks later I got a call from another longtime friend of mine, Jill, who herself had recently gone through a tumultuous divorce, and now worked with me in the same real estate office.

"Have you heard about what Jack is doing? I just talked to Jean, you remember, my friend who teaches at Middletown Middle School? There's a big rumor coming from Jack, and it's all over the schools. At lunch in the faculty room, Jack showed a bunch of photos he had taken of you and Jason coming out of Jason's house...and he had written filthy stuff on the back side of each one!"

"Oh, my God!"

"But, that's not all!" Jill said breathlessly. "That S.O.B. has been stalking you for over a month and a half! He showed the whole faculty detailed notes that he kept on a calendar for every single day—your every move, Gracie! Especially every time you went to the club or to Jason's house. He's tryin' to make you look like some kind of slut! The whole faculty was astounded that he would do such a thing—and that he would show everyone!"

"Oh, no!"

"The principal came in and sent him home! He told him to stay there until he could get a grip on himself."

The phone grew heavy in my hand. My knees threatened to buckle. I ended our conversation and barely managed to get the receiver back in its cradle on the wall. I collapsed on the sofa and sobbed. What more does he want? What is wrong with him?

Had I done the wrong thing? I should never have started all this. My old patterns of guilt welled up. He is so messed up inside. Should I have stayed with him? Tried to help him? Stuck it out? Just as I was starting to feel paralyzed, I caught myself. No! That was the old Grace. I fought off my old guilt. If he could have been helped, it would have already happened. I tried. You can't help someone who doesn't want help.

The next morning, before I could call Jason to warn him about Jack's absurd behavior, Jason called me. Jack had talked to Jason's wife accusing Jason and me of having an affair. My heart sank. I felt so sad for Jason. I also knew I would miss singing with him because I had begun to count Friday nights to lift my spirits. "I'm so sorry you're involved in all of this Jason. You took a chance on being my friend and now look at what has happened. I guess we shouldn't get together again."

"I'll be damned if I'll let them dictate how I run my life," he snapped. "I told her we're just friends and nothin' was goin' on. We haven't done anything wrong...and even if anything was goin' on between us, it's none of their goddamn business!" That was the first time I'd ever heard him swear, especially regarding his wife. He still loved her.

"Well, if you're willing to ignore them, I can too."

"See you Friday," Jason said. "Don't worry, I know how to handle myself. I've met up with a few tough guys in my day. We'll get through this."

The next Friday, Jason finished his last dinner set at the club by nine o'clock, and I met him at his house at ten. Singing with Jason wasn't quite the same that night. I was a little on edge, and he didn't seem his usual self. But, as the evening progressed, the music lifted our spirits, and we were soon back in old form. We sang our favorite songs for two hours. I found myself snatching glances at the clock, becoming a little nervous. The idea of Jack, hovering outside Jason's house, unnerved me. Surely, after the scandal he'd caused, he wouldn't try again. But, I kept imagining him beyond the window in the black night.

Before midnight, I succumbed to my skittishness and decided to leave. Jason insisted on walking me to my car, which I had parked in his garage. I got into the driver's seat. Just as Jason lifted the garage door, a car in the alley across the street facing the garage blasted a beam of light at us, illuminating the garage.

"Hey lov'ah-boy, what'cha doin'?" shouted a voice from the car.

"It's Jack," I called out to Jason, shaking. "And it's late so he's probably been drinking! There's no telling what he might do. If I called the police, like that night my father beat me and the police came, I was afraid of what Jack might do after they were gone.

"Slide over," Jason ordered. "I'll drive. I know somethin' bout losin' idiots like him. I did a little race car drivin' in my earlier days." I sat frozen as he jammed my Volvo into reverse and screeched out of the garage and down a county road in a different direction than I would have gone. Oh, God, no! Jason's taking us to the back roads. If Jack does catch up with us, there will be no one to help us or be an eyewitness to Jack's behavior.

I looked ahead at the pitch-black road and then back at Jack's fast-in-pursuit white Pontiac. He was practically on our bumper. Why was he chasing us? What was he planning to do? Every turn Jason made, Jack made. Jason did a full U-turn in the middle of the road. So did Jack. My throat was so dry, I couldn't speak. If Jack was willing to endanger my life, what would happen next? Jason was now racing my beautiful car through cornfields!

"I know where I'm going," Jason shouted, as if reading my mind. "This field opens out to the highway. I think I can lose him in here." I didn't want to look anymore. I huddled down in the seat to keep from bouncing. Still, I rolled around like a sack of potatoes. I knew, if Jack wasn't enraged before he began to chase us, he was beyond control now. We must have driven every inch of that corn field, turning and twisting. Once, I thought we might tip over. It was surreal.

The front tires rolled up over a big dirt shoulder with a jerky thud—then the back tires. Suddenly, the ride smoothed out. We had made it to the highway. Jason glanced into the rearview mirror, the side mirrors, and back to the road ahead of us.

"I think we did it. I think we lost him."

Slowly, I inched my way back up into a sitting position. There were no lights. Oh, please don't let there be any lights. I checked the side mirror.

Then I saw it! The road sign! The road sign with the state highway number on it...144. The same sign had been in my vision at the mental hospital—twenty-two years ago! It was as if I had seen a movie preview and now it was time for its showing in the theater.

At that very moment, the glare of car lights reflected in the mirrors—and the glare was getting brighter. Within seconds, I could see the hood of Jack's Pontiac. But the road sign...that symbol appearing in the midst of my terror set off a sudden calmness within me. A deep quiet. For an instant, everything stopped. I had an unwavering sense of living my own destiny. Once again, I knew this horrendous time was supposed to occur. I knew that it was part of some plan larger than me, or my concerns. An unexpected strength energized me. Like a monolith—a marker from the unknown, this was a *signpost* radiating a message of assurance.

All at once, I knew what to do. "Jason," I said firmly, "Drive right into the center of town and down Market Street. There are lots of police cars patrolling there on Friday nights 'cause the kids are all out on the streets after the cafes close." Nodding his agreement, Jason veered onto the road that led into town.

Jack caught on to what we were doing. After we entered Market Street, he only followed us for a few blocks before he dropped out of sight. Still, we cruised in town for a good half hour just to be sure. Jason parked my car in my assigned space at my apartment, and he hurried me up the back three flights of stairs. He checked all of the rooms and the locks in my apartment before he made a call to the night desk at the local police station. They dispatched a patrol car to scout the area for a few hours. Satisfied, he gave me a big hug and assured me I was safe. "I'll catch a cab home. I'll be fine," he said. "Don't worry. Jack won't bother me. He only picks on girls."

I undressed for bed, still shaken and feeling like I had just stepped out of a crime report or a mystery novel. Seeing the actual road sign that I'd envisioned years ago in the mental hospital while fleeing from Jack in a frightening car chase gave the night an otherworldly dimension—like a dream. A dream of wonderment. The sublime and the ridiculous at once. After all that had happened I should have been terrified. I wasn't. I knew I was going to be all right.

I knew that other-worldly feeling. It had happened to me when, during a time of personal crisis, I'd first seen the evergreen trees lining Penny's driveway. This was not the first time I'd actually experienced something I had seen in my visions in the mental hospital. It had happened again. A *sign* along the road in the middle of a nightmare. A signpost of assurance from … a spirit? From God?

The next morning around 7:30, with orange juice in hand to revive me, I unbolted the kitchen door and pulled it open to let in the fresh morning air. A note was taped to the screen door. I grew cold and weak as I read it. "Eventually I will catch up with you, you …" The rest of what Jack had written was pure filth.

That was a beautiful, warm, Indian summer day. Dressed in a halter top and shorts, I took a book out to the deck to try and relax. Still drained and emotionally frayed from the events of the night before, I drifted off to sleep on a blanket. I thought I was dreaming when, out of nowhere, an image appeared over me. There stood an Asian girl, about twenty years old, dressed in an elegant, ornate, blue and green silk kimono. She looked like an angel. I sat up so fast I startled her. How could she have climbed the three flights of wooden stairs to my deck without hearing her?

"Please, madam, I only want to provide you with these beautiful scrolls for your pleasure. Do you care to purchase them for the beautification of your home and your life?" Her voice sounded airy and serene.

I blinked hard, checking my reality. Yes, I was awake. I could hardly talk. This was so unlikely. Our town was largely Caucasian, with a small African-American community on South Street. Rarely, if ever, did we see anyone of Asian heritage in our community. I was so startled, I didn't even consider saying no. I obediently pried myself off the floor and dashed in to get the twenty dollars she asked for, even though money was tight. She left as quickly as she'd arrived.

I stared at the scrolls, wondering what had just happened. Still lying on the deck where she left them, I observed the oriental landscape and other details of the twin bamboo grass wall hangings.

Featured on one was a broad, open pavilion built upon a lattice work of bamboo. In the center, a lone figure resembling a Buddhist monk sat meditatively at a table. Resting near him upon a broad corner of a porch railing was a fragile feminine figure. A light green shawl protected her arms which wrapped around her body, as it draped down over her long white skirt. Her gaze was directed somewhere far off into the distance, as though extending herself to the unknown for answers.

On the second scroll, the same female figure crossed a small foot bridge that led from one shore to another. The bridge connected to a path that led into a cozy, green fenced yard and continued on to a charming, simple dwelling. The gate of the fence was wide open. It appeared, looking at the scrolls side by side, that this lovely female, after some contemplation, had made a purposeful decision. She had left the shore pictured on the first scroll, and was making her way on the second scroll to a place of comfort and protection.

As I took in these images, they spoke to me. I could see that they mirrored my own inner transition. In a similar, less dramatic way than my own painting, these scrolls proclaimed my subconscious realization that I had come to after finding the help of Al-Anon and counseling. *The realization that I was crossing a bridge. The* exchange between me and the scrolls affirmed that I was emerging from lifelong beliefs rooted in helplessness and hopelessness into brand-new possibilities.

For all of my childhood and all of my adult life, I had been a victim of oppression and my own disempowered thinking. Yet, even in the face of what had gone on during the last few days, I had not let fear and uncertainty lead me back to my old, victimized ways of thinking and being. Not only had I found the courage to leave Jack, but I was leaving that world of helpless thinking behind, too.

Those simple scrolls came to me in such an unexpected way and they visually heralded my emerging strength from a new place of self-worth. *A spirit marker! They* confirmed my transformation; they inspired me to forge ahead. They validated my spirit!

I loved the symbolism of crossing a bridge, leaving the old and going on into new vistas, new opportunities, and a new me. With deeply felt assurance, I immediately hung them in my long hallway, in the glow of a bank of light-filled windows where I could enjoy them each day.

That evening proved to also be amazing. Jane, my counselor friend, invited me to Bushwaller's, a trendy restaurant in town, to meet an artist friend, Beth, who had come to market her work. The evening was filled with lively conversation, laughter and a little wine, and it was good medicine for me. It took my mind off the bizarre last few days.

As we chatted with our coffee, Jane asked, "Did you know that Beth is psychic?" That made me a little uncomfortable; I'd had enough mystery in the last few months. And, even though I rarely thought about Daddy's fanatical religious ranting, his warnings had made me skeptical of the claims of "charlatans."

"Yes, Grace," Beth said softly, almost intimately. "I feel I must tell you that I have a very strong feeling about you that I shouldn't ignore. I'd like to give you a book to read. It could be central to your path in life."

My path in life? I mostly focused on getting through each day, but her comment prompted me to consider that I might indeed be on a path. I didn't know why, or exactly where the path would take me, but I longed to be led. And I knew where I wanted to be taken. I wanted to once again feel the innocence, the beauty that had come to me in my kaleidoscopic visionary world at the age of twenty-two.

"Stop back at Jane's with me before you go home and I'll get it for you. It's among the things I packed up from my apartment when I lived here. Jane's been keeping them for me."

Later, dressed in my warm flannel nightgown, I sat down on the edge of my bed and scanned the cover of the book with confused curiosity: *Man and His Symbols* by Carl G. Jung.

I was somewhat familiar with Carl Jung's work from college. A colleague of Freud's, he had written twenty-two volumes of his theories on everything from symbols to synchronicity. The later term he coined in reference to the experience of unlikely events occurring together by chance, yet coming together in a meaningful way. In my psychology classes I had been especially drawn to his innovative ideas…synchronicity, as well as the concept of a collective consciousness shared by all humanity. For some reason, these ideas had unusually inspired me at the time. I could still recall the very moment when Dr. Powell introduced Jung's term, *collective consciousness.* I stopped hearing the next part of his lecture. The words struck a chord and caused a deep stirring within me. Like a vaguely familiar memory.

And then came a faint memory of a quotation of Jung's that Dr. Powell had often used. Something about symbols being a psychological way to change or transform the process of thought. "Symbols are the psychological mechanism for transforming energy." Yes, that was it. I jotted it down in the front of the book to be sure I would remember it. I scooted back on the bed and leaned against my propped up pillows to think about Jung's statement.

A psychological *mechanism?* So did that mean that anything considered as a symbol held the potential to alter or change thinking? And *energy* is a process or evolution of understanding in one's mind?

I paused at one example in Jung's book. A picture of a king who had fallen ill. It read, "...a common symbolic image of emptiness and boredom." Reading on, I realized that Jung believed that for some, the picture could conjure a suppressed emotion or a memory from the *subconscious* mind and make a connection in the *conscious* mind, thus stimulating a greater understanding or awareness about something that might be going on in one's life. I couldn't help but think of the scrolls I had just hung and what they meant to me—how they seemed to declare something taking place within me.

Jung also believed that we need not regard ourselves as simply *one-dimensional* beings, but rather beings of *multiple dimensions*. Was there knowledge held in our subconscious mind that could be accessed by the conscious mind—through symbols?

I thought of the beautiful kaleidoscopic light and images that had come to me years ago. Had they been lodged in my subconscious? Had they *always* been there? That experience definitely felt like being in another dimension. Suddenly, I had a moment of clarity. That is *exactly* what seemed to have happened to me with my own painting—the one of the lamp with the bare light bulb. Perhaps *that* had been from my subconscious mind. It had certainly projected meaning to me. Somehow, as I had absorbed the image emerging on the canvas in front of me, it had expressed an inner knowledge, a wisdom rooted within me...within my own subconscious. The art had stimulated my conscious mind. Even though the message of eventual separation had been difficult to accept, its presence had lifted my spirit. The symbolic art emotionally supported me at a traumatic time in my life—my separation from all that I thought I knew. And yet, when the transition had been completed, I knew my spirit had been lifted and supported through it by this previous "aha" moment.

I had had a *light bulb moment*! I laughed aloud at the connection. What a coincidence that my painting was of a lamp with a bare light bulb! My light bulb moment had provided the power to give me courage when it was needed. Just like the decorative scrolls, my own painting had been a spirit marker. A signpost of assurance along the way. Assurance that separation from Jack was for my own good. I was actually being released into a better place in life than I had ever been, in spite of the stumbling blocks I experienced while living through the waiting period for the divorce.

But *why* was this happening? And why was it happening to *me?* Where would the symbols lead me? So, what is this thing we call the subconscious? What does subconscious mean? How does the subconscious know anything? Am *I* pre-programmed? If so, by whom or what? And also, why, as a young woman, was I given glimpses of another world dimension? Why was I allowed to see things that actually came into my life experience?

Am I special? Am I different?

What would happen if I talked about this to other people? Would they think I was crazy?

Am I crazy?

These were all very personal and important questions.

I thumbed idly through my Jung book. Were the answers there? Weary from the stress of the last few days and mellowed by Merlot at dinner, I found further exploration too much of a challenge to my already overtaxed brain. I placed the book on the night stand beside my bed and succumbed to the warmth of my cozy comforter.

CHAPTER 7

The Dream Becomes a Nightmare

It was June already, four months since I had left Jack. I had been struggling to make a living in real estate, but it was becoming harder than ever. The country remained in a recession and by then mortgage interest rates had risen to twenty-two percent. There were few buyers and even fewer houses on the market. It was obvious I was going to have to do something to supplement my income until I received my divorce settlement. I called my lawyer every few weeks, but nothing seemed to be moving. "We can't do anything except itemize a list of the mutual property, unless he changes his mind. Only then could the longer waiting period be waived." I knew there was little to no chance of that happening. Jack had complete control.

Then came the letter from Bank of America. It informed me that I owed sixty-nine dollars every month until the government student loan for my college education of fifteen thousand dollars was paid off! This payment had always come out of Jack's and my household money. "Yes, but only your signature is on the loan, Mrs. Cadwell," the loan officer said. "You are the only one liable for repayment."

And then I remembered. When the loan was set up, Jack had said, "You're into women's lib...you sign it. You don't need me." And I did. How dumb! How gullible! How devious! And to think, our family income had paid for his master's degree and many academic credits beyond! I had even worked in the summers to supplement our income because I felt guilty about taking money out of our account to pay for school—plus, that time in school could have been used for making money.

That was the last straw. I needed to do something else. I decided to apply for what I had been trained to do—a teaching position. But, my certification had expired. In Maryland, teachers were required to update their certificates with additional credits every two years. I had to go back to Hood College for six more credits. I could do it in one summer, but that meant I needed tuition money. In the past two months, I had not seen or been contacted by Jack. Maybe he had cooled down. Maybe I could reason with him and sway him to understand my position. He might at least consider loaning me the money. I stewed for two days. Finally, swallowing my pride and breaking the silence, I nervously picked up the receiver.

"Nope, I got bills to pay. No one's givin' me any handouts. Why should I give it to you? So you can gadabout?"

Nothing was going to change his mind. I quickly ended the conversation so as not to provoke him. My anger mounted. A large lump was building in my throat. In fact, it was there most of the time now. I missed the lighthearted release of singing with Jason. After Jack's last episode of stalking and the car chase, he had succeeded in making it simply not worth it. Jason and I had decided to discontinue our singing.

Two weeks later, through some divine providence, I sold a townhouse that I had listed. I received both the listing and the selling commissions. Thankfully, it covered tuition and living expenses through the summer. Since returning to school was necessary, I registered at Hood for two classes that could also be applied to a master's degree program in counseling. It was hard. I had little motivation. I didn't want to teach. I wanted to leave Maryland. I longed to return to California. I felt as though I'd slipped into a void. I didn't miss Jack, but I missed my children.

The children had each responded differently when they heard the news of our separation. Jennifer did not seem surprised. I think she had already begun to get a sense of what was happening when she learned I had moved out to stay at Mona's for six weeks. Her reaction was to console both parents. I could see she went to great lengths not to take sides. She was already making her life. I took comfort that she had Amy, her best girlfriend, to confide in, even if Jennifer and my communication was not at all what I wanted it to be.

On the other hand, I knew David would take it hard. I exaggerated the necessity for him to come home, and he took a ten-day emergency leave from the Air Force. I stressed how much I needed him. I was sure that to be present and to experience the transition himself would help him to adjust to this life-altering change in his world. He had been gone for the best part of three years. Even though it was very hard for him, he, too, tried not to take sides. I felt mournful for my children. I believed I had failed them, but I had to save myself. Neither one ever made me feel wrong or bad about leaving their father.

I had left our home without any of my books. I really needed some of them as resources now that I was back in school. It took almost a month for Jack to agree to give them to me. I was grateful that David was willing to help. He hauled them over to me in his car; five cardboard boxes filled to the brim. Fondly, and with renewed enthusiasm, I started to sort through my old paper friends. I temporarily stored them on the floor in the giant shared-tenant garage. It was nearly dusk and the high, narrow windows near the sixteen-foot ceiling of the enormous garage let in beams of light, illuminating floating particles of dust in the air. As I opened the first book, I found three small notes tucked randomly among the pages.

So, Dearie, how does it feel to be the town whore? Did you get a little last night? Did you give him a blow job? How many dudes did you ride? Bet-cha sucked....

I crumpled the paper and threw it across the garage floor like a snake that had bitten me. The next note: Was he big enough for you, you cunt? Now you're getting what you always wanted. You always wanted it, didn't you, you bitch? Did he pay ya before or....

I tore it to shreds. I tore the next one without reading it. Obsessed, I grabbed another book—four notes in that one. Feeling crazed, I shook open book after book, holding them upside down, front and back cover in each hand, and let the notes fall to the ground, unread. Every book contained his filthy thoughts! Five cardboard boxes! How long must it have taken him to do this? He had to have spent night after night scrawling out these defiling accusations. I wondered what his teaching colleagues would think of him if they knew.

My heart turned to stone in my chest. Of everything that he had done in betrayal of our marriage since I'd left him, somehow this hit me the hardest. I felt so dirty. Is this what he is saying about me? Is this what others think of me? I was horrified. Shaken to the core, my knees started to buckle. I stood in the middle of a sea of boxes. The garage gripped me, cavernous and cold. I had never felt so isolated, so alone. Was he trying to drive me crazy? The pain of my thoughts became unbearable. I couldn't focus on the reality of what had taken place. In a silent stupor, I stumbled in slow motion between the boxes. A painful realization was coming to me. I couldn't do this alone anymore. I have to find a way to get help for myself.

"Grace, I'm so glad you came in to see me again," my therapist Denise said, after I revealed only a small portion of Jack's crazed behavior since our separation. "We won't worry about the financial part right now. You can pay me after the divorce is settled, because you can't go through this alone—you can't go through this alone." I collapsed into a heap and sobbed. A tidal wave of pent-up hurt, anger, confusion, and fear gushed out of me. I had found an ally. She understood. My attorney had brushed it off while reminding me I was the one who had left the home.

At Denise's recommendation, I enrolled with Marjorie in an eight-week social services course that focused on the hidden effects of alcohol on relationships. I went back to the Al-Anon group as well. The perspectives I gained from counseling and these supportive groups over the next year and a half became the very substance and sustenance of my life.

I never would have thought of myself as *battered,* a term just beginning to be known and used in the 1980's. It seemed to me then that this kind of label could not be part of an educated, middle-class, "white-collar" family. Denise helped me to see clearly the patterns of verbal, emotional, physical and sexual abuse that were Jack's ways of intimidating me in an attempt to gain and keep control. Our marriage had been so much more complicated than just a rocky relationship, which was the way I had viewed it. I remembered what a break through it was for me, at the Al-Anon group, when it became evident that so many aspects of my troubled life were also being experienced by people from every walk of life.

Alcohol is often a big factor but the substance is only the symptom, Denise explained. The batterer's behavior was often the result of the denial of a deeper cause, and the batterer typically sufferers from low self-esteem and insecurity. Letting his anger build up until he exploded, being unwilling to talk things out, being set in his ways, having negative and inflexible views of the world, and demanding sex as an act of aggression, were all faulty attempts by Jack to maintain his self esteem and to feel powerful by controlling me.

I was completely reevaluating my perspective on how I saw him—and most of all, how I saw myself. Like the woman in my scrolls, I was finding the courage to keep on walking. Walking across that bridge into the unknown, trusting that my life would get better.

I was learning to have respect for myself for my past efforts. Even though I might have acted on flawed reasoning, I saw that I had possessed the strength to adhere to my standards and values. I'd extended myself, trying to prop up our marriage, including giving up a promising career. By taking a newly-educated look at my own dysfunctional behavior and that of those around me, I could release guilt and shame that I'd carried all of my life for as far back as I could remember.

Denise helped me to see the strength within myself as I had gone through it all. Over the following months of counseling and guided introspection, I realized I was giving birth to a new me. This was a *new dimension.* A new dimension of me. And I was uplifted daily with soothing reassurance as I walked past the two scrolls in my sunny hallway before I went out into the world. I was indeed crossing a bridge into a new world. Just looking at those scrolls gave me courage.

By August, when my summer school classes were finally finished, I had managed to rally myself enough to earn good grades.

Now, as I looked forward to a full-time teaching position, I knew I could earn an adequate income and lower my stress while I waited for time to pass.

I began to search for a teaching position, but encountered cool reception. From all my old connections in education, I received only vague responses expressing uncertainty about any possibilities of a teaching position.

One day on my way out of the educational administration building where I had dropped off paperwork for a job application, I ran into my friend, Mona. Life had been so complicated I hadn't seen much of her since the day she invited Jane and me to lunch and they confessed what they knew about Jack's extramarital activities. Upon hearing my plight, she invited me to go for coffee.

"Grace, I didn't want to tell you, but when you withdrew from our bridge group after you two separated, Jack stayed. He kept bringing other women to take your place. He solicited everyone's pity, blowing up the story that he had been abandoned! And he took every chance he got, as only he could, to make you look like a cheap you-know-what. I defended you, but some of the guys wanted to believe it. They're such damned chauvinists!"

Those "guys" in my bridge group included the superintendent, assistant superintendent, and controller of the board of education, along with a few very influential teachers. I had done what I thought was proper by withdrawing from the *couples* bridge group once we separated. But Jack had stayed. It was the same group that I had cajoled and coaxed him to be part of—I had begged him to learn to play bridge and now I had been blackballed by my own husband.

With only two weeks left until school began, I needed a job. In a stormy act of utter fury, I made an appointment, dressed in my best suit, and marched into a meeting with my former friend, Doug Koinst, the assistant superintendent of schools. I decided to tell him a little about the other side of Jack. I gambled, hoping he would believe me and not Jack. Then, I did just what I didn't want to do. I began to cry. Nevertheless, he appeared to be quite sympathetic and insisted that he and his wife were there for me. He said he would see what he could do.

By the time school started, I had a half-day job teaching English to alternative classes of seventh-grade boys who had a third grade reading level. These children had been significantly unsuccessful in the mainstream classroom and had been tested and identified mostly as aphasic, dyslexic and attention deficit disorder students. Since special education students were just starting to be given separate programs, these boys had not received help earlier and had developed extreme behaviors, acting out to divert attention away from their inadequacies. I never knew which of my long-haired, Led Zeppelin, tee-shirt-clad boys with their key chains dangling between their front and back pockets were drug-free. It was a job no one else wanted and I earned half the salary I was expecting. I would need to stay in real estate part-time, as well.

I opened my classroom at 7:30 a.m., taught until noon, grabbed a quick lunch, then spent six to eight hours in The Olde Towne Realty office showing properties or doing paperwork. I wrote lesson plans for my classes after I got home. It was exhausting. I had transferred my real estate license to a brokerage that represented Sotheby's, and I specialized in homes in the Historical District in the hope of tapping into a little bit of that upscale business.

That summer I sold two condominiums, netting only three percent commission for a new home sale, rather than the usual six percent for resale homes. I also sold one Federal-style historical townhouse, for which I had to reduce my commission—something we all were doing in order to close a sale. The real estate market, like the country's economy, continued to spiral downward.

Sitting on my phone stool in my kitchen, my daughter announced with a big grin that she and Steven, whom she had been dating for two years, were going to be married. I could feel her expectation that I would be thrilled. Since she had moved to Baltimore, I had seen very little of her. I was really happy that it would mean we would be together again for a little while to plan her wedding. But it was a bittersweet challenge. Like every mother, I had always wanted her wedding to be a memorable and harmonious time of joy. For me, it was the worst time ever to meet the emotional demands of planning a wedding. Not to mention trying to coordinate something with Jack. However, the hardest part was that it brought back all of the hope and expectations I'd had when I'd married Jack.

But her wedding wasn't about me. It was about Jennifer. It was the end of the summer, and they had set the date for the last week of September.

Gathering every ounce of energy and spirit I had, I launched into the plans. We agreed that she would handle the money end of it with her dad, and I would help her do all the rest. His financial contribution turned out to be quite sparse, and once again my good and creative friends, Jane, Jill, and Mona pitched in to help.

Jennifer decided upon a beautiful state park chapel in the woods. She talked her dad into splurging on a long, white-lace gown, with a flattering sweetheart neckline and a Southern belle brimmed hat. A very beautiful young woman, she looked absolutely gorgeous. My friends and I planned and prepared a sumptuous buffet for about sixty guests that would follow the ceremony. I braced myself to make it a happy occasion for Jennifer's sake. I knew it would bring Jack and me together for the first time in over a year and a half.

I met him with a simple greeting. He ignored me, as though I hadn't spoken.

The ceremony was simple, as Jennifer wanted, and it was truly lovely. After the reception and dinner, the guests all gathered outside at the bottom of the stairs to shower the newlyweds with rice from their handmade net pouches. Jack was not among them. This was a time of jubilation, the moment of well-wishing and a joyous farewell—how could he not be there for her? I saw her side glances as she searched the crowd.

When Jennifer and Steven drove away, I returned to the hall to take part in the long cleanup ahead. I wasn't sure what I was seeing when I spied something covering the back of one of the folding chairs beside the buffet table. As I moved closer, it became pathetically evident. Draped with intentional flare over the chair was Jack's tuxedo. A silent, brazen statement. I knew it was his dramatic way of saying he had done his duty and that's all I would ever get from him.

Later, I opened my apartment screen door long after midnight when everything from the wedding had been cleaned up and put back in its place. A note fell to the floor. It was another threatening note from Jack. "You will never get any fuckin' money—or anything else—out of me."

Filing for a restraining order against him was not an option—Jack always had a way of getting around boundaries. I would be living in greater fear. Besides, it wouldn't change the three-year waiting period until the disillusionment of the divorce.

I did finally get a full-time teaching assignment that next fall. I assumed it was because my references had been good. I had created some innovative teaching situations with my seventh-grade boys, including writing pen pal letters to seniors in an assisted living center. We even got our whole group's picture in the paper when I took them to the senior center to meet their pen pals. Still, the salary was low as I had lost my tenure when I had retired. I was back at the bottom of the pay scale. Ironically, my new teaching job turned out to be in the very same elementary school that my own children had attended, only three miles away from our Meadow Crest home.

The job was literally an unprecedented challenge. Waverly Elementary had become a mainstreaming school for students who had graduated from Rock Creek, a newly-built, experiential facility for severely handicapped students. I was being asked to teach a pilot project. Instead of students coming in rotation each hour like the rest of the classes, I would have the same thirteen mainstreaming, severely handicapped students for the entire day. In handicap identifications, they ran the gamut from mildly autistic to Down Syndrome, to severely hyperactive, aphasic, learning disabled and emotionally disturbed. I had to develop four reading groups, three math groups, and try to create social studies and science projects to target the interests of the majority. Even recess duty was up to me. And I was assigned only a part-time aide.

I wanted to believe I was given this assignment because I was an experienced teacher. Deep down however, I suspected it was just another assignment that no one else wanted.

Even though I had threaded myself in and out of some completely fatiguing situations, I had not known the true meaning of exhaustion until then. I was depressed and tired when I went to bed, and I was tired and depressed when I woke up. I lived for the weekends to be with Jane and a few friends I had made in my office at Olde Towne Realty. I had very little time or energy to be involved in real estate. I was isolated five days a week with my desperately needy students. They were expecting me to create miracles. My body ached from stress. I was becoming chronically ill. By November, I was on my third bout with strep with many more rounds of penicillin.

Profoundly weary, I was further devastated being caught in the vice grip from Jack delaying my divorce.

My teaching position was one of those administrative plans that looked good on paper, but it could not have been carried out with less than ten students and two full-time aides. I was obliged to become a glorified babysitter. I tried my best, but the low level of achievement, compared to the endless amount of preparation and time I was investing took its toll.

When the ear, nose and throat doctor insisted I get my tonsils removed or face a more dangerous strep disorder, Type A, I followed his advice. At the age of forty-five, I decided to use the spring break that next February to have a tonsillectomy.

Returning to my classroom was like entering an alien planet. I loved my students and had strong empathy for their severe needs, but it had become evident to me and my supervisors during the previous months that the pilot program was not working. No matter what techniques or strategies I tried for my severely handicapped students, their low level of aptitude for achievement, combined with multiple needs inappropriately grouped together in one classroom, had brought my students and me little to no success or sense of satisfaction. I felt deeply frustrated.

Still, since it was only mid-year and major curriculum changes were not made until the fall, I was duty-bound to cope with the arrangement that had been set up along with the impossible expectations. Throughout my day, there was no one to relate to about my concerns. There was no time to connect and share my problems with my colleagues. I was isolated in one room with a small adjoining playground where I also ate my lunch. I knew I was a good teacher, but no one could have met this challenge. These kids needed a miracle, and so did I. Some of the faculty expressed their condolences from time to time as I stood with the children while they boarded their buses. I felt their unvoiced relief that it was me, and not them. Trapped in a downward spiral, I didn't know where to turn.

CHAPTER 8

A Dream Ends

It was a dismal Sunday morning in March, and so far I'd spent the entire weekend in bed—not the first time. It was nearly two and a half years since my separation from Jack, and still no divorce settlement. My physical strength returned slowly after the tonsillectomy, and I had to force myself to eat. But my despair deepened.

Despondent and angry, I threw back the bed covers, grabbed a pillow, and flung it to the floor in frustration. I sank back onto the bed, opened my arms and extended my legs. In that moment, I felt drained of energy and hope. As I stared at the ceiling, I wanted to surrender. To surrender to something, but what?

My gaze searched the ceiling until my eyes fixed on a point at the upper right-hand corner where the wall met the ceiling. A corner—similar to the one I'd stared into twenty years earlier when I was suddenly drawn to the ecstasy of the kaleidoscopic light that night on the couch in our converted barracks apartment at the age of twenty-two.

I no longer feared the memory. Neither did I feel tempted to abandon myself and slip through the cracks as I had done before. Yet, I ached for the deep peace that I'd once found in that light. In that place of serenity, I had become aware of joy. I knew that was the real me.

The real me possessed no body. In that reality I experienced no concerns. I had no judgments or bad feelings. Fears disappeared. I just was. Would I ever feel like that again? Could I ever in my lifetime experience that harmonious feeling?

My sadness deepened until it was unbearable. I forced myself to move. Turning over, I drew up the bed covers. Resting my head on two pillows, I impulsively turned on the TV and mindlessly flipped through the channels. Sunday morning... television evangelists! They reminded me of Daddy as he wailed Bible quotes, hurling his message of damnation and pious platitudes at us.

I found a program broadcast from California. I left it there, I think, because I loved California so much. The congregation was singing "Love Lifted Me," an old hymn Mama used to sing while she cooked. She couldn't really sing. She wailed, but I found comfort in her occasional spurts of inspiration.

A white-haired minister announced that his ministry was based on Dr. Norman Vincent Peale's principles of the power of positive thinking. I was familiar with Dr. Peale's philosophy, having been drawn to the simplicity and optimism of his teachings. So much so that I'd made it a point to attend Dr. Peale's church in New York when Jack and I had chaperoned one of his graduating classes on their senior field trip to the "Big Apple."

"Tough times don't last, but tough people do," the minister began. His words flowed over me like salve to my wounded heart. Tears filled my eyes, and I stayed to listen as he spoke about, "How You Can Have the Power to Cope." What timing. I knew it was trite, but I felt as though his message had been designed for me.

"What are the deepest needs in human life?" he asked. "Let me tell you. Sigmund Freud said the will to pleasure or sensuality is the primary stimulus of the human life. You might define it in erotic terms, or other terms of sensuality, but sensuality is a profound need. Freud called it the ultimate need. Adler came along and said, 'No, Freud, it's not true. More than the will to pleasure is the will to power. The need to be in control and up at bat is the deepest need." He paused, and smiled. "Now, Viktor Frankl says it's not the will to pleasure, or the will to power. He asserts that the deepest human need is *the need to see meaning in what you are doing.*"

These references took me back to my favorite class in college—psychology of personality. Viktor Frankl's theory and model of therapy were a result of his horrific experiences and imprisonment in Nazi death camps.

"To live a day of life and see no meaning in it, no purpose in it, is dreadful," the minister continued. "One man told me life is so meaningless, it's like sticking a finger in a bucket of water and then pulling it out again; there's no hole left afterward! 'I feel I could die today,' he said, 'and no one would miss me. Life has no meaning.'

I looked away. I gazed out the window and down to the street. Cars cruised by. A couple holding hands ambled along the sidewalk, carrying cups of Sunday morning coffee. Would anyone miss me? I wondered.

"I once said to Dr. Frankl," the minister continued, "even meaning is meaningless unless it feeds my self-esteem. Because the deepest need—deeper than sensuality, deeper than status or power, deeper than significance, is self-esteem. I must feel that I am worth something. And so do you. Our needs stem from our deep need to feel worthy."

These words were profoundly true for me. I needed to see purpose in what I did. I longed to feel worthwhile. I knew I was headed down a dangerously destructive path, to a totally meaninglessness existence. I had to do something to help myself.

"Turn your scars into stars," the minister advised.

By damn, I will!

In a flash, his timeless cliché stirred life within me. I called the number on the screen for a copy of his sermon. For three weeks, I read it repeatedly, working up the courage to face my situation and decide what it was that I needed to do to change it. Once again I had succumbed to low self-esteem. The minister's advice was sound. I determined to turn my life around—to find authenticity and meaning.

On the last day of March, I went to the board of education's administration building and filed the forms to submit my resignation. I had never viewed myself as a quitter. But I needed to save myself, and my life. I hungered for validation of myself, my life, my very existence. As I took this leap of faith, I knew I couldn't achieve any goal without confidence in myself—as a person and as a professional.

I committed to making a success in real estate despite the recession. I decided to trust myself. Each day the scrolls on my apartment wall reminded me that I was still crossing a bridge. They empowered me to believe that I would reach the other side. I determined I would not look back. I simply did what was necessary. I let the door close behind me.

A new door had opened. I'd made the right decision! Slowly and steadily, with a lot of legwork and telephone soliciting, I built my business. Within a few months I could meet my financial obligations—and purchase two new suits.

To my delight, I had reaped another gain—the satisfaction of meeting the needs of my clients and their families. I knew the town well, and I found it inspiring that I was making a difference by genuinely welcoming newcomers to our community. I became a one-woman tourist bureau for our quaint, newly-declared historical town, and I enjoyed going the extra mile to help my clients settle in. Even my broker, proud of my achievements with my clients, appointed me as a member of the board of realtors' ethics committee.

My sense of self-worth grew, nurturing me towards rebirth to discover newness of life. And each day, I continued to derive a concentrated dose of bravery from within the scroll images. By following my heart, I learned to trust myself and to nurture my own self-esteem.

It took me two weeks to secure an appointment with the attorney I'd hired over a year ago at the law offices of Spillman, Hanks & Wettle. I appealed to Jerry Spillman to move forward on the process. I urged him to put together whatever would be required to make the case to secure an equitable divorce agreement for what I rightfully deserved; for what I had helped to build and maintain during our marriage.

Jerry wasn't really interested. I could tell from our previous conversations that he had made up his mind I would be lucky to receive half of the value of our home and little else. He barely gave me his full attention. It had been two years and six months since I filed for a divorce from Jack. Only six months to go.

I hated that it had come to this. Why couldn't everything just be divided in half? How could Maryland divorce law be based on the assumption that our assets belonged to Jack because I had chosen to leave? Why should I be required to show just cause? In addition, I had to prove dire need and appear nearly destitute in order to receive any monetary award.

Early on a Friday afternoon, while on an errand to the courthouse to verify information on the deed of a land parcel I was negotiating for a client, I made a shocking discovery. As I stepped up to the counter to pick up the land document, Molly, the county clerk, commented innocently.

"Grace, I see your divorce trial was just posted on the docket. Are you anxious about that?"

"My divorce trial?" Completely stunned, I sputtered, "Oh—uh, well, I'm not exactly looking forward to it." I quickly recovered. I had by this time learned to carefully consider those with whom I shared confidential information.

What divorce trial? Jerry had led me to believe we would have a routine settlement in his office. What the hell was Jack up to now? I poked around until Molly was attending the next person in line so she wouldn't notice as I made my way to the posted courtroom calendar. There it was.

Jack Cadwell versus Grace Cadwell in the matter of matrimonial dissolution, on the 13th day of July, 1983. The Honorable Jacob Angleberger presiding.

Why the hell hadn't I been informed? Why was I paying a lawyer for every dammed phone call I made to him if he couldn't even call to notify me that Jack had managed to set up a divorce trial?

"It was just filed on Wednesday, Grace. There is a notice in the mail from our office. You should receive it by tomorrow," said my obviously irritated attorney, Jerry Spillman, when I called him from my kitchen phone.

"Why didn't you notify me right away? What are we going to do? How are you going to defend me? What does this mean? Why is there a trial happening now?"

"Come into my office on Monday morning around ten. We'll talk about it. I'm sorry, Grace, I have to be in court in ten minutes." He ended the call without waiting for my reply.

Immediately I called my friend, Jill, who worked with me at Olde Towne Realty. She always knew the latest scoop on everything.

"Good God, Grace!" she wailed. "Give me an hour. I'll call you back."

Forty-five minutes later the phone rang. "Well, Grace, it seems Jack and his cozy criminal trial lawyer, Nikirk, have cooked up a lawsuit to award Jack the house and his entire retirement pension." Jill's normally sultry voice sounded like a squeal and contained as much outrage as I felt.

She continued, "Get this! The scuttlebutt is that he just wants to get you on the witness stand so he can call you a whore in public. That's all he can talk about. The scum bucket is a weirdo, Grace. He's totally bonkers!"

As enraged as I was, I was not as shocked as I might have been a year ago. I'd come to understand this was Jack, and I doubted he would change. "What am I going do, Jill? I have to fight this."

"Why don't you go to family court and get a look at this judge. See how he operates. Use every trick you can find. When I went through my divorce, my lawyer told me that sometimes even little tricks like wearing white gloves can sway a judge's opinion—it makes you look innocent, even frail.

My God! My survival is dependent on white gloves! I fought for courage as I climbed the courthouse steps the next Monday afternoon. Just that morning my attorney had attempted to persuade me that he was doing his best. "Good news, Grace. The state of Maryland has repealed the three-year waiting period for involuntary separation. You don't have to wait any longer."

Great! After two and a half years, I don't have to wait. But what good is that if I don't have the money for a fresh start in California, and Jack is suing *me*? Then he said, "Well, we're going to have to show just cause for the charge of abandonment…and it's hard to counter with abuse charges unless you have witnesses. We'd have to prove that his actions compelled you to leave for your safety. Our best chance is to plead irreconcilable differences and hope for an even split on the house. But you shouldn't expect any of his accrued pension account. You know, Grace, if you take away a chunk of that, it won't even leave enough to bury him."

Livid, I shot back," Bury him! Bury *him*! Jerry, I'm going to need burying too one of these days. What about me? I thought it was a family budget. I managed and cared for his needs. I planned, designed, and artfully decorated our home which definitely created a greater market value on the property. I did my very best to care for the children, and, held a job while he got his Master's degree… and that accruing pension. I thought you were trying to help *me!*" I loathed the presumptuous concept of male entitlement.

Once inside the courthouse, I found the number of Judge Angleberger's courtroom on the daily roster and headed for the mahogany-paneled double doors of Courtroom Two. A clerk halted me, questioning me about my business there. I thought fast, and then lied, "I'm taking a course in legal proceedings at Hood College. I heard Angleberger is an excellent judge, and I just want to observe while he was presiding."

"He certainly is, honey, and you're welcome to stay. But if you really want to see a hot trial, you should come back in July. That Cadwell versus Cadwell case is gonna be a doozy."

"Thanks." I mumbled, turned on my heel, and walked out the door.

Numbly, I found my way back to my car. I couldn't wait to get out of there. This was worse than I'd thought. I felt like a witch from Salem, about to be burned at the stake. I knew then that I had to do something drastic.

The trial was nearly four months away. Two weeks later I met with my attorney. I appealed to him to help me compile some kind of evidence of Jack's maliciousness, or even of the slander and defamation of character I'd endured since leaving him. Jerry shuffled papers, barely looking up from his desk. He'd already made up his mind.

"Here's a copy of an appraisal we just received on your home." Jerry slid a document across his desk.

I immediately protested when I saw the figure. As a realtor, I knew what our house was worth. This appraisal was at least twenty-five thousand dollars undervalued—a significant sum relative to the price of homes in Maryland during the 1980's. "They claim the house is run down, even the deck is rotting," Jerry said. I guess he doesn't have a whole lot of money to fix it up; says he has to pay his lawyer." My blood boiled, making me stammer as I spoke.

Jack had built that deck and he could easily repair it himself in a day or two.

Then I realized why he'd let it rot. If I were awarded half of the appraised value, it would be half of a depleted value, not the true value. Would this insanity ever end?

"Jerry, I need evidence of this deterioration. I want to take photos to show he's doing this on purpose, and to prove he can do the repairs. Won't that at least show his deceitful intentions?"

"Grace, if you're asking my advice, I recommend against it. You would be trespassing."

"What are you talking about? My name is on the deed. That is my home, too."

"Yes, but you've officially 'abandoned the domestic domicile.'" He made quote signs in the air with his fingers. "You have established another residence."

"Yes, but that doesn't change the fact that my name is on the deed!"

My words fell on deaf ears. I left his office filled with rage, my high heels clicking with determination as I sprinted across the fountain plaza and the two blocks to Olde Towne Realty. My broker's office door was open. I walked in and sat down, as I often did whenever I needed his business advice. This, of course, was different business. Brady graciously listened to me.

"Brady! You are an appraiser. You could do an appraisal for me as part of my evidence, and I could take the photographs. You would be doing your job, and I would be the only one taking a chance. Besides, I would be afraid to enter the house alone. Jack might come home while I'm there."

It took Brady several days to give in to my pleas for help. "Set up the appointment with your husband and put it on my calendar," he said.

"I will," I lied. I didn't intend to tell Jack what I planned. He would never cooperate, and I would never get any pictures. I didn't like deceiving Brady, but I was desperate. I scheduled our visit for the late morning, because Jack should be at school teaching.

That morning, the closer we got to the house the colder my hands became. I nervously chattered to Brady, looking for any excuse to laugh. Tumultuous emotions simmered inside me. A sickening wave of nostalgia overcame me as I saw the yard where my children had played. Instead of the rich green landscape, the lawn looked unkempt with its large brown spots of dead grass. Beside the driveway an old wheelbarrow lay upside down atop a pile of gravel, alongside a disorderly pile of firewood. My flower bed beneath the kitchen window had deteriorated to dried weeds. This was not the home I remembered. The cedar siding, faded now, was in dire need of resealing.

As we neared the kitchen window I caught a glimpse of our spinet piano. A flashback brought back the night Jack had locked me out of the house—the same night he had discovered that I was attending Al-Anon meetings. He sat at the piano, his scotch perched on a corner, playing my favorite songs, completely ignoring me as I knocked calling out to him from the front porch. I had spent that night at a friend's house.

I wanted to turn and run. I really didn't want to go back into that house again. But, I'd come this far, and I would do whatever it took to help myself.

Brady lifted the manually-operated garage door and an irrational image swept over me of poisonous bats flying out into our faces. Suddenly, the truth hit me. I was actually afraid to go back into my own home. Brady turned the knob to open the door into the kitchen. It was unlocked. Oh, thank God!

But of course, why would he keep the kitchen door into the garage locked? Jack wouldn't expect me to do anything as gutsy as this. I went straight through the living room to the deck, and it was worse than I imagined. Several boards had nearly rotted through, and the neglected redwood was ashen gray. I began to photograph anything and everything. We worked our way through the bedrooms and headed downstairs. The family room carpet was dingy and frayed. I stared at the mammoth floor to ceiling stone fireplace Jack had built and remembered the family time capsule we had all compiled and buried inside the hearth; mementos from each of the four of us along with a newspaper to mark the date. My heart wrenched, and I swallowed back the tears threatening to choke me.

I moved on to our master bedroom. I stopped in my tracks. There on my long mahogany dressing table was a nine by 12 inch framed picture of a brunette woman with short dark hair. Definitely not me. It was surrounded by hair curlers and makeup. Beside the bed were two undeniably feminine fuzzy pink slippers. Swallowing hard, I snapped picture after picture, taking duplicates just to make sure. I didn't miss anything.

As I made my way into the bathroom, I almost missed it. Indisputable evidence that Jack was involved in a sexual relationship with another woman. A light blue, lacy night gown dangled from a hook. I felt like some shabby actor in a B-movie as I snapped three pictures of the thing. What had I come to?

I didn't know how much weight those pictures would have, but if he intended to try to discredit me, I could counter his accusations with his adultery.

I didn't show the pictures in advance to Jerry, my attorney. I'd lost all confidence in him. I waited for the day of the deposition, a time set up by the court for each of our attorneys to meet along with the two of us to take our testimony. It was part of protocol as a final attempt at an out-of-court settlement.

The deposition was on May 29, at 11:00 a.m. I didn't know what to expect. I awoke feeling a heavy blanket of darkness encapsulating me. Ironically, a solar eclipse was to take place at 11:59 a.m. that same day. Even the earth was going to block out the light. I dreaded having to come face to face with Jack again. I hadn't seen him since Jennifer's wedding. But I needn't have worried. Jack and his lawyer were already there when I arrived, and they had chosen to remain cloistered in an adjoining room.

Jerry sat slumped behind a small table in our appointed conference room. It soon became evident that he was resigned to go to trial. I reached into my purse and pulled out the white envelope that held my entire defense strategy. I arranged each picture on the table. He sat upright. "Where on earth did you get these?"

"I did what you told me *not* to do. I took them."

"I don't think I want to know any more," he said, scooping them up. "Wait here. I'll be back."

It seemed like hours, when in twenty minutes he finally burst into the room. "Well, I did it," he said breathlessly. "He's going to refinance and buy out your half of the property. You'll probably receive half of his pension. We're working it out."

"We don't have to go to court?" I asked in a shocked voice.

"That's right. It's all over but the details."

"What happened? What did he say when he saw the photos?"

"He said, 'Well, I'll be,'" then nodded at his lawyer. I can tell you one thing, he sure didn't look very happy.

It was true! All he wanted was to embarrass and degrade me. He knew he couldn't look credible with this evidence? "Was that it?" I persisted.

"Yeah, sure looks like it."

"*You* didn't do it—the pictures did it! I'm getting my divorce because *I* took matters into my own hands!" I prodded, exhilarated by the success I had engineered.

"You'll need to meet me here next Thursday, and we will cut you a check for the settlement amount," he said, ignoring my last comment. "Is there anything else I can do for you, Mrs. Cadwell?"

"Yes. You can provide me with the correct form to legally change my name. I no longer wish to be Mrs. Cadwell. I'm taking back the name I came into this world with. As of right now, I am Grace Worley."

I fairly floated out into the waiting room. A sensation of sweet relief, as if I had just been released from jail, soared through my entire body. I stepped out onto the quaint veranda of the eighteenth century law building and took in a deep breath of fresh air. It was the sweetest air I had ever inhaled. I'd been gutsy, and it had paid off! Congratulations Grace!

Just then, an office secretary came out to join me. "Here," she said, "use this envelope with the pin hole in it. Be careful, don't look directly at it—the sun. It's happening! We're having a solar eclipse."

The forces of nature seemed to be sanctifying my moment of justice and freedom—and courage. A long-awaited moment. I had experienced a miracle. I had *created* a miracle. Never mind that this eclipse was an occurrence predicted by scientists. This was my moment of victory. I had come through the darkness. I could see the light. I had endured. I had overcome. And furthermore, I had made it happen. *Me!*

For a split second I teetered, grasping for the railing. A bittersweet gush of adrenaline exploded in my head, star-bursting-like fireworks seemed to shoot through my body. Words echoed in my ears. I saw a flash. An image. Me. Back in the mental hospital, twenty-three years earlier. The moment during which I awakened from my visions. That moment when the nurse and Jack stood over me—a stricken look on his face. I had been muttering words that I later denied saying to him because I couldn't make any sense out of them then. The words were... *"Thank God, I'm going to get my divorce."*

Oh, dear God. What profound meaning those words finally held for me on that day. The earth would keep on turning. The *light* returned again. What is this wondrous, abiding *light* that walks along with me in my mind?

CHAPTER 9

A Dream Begins

Signaled for departure from the gate, our plane bound for Los Angeles, California taxied down the Dulles Airport runway to assume its position in line for takeoff. Jennifer and her husband, Steven, had become more like friends than spouses. After a year of marriage they agreed on an annulment. I wondered if Jennifer's decision to marry had been a rebound from the shock of the divorce, but I never asked her. Either way, she and Steven forged a deep friendship. I was absolutely elated when she made the decision to move to California with me. I was so grateful for the opportunity for us to become closer. Everything was changing.

Jennifer and I sat, side by side, holding our simple gifts of sentiment in our laps like two refugees. Jennifer had humored me, and we each sat with delicate bunches of shamrocks, the roots of which I had carefully wrapped in soaked napkins, sealed with plastic bags, then bound tenderly with rubber bands. They were from a lush mother plant that had adorned my kitchen counter in my Maryland apartment for three years. They would be my heartfelt gift to my family.

I hoped the shamrock, a legendary symbol of good luck, might also become a mutual token of bonding between all of us. I had daydreamed for so long about what it might be like to interact on a daily basis with my sisters and their families; loved ones with shared histories and compassion for one another. Now I was ecstatic to finally have the chance.

The task of cleaning out, packing, and making the arrangements to leave Maryland had taken on a ritualistic cadence, as though I had reached some maturational rite of passage. I had chosen and framed two outstanding pieces of art done by Jennifer and David in elementary school to take with me as a loving tribute to them in my new life. I had gathered up my silver jewelry, which held sad memories of the past, along with charms from bracelets Jack had bought for my birthdays and our anniversaries. Those charms aroused memories of stressful times when I'd forced myself to pretend that everything was fine, hoping that someday it would be. I saved only the charms from the children and my California family.

I took the rest to be melded into one abstract nugget. Transformed into a flower-like pendant, I placed the newly-wedded amalgam on a sparkly, fresh, eighteen-inch silver chain. No longer did dark energies live within me, I had transformed them. I'd emerged intact. Forged in fire, I had survived.

I had also arranged a final appointment with my counselor, Marjorie, at the Mental Health Association. She'd guided me through the fog into deeper recognition of the damage to all our lives caused by Jack's alcoholic personality. Arriving there, I placed my painting of the light bulb on Marjorie's desk. It was the one I had done in an exhausted frenzy nearly ten years earlier. The one that reflected to me that everything in my life would be torn apart, lost. And it had been. I no longer wanted or needed that painting.

Looking at it reminded me of a past I wanted to forget. I'd shared my inner knowing about the painting with Marjorie. My knowing that I could read my own future in it. She didn't think I was crazy. She commended me for my bravery, and regarded me as a sensitive, intuitive person. For that one vote of confidence, I would always feel gratitude.

Although I didn't want those memories with me, for some reason, I couldn't completely surrender the painting. I took a picture of it and tucked it away in a white envelope and slipped it inside a photo album.

After the divorce, everything had seemed to fall into place. However, my freedom was punctuated with bitter sweetness in knowing I would not be near my son. Having served four years in the Air Force, he had returned home to his dad, to make another try in community college for an education. I felt guilty leaving him even though he was by then twenty-six years old. Still, I believed he was in the right place. His greatest challenge lay with his father.

Our 747 surged forward into flight. With a grateful sigh, I relinquished control of the next few hours. I loved looking out the window, drinking in the panoramic views of the world below. At that moment, nothing down there could demand anything of me. Soon enough there would be many decisions to be made.

Packed in the coast-to-coast moving van I'd hired, some-where below me on the highway enroute to California, were the two Asian scrolls. I could still remember how startled I was when the beautiful young girl had materialized on my deck. The scrolls had become symbolic of my growing strength and self-confidence. No longer was I prone to a victim mentality. I vowed to allow myself to be treated only with respect. With the help of Al-Anon, Denise, my counselor, and Marjorie's tutoring about alcoholism, I now stood on new ground. However, the scrolls also conveyed a subtle feeling of unfinished business. Something larger loomed ahead. Trusting in my intuition, I'd decided not to discard the scrolls.

But now, my life was on a brand new track. Maybe the time had finally come for me to learn how to enjoy the little things. A time to play. A time to laugh more. To discover what it is to be "nor-mal"…that state of being I had wondered about so many times grow-ing up. Oh, God, I hoped it was true.

I stood on the threshold of my own independence in a place of personal power. The place I'd sought since leaving home at nineteen. I was forty-six—and finally I could be the master of my own fate. Free to act upon my own will and desires. It was intoxicating.

Our flight arrived a half an hour early. Surrounded by our luggage and holding our thirsty shamrocks, Jennifer and I sat in the terminal and waited for my sister, Mickey, to pick us up. There was magic in the air. Even in the airport I could feel the delicious, arid dryness of a California autumn.

We were fascinated by the L.A. glamour parading past us. We playfully took turns spotting the Hollywood types. Jennifer had not seen her Aunt Mickey since the time she was in high school when she, her dad and I had come out to California for a visit. Jennifer drew my attention to a gorgeous reddish brunette moving through the terminal toward us. It was Mickey…complexion glowing, dressed in a copper-colored dress to compliment her reddish, brunette hair, with her perfect legs ending in stiletto heels; she looked like a movie star.

There were happy, spontaneous hugs all around. Mickey stuffed us and our luggage into her baby-blue 450 SL Mercedes convertible. She whisked us off to her stately, well appointed, 3,500 square foot home in Lemon Heights, which perched on a hillside with a commanding view of the lush Orange County valley and a sweeping vista of the ocean. That evening we could see Tinkerbell fluttering over the twilight sky fireworks, as Disneyland held its Main Street parade.

What a contrast in lifestyle this was to the cramped quarters of our growing up years when Mickey and I slept in the same bed. Mickey prepared a delicious dinner for all of the family present to greet us. Prime rib and Yorkshire pudding. Daddy died in 1973, and Mama had changed dramatically. The need to survive forced her to discover her strength. She had managed her own beauty shop for ten years, and just in the prior year, re-married a tall, gentle, sweet man who owned a farm in the Chino Valley. I was so proud and happy for her.

On the other hand, my younger sister Sue, had, like me, fallen into an abusive marriage. Married to a hot-headed Italian from New Jersey, they lived in San Diego. She struggled to maintain some normalcy for her two boys, ages eight and ten, who also came to Mickey's to greet us. Her husband did not come.

Fortunately, after Mickey had divorced her children's father when they were preteens, their dad had maintained a fully supportive relationship with their children. Her daughter, Kate, and son, Josh, were outgoing young adults.

As we ate, then cleared and washed dishes, we talked and laughed. We caught up on our lives and the evening included the bittersweet exchange of good and bad fortune. I was a little let down when no one asked about my last few years in Maryland. Perhaps they didn't want to feel anymore sadness.

During most of our childhood, Mickey was shy, unsociable, and intimidated by my drive for good grades and an active social life. Sadly, Mama's misguided criticism of Mickey entailed questions like, "Why can't you be like Grace? And why can't you spell like Grace?" Making matters worse, Mama insisted that Mickey accompany me when I went out to play, so Mickey felt like an unwanted tag-along and I resented not being able to be on my own. Not the best breeding ground for sisterly love.

Still, the bond created by our endurance of Daddy's abuse and angry tirades throughout our childhood ran deep. During our own parenting years, via letters, phone calls and occasional visits, we shared the joys of our children and our domestic accomplishments.

It was apparent to me that the family now revered Mickey as a matriarch. Sue idolized her. A chorus of praise for her and her accomplishments rang throughout the evening reunion. She had worked her way up to become the manager of a fashionable art gallery in Newport Beach. While I envied Mickey's glamorous lifestyle, I was truly proud of her, and of her success.

It was 1984 and I was in California! Each day when I awakened, I was still in California! The world was mine for the living. All I wanted out of this part of my life was to savor my autonomy and to enjoy living! Of course, there were a few little details I would have to take care of first—a job, transportation, a place to live. Everything in California was at least triple the cost of East Coast living. My settlement of twenty-five thousand dollars, which had seemed substantial in Maryland in the 80's, would not go very far in California.

I loved the little Volvo I'd had in Maryland, and I wanted to find another one. Stepping onto a used car lot in California as a single woman was like swimming into a school of piranhas. I enlisted Joe, Mickey's new friend and sometimes date, to shield me. I fell in love with a burnt orange 1979 Volvo 240 DL sedan, with an automatic sun roof and gold wire hubcaps. And the price was right. Jennifer called it, "Mom's ambulance." She, on the other hand, became impassioned with a practically new Jeep. I gave her the down payment, wanting her to be as happy and as excited about her new life as her mother. So I took the risk. She went all the way, getting California vanity plates that read, *JENSJEEP.*

As I reflected upon the past years of my life, I was deeply, and profoundly grateful for somehow being rescued by an elusive "inner sight," as well as for my growing awareness of a kind of "symbolism." Some almighty force I didn't understand had reached out to me during those painful times. I was finally leaving my dark past behind—at last! I anticipated very little likelihood for the continuing need for such divine intervention. It was the 1980's and I happily embraced our country's mood to have a good time. I could not know that that would be when the real synchronicity would begin. Little did I even suspect that my life, my world, would be catapulted at warp speed.

Although I knew I should focus my efforts on finding employment and a place to live, it was the weekend, and I decided to treat myself to a day of exploration, heading aimlessly southward along the beach, cruising wide-eyed through both quaint and elegant communities. Only once or twice had I ever visited the beach while growing up, so the new resorts, shops and parks seemed so delicious.

The coastal highway curved ever southward, turning me out into a small, quaint harbor community. Buildings and small retail stores painted chalky blue and trimmed in crisp, clean white hinted strongly of a New England fishing village. With the ocean to my right and a hillside on my left, I rounded a curve in the road. Suddenly, as if it were the most natural thing, I heard a voice in the car that said, "Where are the houses? Where are the pink houses?" I looked to my left at a balding, dry, grass-covered hillside. No houses. Oh, my God. Why was I looking for houses?

Then I realized the voice was my own. Out loud *I* had said, "Where are the houses?" Why had I done this? The voice didn't sound like me. It didn't even feel like me. It came from somewhere else. Now what the hell was happening to me? Some part of me, a totally unknown me, was directing. Oh, my God, this was scary strange.

Then, as if of its own volition, my car stopped before a Century 21 real estate office. I didn't know why, but I felt compelled to investigate. I also felt slightly disengaged; almost as if I had become a character in a story or a play and had just stepped in to assume my part. Oh well, there's no harm in asking, I said to myself. After all, I did need to find a place to live.

"Ms. Worley, I'm sorry," the rental agent empathetically stated. "There just isn't any place in this seaside area to rent that is within your budget." I could tell she genuinely liked me. As I turned around to leave, she remarked, "Did you say you're a teacher? I've just remembered an investor who's had really bad luck with three young tenants that ran out on him. Why don't we find out if he might consider you because of your maturity and reliability ...?"

Hanging up the phone and grabbing the keys from the pegboard on the wall, she said, "Come on, let's go. He says he will try to work with you." In only a few minutes we were there, just a half mile from the ocean and one left turn off the coast highway. A small winding creek ran over big rocks with little wooden foot bridges branching throughout the charming harbor condominium community. As dusk settled in, we walked passed a lighted, kidney-shaped swimming pool with a spa at one end. I looked up to see the fading beams of fall sunlight piercing through the limbs of colorful plum trees, and inhaled the fresh smell of pine from the evergreen trees. Begonias and impatiens covered the ground, and I had a rush of nostalgia. Yes, it was beautiful—but there was more. There was sweetness, and it was familiar!

Just to the southeast side of the pool, the walkway rounded into an alcove leading to a front door. The realtor turned the key in the lock. "It's really small," she explained. "It's a studio plan but it has everything you might need—an L-shaped living room, dining room, bedroom, walk-in closet, kitchen, small patio and a laundry closet— all tucked into 900 square feet."

I stepped inside and my knees wobbled. I've been here before, I realized. What was this feeling? Was it déjà vu? Maybe it would pass. Part of me was outside of myself.

Hardly able to concentrate on her comments, I made an earnest effort to be logical. This was almost an hour away from Mickey and any area of probable employment. It was not nearly as big as I had hoped I would find, and there was only one sliding glass door and one bedroom window to let in the light. I had planned to undertake a thorough search on Monday to find the most suitable place I could possibly afford. Although I'd love to be near the water, I'd never thought about living near the beach. I struggled to resist an absurd yearning to curl up and nestle like a kitten on the floor.

"Mr. Hearldson said he would actually cut the rent in half. He would accept $500 a month. Can you manage that?"

As if in a daze, I heard myself reply. "I'll just have to."

"A condo in a beach town! Nine hundred square feet! You won't have room to turn around." Mickey looked horrified, but I didn't try to explain. I couldn't explain my choice to myself.

"Why Dana Point?" she asked. "Is it the fancy beach town's address?"

What had I done? Had I even done it? That Sunday excursion seemed like a mystery ebbing and flowing in my mind. Had I been intoxicated with the scenery, the potential of an all-new life? Was I overstressed? In the past, those experiences of intuiting a "knowing" or a sense of "presence" seemed to arise to help me out of the darkness and pain of my life. But this was now. My new life. To my surprise, strange things were *still* happening to me.

My mystical day of events that Sunday was different. This time I felt a calmness. I felt like I was coming home. Yet, I didn't know where *home* was. The condo? There was serenity, a deep sense of union with…something? The community? Myself?

Inhaling deeply, I stretched my legs and rested my feet on Mickey's ottoman. I released a grateful sigh, knowing the darkness was behind me. Whatever this new presence was, I was thankful for the peace it was bringing into my life.

A few days later the Mayflower moving van rolled into Orange County. Jennifer's and my things, combined, only took up one-fourth of it

Humble as my belongings were, I couldn't bear the idea of starting over without my possessions, despite the expense of moving them. I watched anxiously as a burly Iranian man and a Mexican teenager unloaded the van. I was comforted by the sight of my two-piece rust and beige brocade sectionals, my glass and clear-finished wicker dining room set, and especially my silky, beige-shellacked wormy chestnut five-drawer desk. With them, I felt I belonged somewhere.

Fortunately there was little to no damage to anything and the set-up took only a fraction of the time it had taken to sort it all out and pack it up. I knew I was home after the movers assembled the humble metal bed frame, mattress, and box springs I'd bought when I moved into my Maryland apartment. In a nesting frenzy, I arranged the end tables and smaller pieces, and then I unpacked and organized most of my personal items. Everything had fit into the condo as though it had been custom ordered.

Tired and happy, I locked the door on any remaining clutter, and hopped into my Volvo to discover a little bit about this place that had so magnetized me. The sun was about to set. I wanted to see all that I could before dark.

Turning left out of the complex toward the ocean and feeling the coziness of my location nestled between lovely grassy hillsides and the ocean, a buzz of euphoria rushed to my temples setting off a nostalgic sense of belonging rippling through me. It penetrated into my very bones. What was it about this place? Why did I feel so alive here? Crossing the coast highway, the road I now lived on curved slightly south, and opened onto a charming harbor ringed with grassy picnic areas and winding walkways. Colorful sails in repose wrapped neatly around masts jutted skyward from the hulls of sailing vessels both luxurious and modest.

I rolled down my window and opened the sunroof. Inhaling deeply, I drew in the salt-laden sea air. I looked to my right. Without warning, a contraction of sorrow from the pit of my belly rolled up my body and into my chest. In a flash, I froze in the grip of bitter remorse. My shoulders slumped and wails of mourning poured from me. The moans moving through me were not my own. I wailed like a wounded animal. A dam was breaking inside of me. Over and over, I sobbed, "Oh, my God, Oh, my God." What is happening to me? Who is this person inside of me?" Groans and sobs consumed me in a tone at least an octave below my natural voice. Something ancient seemed to be washing through me.

The car, barely moving, rolled along the curving road leading out to a point. On my left, I was four-hundred yards or so away from the ocean, yet I felt confined by the massive cliff wall on my right side.

Scenes were being projected in my head—a large wigwam village with smoke rising from campfires and children playing flashed before my eyes. They dissolved as soon as they came...then there were images of Indian mothers grinding corn on rocks. In a rite of passage, within of one of the teepees, an old woman taught a young brave the art of lovemaking in preparation for his wedding night. I saw each vivid scene.

Then, everything changed. I witnessed women struggling, men fighting and killing, bodies sprawled on the ground. The scene changed yet again. With unsympathetic finality the ocean crashed onto the land, flooding and transporting bodies, animals and tents back out to sea.

Distraught and immersed in confusion, I managed to make my way back to the condo. Heading straight for bed, I collapsed, weeping. Unrecognizable groans mingled with the familiar sound of my own voice as I pleaded directly to the Almighty...show me what this is, show me who I am...oh God, I feel such despair for those people and their terrible devastation. What, for God's sake, is the meaning of all this?

...Finally sleep came, finally relief came.

It was pitch dark when I awoke. I couldn't remember the last time I had eaten. I was starved. Not yet familiar with the switches in my new home, I tripped over a shoe box, barely righting myself as I fumbled for the light. The closest thing to fresh food in my cupboards was canned goods. Opening a can of corn and one of stewed tomatoes, I dumped them into bowls. I ate ravenously, savoring every bite as though I'd never tasted corn or tomatoes.

Undressing and crawling under the covers, I listened to the silence of my new surroundings. Through my opened bedroom window, I could hear a frog croaking rhythmically in the creek a short distance away.

Telling anyone what had happened earlier that evening would have caused serious alarm—perhaps even aroused suspicion that I was going crazy. But I wasn't alarmed. I didn't know why. I wasn't psychic, and what I'd seen wasn't even a vision like the others that I'd had before. It had seemed more like a larger-than-life dream. But somehow, I knew—I had been there before. I had been a part of all that I had seen.

I felt contented, even renewed, because I sensed that something was being released from me that had been suppressing my well-being. And at the same time, something was being awakened. Inside of myself I felt a bravery I didn't know I possessed. I allowed myself to surrender to the mystery of it all.

I mused aloud, "This is something bigger than I am. I don't have to know what it is right now. I'm going to let it show me. I'm going to trust that I will understand somehow, someday." Letting go of confusion and concerns, I surrendered once again into a deep and restful sleep.

With my financial help, Jennifer found a really nice apartment in a new building in Laguna Niguel, just fifteen minutes inland from my condo. To my dismay, Jennifer had not requested any help from me in getting settled. She still seemed to maintain a certain amount of distance. On my first visit to her apartment, I saw that she really didn't need my help, at least for decorating. She had filled her one-bedroom apartment with cheerful flares of red and cobalt blue, right down to a wallpapered breakfast bar and a red wall clock. She proudly showed off her creativity to me. I was proud of her, and so happy to be with her. Plus, I was pleased to learn Jennifer was called back for a second interview with a local college, National University, for a position in their human resources department. She was also looking into schools to be trained as a travel agent.

While still in Maryland, Jennifer and I had each atypically purchased a packaged set of four hundred reproductions of fine art prints, prompted by a dynamic sales woman; our goal being to sell them to commercial offices to make extra money since both of us were single women and needed to support ourselves. My divorce settlement and our decision to leave for California occurred soon after, so we never pursued it. However, she made good use of the colorful prints in her apartment.

So how long does it take to organize and decorate nine-hundred square feet? A lot less time than the 1,800 square feet I'd had in Maryland. But it didn't matter. I was thrilled at the prospect. Within a few days I had arranged my few pieces of furniture and unpacked and organized my kitchen and tiny walk-in closet. I'd bought the perfect piggy-backed washer and dryer that snuggled tightly into the laundry closet off the patio outside the only sliding glass door, which opened to the living room.

Taking a break, I fixed myself a pot of French roast coffee. Mug in hand, I sank down into my sectional to admire my handiwork. Something was missing. The walls. The walls were bare. But, of course—not a problem! I just happened to have a collection of four hundred reproduced prints of some of the finest art! As Jennifer had done, I would decorate my walls with them.

Digging into one of the surplus boxes now stored tightly in the shelf above the washer and dryer, I pulled out the long fat tube. I dumped the rolled up contents onto the floor and playfully sat down in the middle of many prints which were laminated together in numerous long strips. I felt my cheeks flush with the excitement of the challenge. I loved decorating. How in the world would I select from all of these? I only needed a few. My eyes fixed upon a five by seven foot tranquil scene of a docked sailboat in a pier in a harbor. How perfect! I knew I'd selected the right one when I held it up to the wall. Entitled *Safe Harbor,* no other image could have so well expressed my feelings about my cozy new home.

For a limited rectangular wall space in my bathroom, I then chose a picture that was the perfect size; a beautiful Indian maiden with long dark hair held in place by a wide band that circled her forehead. I loved her mysterious and mystical aura.

After unsuccessfully searching for a print I liked to fit a specific narrow wall in my bedroom, I realized I had the perfect solution. I rummaged through the storage boxes and soon found the Asian scrolls I'd brought with me from Maryland. Placing one above the other on the wall, they fit like they belonged there.

Nearly two weeks later, on a Saturday morning, I awakened at 4:15 soaked in perspiration and in a state of torment. Frightful images were racing through my mind as I remembered my dreams. These dreams had begun in my childhood, and had last appeared sporadically during my teens. This night I'd experienced two recurring dreams.

In one, I was in a foreign land, when I suddenly fell backwards into turbulent greenish-black water. I saw the face of a man suspended above me in the water. I was trying to communicate something to him but the swift currents plunged us deeper into a whirling, watery darkness. That was when I would always awaken.

But no sooner had I gone back to sleep when the other dream came. I was an Indian maiden and I was running for my life, racing through tall corn fields as a band of Indian warriors chased me. The dream always ended before they caught me—although I knew I would be caught. When I awakened, my heart pounded out of my chest. I threw off the comforter and jumped up to change my gown. No sense in trying to go back to sleep. I was more awake than I would have been after three cups of black coffee.

I returned to bed with a glass of water and my journal, propping myself up with pillows. I had been journaling a lot lately. I knew that Jane, my psychologist friend in Maryland, would have been proud of me. Putting my feelings on paper helped me to be free of them. At least, for awhile. I poured my emotions out on the writing tablet:

"...It feels as though something inside me is swelling, rumbling; dredging up a deep, dark, sludge that lay within me. As if washing me out...so that all of me can be brought to a new level of peace. A peace I am just getting a taste of in my new life. Could I ever hope for peace as complete as that which I had found in my kaleidoscopic visions? The deep panic I feel in these dreams is like the emotional darkness I had in the harbor. Strange as it may seem though, even with all that has happened, I still sense that same growing, abiding calm."

Sitting on my front porch with the Monday morning *Orange County Register* newspaper and my extra-strong, French-roast coffee, I scanned the employment section. Mentally taking stock as I relaxed in the warm fall sun, it shocked me a little to realize that it had been less than three weeks since my return to California on October 22, 1984.

I had already made a few potential job contacts, so I left the sliding glass door open in case the phone rang. Although I had managed to inquire about work, it had been difficult to center myself after the disorienting experience in the harbor. I felt enveloped by a vague, even rather euphoric, and "certifiably" mystifying daze.

Neither my degree in education nor my license as a realtor would be valid in California. To get California teaching certification would cost me nearly a year of time in courses, most of which I had already taken, and thousands of dollars. I could not afford to live without a full income, and I was still emotionally exhausted from the prolonged divorce. I had neither the time, the money, nor the stamina to undertake such ambitious career adjustments.

Truth was, I wanted to simplify my life and have less responsibility. I wanted to make a decent living and have some time to relax, to renew myself, to have some fun. At least for a little while. No evenings filled with homework to correct or PTA meetings and parent conferences to attend; no property to show on weekends or open houses to host. This was the first time that my life was completely mine to live.

I wondered about an office job. Surely an educated and experienced woman could find something worthwhile. But then I realized that not wanting to teach or to practice real estate, I was somewhat out of the mainstream. My past strengths and hard-earned accomplishments and esteem would not be part of my new life. In that moment I felt a twinge of anonymity. A little lonely. And my female hormones were kicking in. I longed for a loving companion.

Why not? I was an attractive, forty-six-year-old blonde, with a trim figure and a sunny smile. Men were drawn to me. Immediately having second thoughts, I checked myself, remembering that I knew I could be content with life on my own. Still, I looked forward to the possibility of the joy of a healthy partnership.

Restless, I walked around the corner to water the geraniums just outside my front door. Then—there it was again. A feeling. A knowing that a man would come and stand right there on my doorstep someday. I would open the door, and he would be there. He would become my partner.

Then, there was more. I lifted my eyes to look at the number beside my condo door. Number fifty-two. As trite or obvious as it may seem, I suddenly *knew* it was a light bulb moment. I would be fifty-two years old when that happened. *Oh, dear,* I thought. *That was five years away.*

CHAPTER 10

The Dream Begins to Transform

It was becoming evident that trusting my inner knowing had become an essential part of me. My first visions at twenty-two had shifted my reality. Without the manifestations of the visions from twenty-four years ago, I might have blocked out or convinced myself to overlook these more recent insights. I might have persuaded myself to ignore the images I saw of the vivid pink houses, of which there were none, and the scenes in the harbor of an earlier time, and the insight that the number on my front door was some sort of pronouncement of the age I would be when I married again. I could have disregarded those more recent mental images as simply flashes of déjà vu, and convinced myself I was just imagining things. But, now I didn't.

I'd believed in the signposts that had nurtured me through my troubled past. Even though these recent events and insights hadn't come from visions in a mental hospital, I trusted that some kind of transformation was going on within me. And, I trusted that it was good. In my very bones, I knew that my spirit was reaching out for the richness of life.

By staying conscious and not ignoring what I was shown, perhaps I would glimpse clues to my future. In fact, in more and more of these signposts and images, I felt I was in a dream that enveloped both my sleeping and waking hours—a dream of my own life! As if some part of me was watching my life unfold, and I was simply observing.

I decided to keep a regular journal, holding the hope that ongoing recording would eventually reveal a bigger picture. Were these strange experiences in my life a structured maze leading me to a destination? A kind of road map that was nudging me along to some greater part of me?

In late 1984, the world of business was undergoing radical change. Computers and word processors were gobbling up the standard typewriters with which I was so familiar. I was concerned as I prepared myself to enter the job market, but optimistic I had skills that were still marketable. And I felt confident in my ability to learn quickly.

With the help of Peggy, a former business friend in Maryland who owned her own escrow company, I arranged two real estate-related job interviews for the coming weeks. Just prior to leaving Maryland, Peggy and I had had a farewell dinner together. Since I was leaving town, I took a chance and confided in her about the visions from years ago in the mental hospital, and the ways in which they'd rooted in my life. It was freeing to talk openly about it. To my relief, she was completely receptive and without judgment. Peggy gave me the name of a good friend in San Diego, and she urged me to call her, certain we would have a lot in common.

So, I called Peggy's friend, and we agreed to meet that weekend for an early meal, and then a symphony concert. Our lighthearted conversation flowed easily. Gretchen, an extremely pleasant, middle-aged woman with laughing eyes, turned out to be a Jungian therapist. I began to understand why Peggy felt we might enjoy each other.

During dinner it seemed natural to share my experiences with her. Genuinely interested, she asked for details. Before I knew it I'd described the events beginning in the mental institution all the way up to the bizarre episode a few days earlier at the harbor, as well as my recurring dreams.

She encouraged me not to dismiss the significance of these occurrences. "Your journey is still unfolding." She was quite enthusiastic. "Regarding your glimpses of scenes at the harbor and your similar emotions in disturbing dreams, it sounds to me as though you may be trying to recall a past life."

A past life! That was something I knew very little about, except for the then-current number one best seller by Shirley Mclaine, *Out on a Limb*. Past life? The words caused me to stiffen. Daddy would have beaten me without asking questions if I had dared to utter such words. Wicked, evil, the work of the devil, he would have said. I could see his red face and bulging eyes. But my father was gone, and I was making my own decisions. The only thing I did know in my own heart was that what had happened to me did not feel evil or even bad. Mysterious, yes.

"Grace, I have a great idea." We had planned that I would spend the night rather than drive an hour back home. "When we return to the house, would you like to draw from the *I Ching?*"

"What is the *I Ching?*"

"Well, for one thing, Jung used it on occasion with his patients. It is also called *The Book of Changes,* a very ancient book of wisdom. Its roots go back to mythical times, probably before 3,000 B.C. In fact, Taoism and Confucianism have their origins in the *I Ching*"

As she explained, I began to recall a mention of the *I Ching* in my comparative religions class in college. Gretchen continued, "It's a book based on the hypothesis of the *oneness* of man, including the surrounding cosmos. Jung proposed that when anyone consults oracles or uses divining techniques, such as the *I Ching,* to understand meaning in their life, they are using a principle he coined as synchronicity, or meaningful coincidences."

Meaningful coincidences. Synchronicity. The book Beth had given to me in Maryland popped into my head. Jung's *Man and His Symbols.* Beth thought it had a message for me. It had sat on my night stand beside my bed in my Maryland apartment for almost a year and I'd tried to read it a few times, but my mind had been overloaded with the challenges of survival. I told Gretchen about my psychic friend and the book.

"Grace, it seems to me that the awareness of symbols and synchronicity may have a lot to do with your personal path in this lifetime," she continued. What Gretchen said next echoed in my head as she went into the kitchen to prepare tea for us.

She made it a point to explain that a great contribution made by Jung, both to the world of psychology and to the world of science, was to point out the importance and validation of the intuitive life as man's *most distinctive* characteristic. Jung took very seriously the unconscious inner knowledge of human existence—that knowing which can synchronistically inform conscious awareness by way of a physical object, event, or dream. That was actually the message of his quote that I had noted inside his book: *"Symbols are a psychological mechanism that transforms energy."* Mind and matter interacting.

As I processed the validation of what she had just said, a huge wall of previously unrecognized subconscious mental doubt began to crumble; bone deep stress from years of vague disbelief and cross-examining myself. What a comfort to hear words from the likes of Jung, affirming my inner convictions during the long years I'd kept so much bottled up inside of me. For nearly two decades, I realized, a little part of me still couldn't help but wonder if I was crazy.

Ever since that unforgettable day when my subconscious, or perhaps as Jung believed a deeply intuitive part of myself, joyfully envisioned light that contained images of future places and events, and had resulted in my stay in a mental hospital. Then, once some of those images actually took form, their presence caused me to doubt my entire outlook on life.

It had been so mystifying beginning with the evergreen trees, and envisioning the last name of my friend who had betrayed me, and the words predicting my divorce. I'd seen a highway road sign that sixteen years later I was traveling on! Their actual manifestation had brought me comfort and assurance, and also to wonder about some sort of destiny. My visions had also taken some of the sting out of painful events, as when I learned of Jack's infidelity. They had softened the trauma of the terror-filled car chase by Jack. A trust of some undefined purpose was forming. Another expression of my subconscious mind was in my abstract painting of the lamp with the bare light bulb. It was remarkable that my unconscious mind expressed an image on canvas that had *intuitively* carried with it the message of my own torn future. My light bulb moment, gave me courage when my life fell apart. So, all of that was—as Jung stated—my mind inter-acting with physical events or matter!

Suddenly, I realized there were still unmanifested visions from the days before and from during the mental hospital stay. There was the vision of the hot tub in a peaceful setting, unlike the one in our home in Maryland. And the mountain with the multi-lane highway below it, and the long, blank, white sign over it. Did these visions represent additional events, signposts, markers helping me through events yet to come?

My life had become an uncanny mystery. What might this mean for my future? Would there be painful and traumatic occur-rences as there had been in the past?

And, what about the new visionary experiences I had in the last three weeks? I had seen pink houses on a hillside, but there were none. Then there was the almost mystical experience of finding my condo and the strong feeling I had been there before. And, then, upon seeing the address of my condo, I simply knew I would be fifty-two when I remarried. Could these be real and true indications of my future? *Mind and matter interacting?*

What could ever make sense out of my deeply emotional drive to the harbor where I'd envisioned an Indian village from another era, and the tidal wave that followed? Even my recurring dreams seemed connected somehow to this—this energy—this dimension of time that I had fallen into while at the harbor; dreams of drowning, sinking below green-black water; dreams of Indians chasing me. I wondered where one ended and the other began.

I had to resolve that I didn't know … but I would know, when I know.

What I did know was that through all of these years, I had changed so much for the better. In spite of my ongoing bewilderment, I knew my perspective on life had continued to open to a whole new world of possibilities.

I returned to the moment as Gretchen waltzed out of the kitchen with a tray holding two exquisitely hand-painted tea cups and matching tea pot. We drank chamomile tea and nibbled on gin-gerbread, talking until after midnight and exploring a little of the *I*

Ching. At her suggestion, I cast dice producing numbers and then we looked up their significance in the *Book of Changes*. It was difficult to relate to the messages, though, as they were written in the manner of an ancient time and thought.

"Grace, it is believed that even our names have a significant influence in our destiny. Look up the number twenty-two in the book." The heading for number twenty-two was identified simply with the word *Grace*. My name. As I perused the page, my gaze came to rest on the last line. *"Simple grace. No blame."* I really liked that.

The next morning I headed back onto the Pacific Coast Highway to my cozy nest in Dana Point. As I relaxed into the calming coastal scenery, I began to focus on finding a job. I couldn't afford to allow this new dimension of my life to distract me from keeping my feet on the ground. I needed to make some money. The next day was the first of the two interviews I had lined up. I comforted myself that I had used my time wisely, and that three weeks, since October twenty-second, had been a reasonable period of time to settle in to a new way of life.

That's interesting I thought—*the twenty-second... the number twenty-two, which is also the number assigned as Grace in the I Ching*. In fact, I realized that this number had always stood out in my mind, because I'd been twenty-two when I was put in the mental hospital. Even Jennifer's due date to be born had fallen on the twenty-second of September. And, while I was at it, although it had been twenty-five years by the time I was legally divorced, my actual marriage, before the separation, had lasted twenty-two years. Interesting "synchronicity," I mused. Gretchen had also mentioned there were several ancient numerological systems that could be used to divine the meaning in one's life. I decided I would consider the number twenty-two as my own special number.   ႙ ⌀

Tuesday's job interview as office manager for the owner of a real estate development company did not go well. A younger woman who was computer savvy in word processing, database and accounting software received the offer. I spent the rest of the next two weeks on the phone, following up on classified ads and miscellaneous leads. I was becoming anxious and concerned. I needed to generate some income.

Finally, two weeks later, the morning came for my second scheduled interview. I dressed early, choosing my navy blue pin-striped suit and a silky magenta blouse that tied with a bow under my neck. It was one of the two suits I had treated myself to when I had finally made some real estate sales while back in Maryland. Tucking several copies of my typeset resume into an alligator skin pouch, I slipped on conservative pumps and threw my best handbag over my shoulder heading for the covered carport where my sturdy burnt-sienna orange Volvo waited.

I had not yet committed my license plate number to memory. I shall always remember the sudden thrill as I scanned it. Was I seeing what I thought I was seeing? A large percentage of California vehicles carried personalized plates, usually in cleverly-coded numbers and letters. I just took the plates that had come with my car. I stood and stared at my randomly-assigned license plate. It read: 2BEZ422. As plain as day my license plate said, "To Be Easy For Grace (22)"!

Oh, my God. The universe has a sense of humor. A positive symbol! How affirming! How comforting! What fun! God knew I was ready for easy.

That day the interview for the position, which entailed setting up a new office and becoming the bookkeeper and office manager for a mortgage brokerage, went well. My real estate background made me a likely candidate to eventually work into the business as a loan broker. Two days later, I was offered the job. Even though the salary was several thousand less than I'd anticipated, and needed, I accepted it. I felt optimistic there was potential for advancement.

That night I wrote in my journal.

I chuckle every time I think about the coincidence of the cheery message of my license plate. It's beginning to seem like anything and everything could be some sort of symbol to mirror communication back to me. What I love is that the message is always some form of comfort, or maybe even gentle preparation for an upcoming change, like my painting was, or even the number 52 perhaps coming up in my future. Certainly there is something being transformed in me. Something is going on. That much I know. I'm grateful for the comforting messages.

I lifted my gaze to the familiar Asian scrolls on the wall across from the foot of my bed. Why had I felt compelled to bring them from Maryland? The image of the wooden foot bridge hung suspended in my mind as I drifted into a sweet, deep slumber.

My financial situation was becoming quite serious. Each month I had to dip into my tiny savings to pay my bills, even though I carefully watched my spending. Another stress came from the computer skills required on a job I hadn't really mastered. I needed to get up to speed fast. I found myself, risky as it was, literally reading the various software manuals in the car during the nearly one-hour drive to Newport Beach where I worked. Prime time, commuter traffic added half an hour to a normal thirty-minute drive. I was quite happy, however, as I did catch on. I learned the basics of several programs in a few weeks time. Fortunately, I was pretty speedy on the keyboard as well.

My job in the mortgage brokerage was pleasant enough, but the commute lengthened my days. I was up at 5:30 a.m. and often it was 7:00 p.m. before I reached home. This was not turning out to be the easy lifestyle I was seeking. I went to bed tired and got up tired. My recurring dreams became more frequent. The image of the foot bridge pictured on one of the Asian scrolls was hauntingly present both during the day and at night. It repeatedly captured my attention, almost as if it were illuminating, communicating to me, in a *wordless interaction.* Something wanted to emerge. Sometimes I even caught myself talking to the image, asking, "What?" What did it want of me?

That first summer back in California, hungry to learn more about myself and the mysteries of my life, I ventured off one Sunday in 1985 to a health and wellness exposition in Pasadena. I was attracted by some of the speakers' topics like "Truth Heals" and particularly "Discover the Child Within." I keenly recalled the time in the mental hospital twenty-five years earlier, when I'd been swept away into that lovely kaleidoscopic space and discovered a new, carefree part of myself. It was a sweet and simple, childlike innocence. And, at the same time, it was strength. I'd gained a vivid sense of power and passion for life that stayed with me, and I yearned to know more about it.

When I located the booth related to the topic of the child within, a gentle Asian man—Dr. Ishakaki—sat behind a table with a large display of literature. He was an instructor from Chapman College in Orange, and he taught classes in a graduate program called Psychosynthesis.

"The Institute of Psychosynthesis was founded by Roberto Assagioli," he began in response to my query. "Are you familiar with Freud's basic premise, Grace?" Assagioli had been Freud's contemporary, but they split in opposition.

"Yes, I studied psychology in college."

Dr. Ishakaki went on to tell me that Freud's theory of the development of personality was based solely on the libido, or sex drive. By contrast, Assagioli insisted that in order to achieve the goal of a healthy individual, there must be more of an integration, or *synthesis,* of various psychological functions. It was a transpersonal theory, stressing the need of communion with one's higher or *transpersonal* self.

Those terms, higher and transpersonal self…could they be words for that other dimension I had experienced? For what I'd experienced after Jennifer's birth. Or was I stretching credibility because I wanted it to be so?

"Is this a New Age or metaphysical philosophy?" I asked with some skepticism.

He responded enthusiastically telling me that to the contrary, it was a scientific enterprise, not a religion or an ideology. The Institute of Psychosynthesis was an integrated study of the transpersonal self and recognized the importance of other disciplines, including biology, physics, religious and literary studies, sociology, education, and the like.

"So what is the goal of this study?"

Assuring me that I'd asked a fair question, he explained that the principle aims and practice of Psychosynthesis included a comprehensive approach, the goal of which was to eliminate conflicts or obstacles, both conscious and unconscious, that block harmonious development within the human personality. Psychosynthesis applied a variety of psychological disciplines and techniques to stimulate the psychic functions of the parts of the mind that may still be weak and immature.

"A variety of psychological disciplines?"

"Yes," he answered. He then mentioned a few of the pioneers and contributors to the work of transpersonal psychology, like Teilhard de Chardin, Aldous Huxley, Abraham Maslow, Stanislav Grof, and Carl Jung.

I was impressed. These were all names I knew and respected. Some of my favorite theorists, and, of course, Jung. I understood Dr. Ishakaki was there to promote his program, yet confident I had become a pretty good judge of character I felt drawn by his tone of humility. He was easy to talk to.

"What does the term 'transpersonal' actually mean?"

"It refers to beyond the personal in each of us," pointing out that a common assumption in transpersonal psychology is that transpersonal experiences involve a higher mode of consciousness. One in which the ordinary mental or, to use a Freudian term, *egoic* self, is transcended.

I stared at him, a blank look on my face.

He then summarized by telling me that Psychosynthesis and the theory of one's higher or transpersonal self were concerned with those states of mind and processes in which people experience a deeper or wider sense of who they are—a sense of greater connectedness with others, their surroundings, nature or the spiritual dimension.

A connectedness—our surroundings—nature—spiritual dimensions! He had my attention.

Suddenly, I felt comfortable enough to describe to this stranger I might never see again the events involving my original visions, and particularly the euphoric peace, and strength, and beauty I had remembered.

"Oooh," he said, smiling, and obviously excited at what he had heard. "You had a psychic break. How wonderful!"

How wonderful? He thought it was a good thing.

Actually I was comforted by his apparent sincerity and appreciation, and that he recognized my experience. The conversation took on a relaxed flow. I found myself confessing new feelings to him. Feelings I didn't know I had. I wanted to move on to a more creative, satisfying expression of myself. Events in my life had created a subliminal level of anxiety and mental confusion. I wanted to get to the bottom of the cause or the meaning of the unexplainable experiences I'd been having.

Obviously intrigued, he warmly offered a suggestion. He explained that the Institute of Psychosynthesis provided different pathways in post-graduate level courses; training in psychiatry, psychology, psychotherapy, therapeutic counseling, coaching and group work. He suggested that I might want to consider taking the first year of Psychosynthesis.

The curriculum was planned so that entire first year consisted of an introduction to the fundamental concepts of transpersonal psychology, but it also focused on delving into the student's own life. That way, when the student had personally explored—and applied—the principles of the program, they would have a more solid understanding, and would be better prepared to assist others in the same process.

I said nothing. I was shocked at myself for even considering the possibility.

He prompted that taking this first year of study could provide me the opportunity to explore this mystery I was experiencing. And I would be acquiring post-graduate level credits at the same time.

The classes met for a full weekend, once a month for a year, which seemed like a timeframe I could actually manage. He addressed my yearning to know what I had experienced in the kaleidoscopic light as the "innocent" part of myself.

"No matter how distant or evasive it may seem to be, we each have a child within. It is that part of us that is the real self...sometimes called the inner child." He lamented that most everyone learns to be a grown-up but forgets, or denies, that part of themselves. "We're stifled by authority figures and institutions. The focus of Psychosynthesis is to return to one's real self, which is the heart of our authentic power. The vital, natural part of ourselves. Perhaps this is what you have been sensing. It needs exploration and nurturance in order to be accessed."

Although the fee was reasonable, I knew there was no room for anything extra in my budget. Suddenly, I didn't care. I filled out the application for registration having no idea what I was in for.

It was an early Saturday morning in October of 1985, the second weekend of the Psychosynthesis course, when I imagined I was flying over the freeway, exiting onto Highway 22, towards Chapman College. With just one weekend of classes behind me, all I could think about were those sessions. I was delighted to return. I thirsted for it. I'd found an oasis in a hot, dry dessert.

In that first weekend I learned that Psychosynthesis is based on a theory of human development of *sub personalities,* which evolve from habits and patterns that as a whole make up an individual's personality. In order for there to be a *synthesis* of these habits and patterns into one healthy personality, and to live in a reasonable state of peace and harmony, one needs to find the center around which this synthesis can occur. This center is an *inner drive,* or urge, which strives to be known, to be realized and expressed. Dr Ishakaki quoted Jung saying that, "The mind is in an inexorable search for balance."

An inner drive, an urge striving to be expressed certainly described the storm brewing inside of me. I was shifting, changing. Without warning, I could be alternately drawn into rapt visionary moments of the future or swept into deep sorrow from somewhere in the past. My real passion would have been to turn a blind eye to all responsibility and immerse myself fully in pursuit of the beckoning obscurities veiled within me. I was caught in a dilemma of needing to be grounded—to establish a stable new life—amidst the wild pull to venture into the unknown. But in that moment, I was a little nervous about the upcoming classes, recalling how challenged I had felt the prior week in class.

Dr. Ishagaki had made it clear in that first weekend that throughout the program, we were to observe a strict code of confidentiality—this was necessary so that each student could feel safe to share their personal stories. He had asked us each to take a turn talking about our private lives and thoughts in front of the class, as we laid the groundwork for going deeper.

Most of the others shared concerns on a level of occasional despair and unfulfilled dreams, even some on abuse. I shared similar problems, but mine were coupled with descriptions of my stay in the mental hospital, my visions, and then the actual events later in my life.

So, there I was. Determined to finally speak my truth aloud. Not just to a counselor or a close friend, but to a classroom full of eighteen strangers. I spoke openly about extraordinary, unexplainable episodes in my life—about my mental collapse, the visions, the times when the visions actually happened. I even included the abuse I'd been through as a child and in my marriage.

Although, even then, I did not talk about what had happened since my arrival in California—about seeing mysterious pink houses, my condo, and that evening in the harbor. It was too new. Too bizarre, even for a confidential and professional group situation. I was afraid even they might think I was crazy. After all, I didn't really know those people.

I entered the classroom for my second weekend of sessions and found an empty seat in the circle of tables, next to a slightly austere, dark-haired European woman. "Emily" was written on her name tag. Our second weekend session began by working with a technique called guided daydreaming. The person to my right, Emily, became my partner. Dr. Ishagaki said that applying this technique while working with a partner, was a means of establishing communication with our unconscious. In a mock setting, as if we were the client we would eventually be working with, we were asked to close our eyes, relax and imagine ourselves in a peaceful, neutral place such as by the ocean or in a meadow. Then we were to allow ourselves to be whatever comes, especially our feelings, and any symbolic imagery. Afterwards, we were to relay our experience to our assigned partner.

The partner's job was to encourage the process and to help the other move into problem areas so that we could begin to face and resolve them. "Everyone always has something." Dr. Ishagaki assured us. Elaborating, he explained that by tracing back and examining the causes of a situation from the past, one was clearing the way for a more joyful future.

When my turn came, I couldn't relax. I couldn't really find any neutral, safe place in my mind. I didn't know if it was because of Emily's sullen demeanor or my own reluctance to open up. I felt very anxious because in recent weeks the storm in my mind had been magnifying. My nightmare of drowning under dark, cold, turbulent waves of green-black water had returned with more frequency. And to make matters worse, an irrational fear was building inside of me. I couldn't seem to shake a gripping image of inevitable destruction...that an earthquake, accompanied by a tsunami of devastating proportions, was about to strike the seaside of Dana Point where I lived. It would destroy everything and everyone for hundreds of miles. We would all be consumed by the angry ocean. Not only were these fears present at night, they had begun to haunt my daytime hours too. I knew how irrational this all was, but still it consumed me.

When we finished up the first day's sessions, I was disappointed. I had talked around it all. I hadn't really opened up and that was what I had wanted to do most of all.

When I arrived home, my head woozy and my eyes blurring, it was about an hour before one of those blazing, fall coastal sunsets. I changed into a cable-knit turtleneck and tucked my wallet into comfortable culottes. I decided to step out for a salad, and maybe take it down to the harbor. I could sit in the car and eat while I watched the sunset.

I opened the sunroof of my Volvo. The fresh air revived me. I drove down the hill onto the harbor road and as I drove, I recalled my previous visions...then they happened again! The little Indian village and the ensuing watery destruction swelled, filling my mind, but not as vividly as before. Yet the sorrowful tragedy still was all consuming. Again I sobbed! My body shook. Chills ran through me. Even though it was less than a quarter of a mile until the road ended at the ocean, it seemed far, far away. I managed to steer the car to a safe stop at the dead end of the harbor where the road met the ocean.

As I drew closer to the shore, the feelings subsided almost as quickly as they came. It was as though I had just passed through a time warp. I parked facing the ocean at the end of the cliff which wound around behind me. I closed the sunroof and put the heat on full blast to calm the quivering inside of me. Reclining my seat, I closed my eyes.

One underlying feeling pervaded: a sense of familiarity. Like a returning memory. Somehow it was all connected—the visions, the symbols, the painting, finding my condo, even the pink houses. I felt like two people—the one who was in some way joined to these forthcoming insights and the one who lived in an ordinary, work-a-day world. Why couldn't I be like everyone else I knew? Finding a good way to make a living in life? Just being a good person and having some fun once in awhile? I wondered if people's lives and destinies really were preordained. Was mine?

The sun had set. My chills shifted to prickly heat, and my skin was clammy under my sweater. I turned off the heater, put the car in reverse, and headed back up the harbor drive for home. I pressed hard on the accelerator as I passed the cliffs. This time, when the unwelcome rush of terror-filled feelings came, I managed to physically shake them off. As I left the harbor, I didn't feel the same intensity as before.

I felt a lot like Alice in Wonderland. I wondered just how far down this rabbit hole I would fall.

The next morning, Sunday, during our second day of the second weekend of classes at the college, I was paired with a gentle, friendly woman near my age, whose name was Anita. She was lovely with dark red hair and compassionate hazel eyes. She put me at ease by sharing her amazement about the part of my story I had been able to tell the class.

During the morning break we enjoyed a snack out on the campus lawn under a beautiful elm tree. Anita was a social worker and she had a natural personality for helping others. She asked several questions regarding my surprise over my visions, and my surprise later when I actually saw those events occur in my life.

Feeling the stress of the previous evening at the harbor, I opened up to her. I poured out a brief description of the unexplainable events that had occurred since I had returned to California. Particularly the dreams and the trauma I experienced while at the harbor. I even found the courage to tell her of my irrational fear of impending destruction.

"Grace, this class work will help you, I'm quite sure. But if I were you, I would also go to a hypnotist for help. I think there's something inside of you that is ready to come out, and it's too much for you to handle alone." She shared that several of her friends had achieved successful results through hypnosis, and undergone great change. She assured me that they were much happier.

Hypnotism. It alarmed me almost as much as the concept of a past life. My first reaction was to reject her suggestion. My life was unconventional enough as it was without complicating it with additional unknowns.

As if she'd read my mind, Anita spoke about the misconceptions most people had concerning hypnosis, primarily because of the way television, movies, and stage shows portrayed the process. "It's not like you're entering a time machine and find yourself in another time and place with no awareness of the present. Your conscious mind is always aware of the experience. Hypnosis is really self-hypnosis, and as the patient, you control the process. The therapist is merely a guide. In fact, most everyone enters a subtle level of a hypnotic state every day like when we are listening to good music, reading an engrossing book, or even when we drive our cars on familiar routes. It's kind of like being on automatic pilot," she said with a smile.

Feeling a little less defensive, I asked if she really believed hypnosis would help me. She recommended we speak to Dr. Ishagaki, so we found him in the hallway heading back to class.

He assured us that hypnosis was a commonly used method and considered a desirable option by many of the founding theorists of Psychosynthesis. He did caution me to find someone reputable though with good training.

Dr. Ishagaki said that hypnosis helps to access the subconscious part of the mind, lying beneath our ordinary consciousness where mental processes occur without our awareness. It can recall experience, beyond our everyday capabilities in order to help us heal. Our subconscious is not limited by our imposed boundaries of logic, space and time.

That sounded good since my past and present seemed to be blurring together. I felt ready to learn more about my own subconscious thoughts.

As we walked into the classroom, Dr. Ishagaki added that in a state of hypnosis, the subconscious becomes the dominant thinker. And in the subconscious, we can access all of our strengths, without any of our self-imposed limitations.

I became hopeful that I'd found a way to get in touch with whatever was causing my underlying fears. When class ended, I asked Anita for the phone number of her friend's hypnotherapist.

The next evening, after a long, tiring day of duties as office manager in the mortgage brokerage, I sat down at my old, wormywood chestnut desk, staring at my phone. Not only had my job become a tedious grind, the money just wasn't enough. I'd even lost interest in eventually becoming a loan broker. I let the view of the running creek outside my window soothe my spirit. I loved the moments of soft, fading light just before dark. I lamented that only a few weeks remained until the end of Daylight Saving Time. Soon it would be dark when I arrived home from work.

I felt anxious and torn in two very different directions. First, there was the immediate need to earn a good income. Second, there was the relentless need to pursue the mystery of the storm brewing inside of me.

It had only been a few months ago when I chuckled to myself as I leisurely browsed through a department store to buy kitchen cookery for only me. I had relished the simplicity and freedom of my life. No one was demanding anything of me. No one was trying to control me, as in my past. I was looking forward to minimal complications and minimal responsibility. I wanted to live a little. Fun was going to be my watchword.

But now even in my spare time, I was agitated. I had shared a little of my traumatic experience in the harbor with Jennifer, but only vaguely so as not to risk weakening our newly budding relationship. I didn't want her to think I was crazy. However, I couldn't ignore what was happening. I rarely got a good night's sleep. The helplessness that overcame me in my dream of drowning beneath green-black water persisted even through the daytime. I lived under a cloud of vague, expanding fear.

Adding to my emotional burden were feelings of guilt and shame, as if I was involved in those watery deaths. It was irrational. Yet, the feelings had grown as strong as my fear. Why should I feel responsible? Where was this coming from? Why did I feel I'd done something wrong? I was becoming overwhelmed by an expanding certainty of impending doom—and a desperate sense I should be doing something to prevent it. Me! Why me?

Coming back into the present there at my desk, in a state of apprehension I knew that any hypnosis sessions I undertook would need to be paid for on credit, as I'd done when paying tuition for the Psychosynthesis course.

I remembered I had left Jack when I only had $150 in my account, but I managed to survive. If I could do it then, I could do it again I told myself.

I picked up the phone and dialed the number for Dr. Neville Rowe.

"Dr. Rowe is still in session. He should be finished soon." A lovely, petite woman, a little younger than myself, with sky-blue eyes and beautiful blonde hair nearly to her waist, introduced herself to me as Andrea. A family therapist, she shared the office with Dr. Rowe. She served me hot herbal tea, suggesting it might help me relax.

"I guess I am a little nervous. This is my first time." Andrea assured me I couldn't have come to a better person; that he was sensitive and willing to take the time to answer any questions I might have. She told me he was also an author and a speaker, and gave seminars and presentations throughout the country. He had seen and learned a lot in the several decades he had been working with "the multiple dimensions of the human mind." Andrea's light and sunny manner helped me relax. I liked her, and we chatted about her two toddlers and motherhood. I nearly forgot why I was there until it was time for my session to begin.

Neville, as he asked me to call him, was tall, sturdily-built, with dark, thinning hair, probably in his late fifties. "Don't worry," he began jovially. "Not one person I've ever hypnotized has involuntarily barked like a dog or mooed like a cow. I'd like to dispel some myths about hypnotism. There are three things I want you to understand before we begin: you can't become trapped in the hypnotic state, you can come out of hypnosis whenever you want, and you are always in control."

I laughed nervously. "I'm told you do some writing and public speaking as well," I said, trying to avoid the purpose of my visit. I was realizing I feared what I might see during hypnosis.

He volunteered that as his clients worked with him and other self-help professionals, he'd seen people take on a more positive outlook about their own lives, and thus a more optimistic outlook about the world in general. His words and tone reassured me.

He expressed gratitude that now, in the 1980's, more individuals were willing to seek help and face their problems through professional services such as counseling and hypnosis. I knew that I'd certainly been helped by counseling.

"The result most often is a personal clearing of old issues that have nothing to do with the present," he continued. "A sort of a mental cleansing. This in turn creates more emotional availability—more freedom and energy to be willing to take on life's challenges. As long as a person is laden with anxieties and fears, they aren't able or interested in reaching out to others. For instance, if someone's well-being was affected by an emotionally and physically abusive parent, they're not likely to be motivated to head up a drive for funds to help abused children until those painful issues have been examined and released. At that point, the healed traumatic experience can actually serve, and often does, as a motivation to assist others in similar predicaments."

I nodded my understanding, appreciating his thoroughness.

"Personal traumas can become blocks to healthy living. When the blocks have been cleared, there is a natural renewing, and a birth of new spirit and energy. People who discover lost and much-needed parts of themselves reconnect with their own strength."

I listened carefully as he described the state of hypnosis. Neville claimed everyone experiences deep levels of hypnosis daily. One example was our transition between sleeping and waking. We can vividly recall our dreams and accompanying emotions, but only before everyday concerns come back into our minds and obscure them.

As the hypnotic state allows us to access the wisdom housed in our sub consciousness, we sense no boundaries or limits. In this pure subconscious state, we can experience sudden insights and flashes of wisdom, even ones guiding intuition and creativity.

Still sitting rigidly on the edge of my chair, I think Neville sensed my lingering uneasiness. He offered an example—Thomas Edison, inventor of the light bulb, used his own technique to access the hypnotic subconscious stage in order to envision his innovative discoveries. He repeatedly meditated to reach a deeper state of mind—a state of consciousness between sleep and wakefulness. With his arm on a chair, he would hold ball bearings in his hand and if he fell asleep, the ball bearings would drop and rattle in a metal bowl on the floor. In this deep state of mind, ideas and concepts broke through into his conscious awareness, including the one that eventually gave us the light bulb.

What a coincidence that Neville had mentioned a light bulb. A light bulb like in my painting, which had illuminated my own future. That subtle synchronicity was enough to put me in a willing state of readiness for what lay ahead.

There I was on the couch with my eyes closed, just like in the movies. Neville began a vivid guided visualization with suggestive images which led down many steps and through doors deep into the earth, to a completely safe and impenetrable space. I was calm, aware of his voice, and my own body, but kept my hands folded securely over my middle. Although still fearful of what I might see, I somehow managed to give myself permission to be open to whatever I was destined to discover. Neville began to ask questions about where I was, and what I was observing.

Chapter 11

A Dream from the Past

Neville's voice grew distant. Barely aware of my own body, I heard myself describing a foreign, yet strangely familiar, image. Within an instant I saw myself seated in an oversized, ornate, chair chiseled from a massive piece of marble, blending seamlessly into a marble platform and then onto a terraced floor below. My arms rested on the carved sides as I grasped the decorative, claw-shaped ends of the chair arms. I was a woman of power. My God. I was some sort of priestess.

Hearing myself say the word "priestess," it felt like a bolt of lightning had split me in half.

I became aware of a substantial band—a copper tiara, placed tightly on the crown of my head. In the center was an enormous triangular-shaped quartz crystal, mounted on a silver disc. The crystal was positioned low on my forehead, between my eyes. In a flash, somehow I knew it was a device to amplify and actually beam my thoughts at will.

In some mysterious way I had understood in that time, crystal, together with the copper band and silver disc, had the capacity to store mental energy. In amazement, I realized that like a transducer, my very own creative thoughts could influence the form of *all* human thought. I struggled to grasp the fact that the mind that inhabited this being, was also me. As I lay there on that couch, I felt small and helpless—and yet immortal and powerful.

I knew at that time, my thoughts and images could be converted into beams of energy. The beams were sent to receivers at great distances and these receivers were the waiting open minds of others! They converted the beams into their interpretation of images and thoughts, like mental projection.

How could I know this? Was this part of history? Was it even part of this planet? Yet, I had no doubt about it. It was common knowledge that those of us in that land possessed the ability to have our minds joined. We controlled the motion of the changing forces that created and destroyed.

With an unexplainable certainty, I knew that I, along with other priestesses, was a woman who had developed strong mystical powers for the advancement of the land. It was power to remotely amplify others' visionary thoughts of goodwill, power to amplify healing bodily energies of others, and power to amplify the physical efforts of the people into superhuman strength. And this mental strength, when combined with others, was capable of moving giant objects for the building of magnificent structures.

As though it were completely natural, I knew I could accomplish these feats not only with focused mental thought but with specific vocal sounds. My own sound vibrations could also be amplified through the purest crystals.

My thoughts! *My* sounds!

Suddenly, I felt the weight of a copper rod with a long cylindrical crystal on one end lying across my lap. A large carnelian stone was mounted on its other end. I knew this was a rod of grand power. It was always with me, a part of me. I picked it up and within the mental imagery of hypnosis, I experienced a powerful vibration of proverbial kinship. I instantly knew that by pointing it I could magnify and project my own thought energy and visualization in any direction through the crystal tipped, copper rod.

Gasping for a breath, I rolled my body away from Neville, signaling my need for a time out. I wanted the assurance of knowing I was still in his office. This was too much to grasp all at once. Finally, after a few deep breaths, I summoned the courage to focus again. Neville promptly guided me back to that incredible place.

I understood that when I clearly focused my attention, the rod switched from passively radiating energy to generating an active energy beam. Amazed, I realized that even the intensity and distance of the beam could be determined by my decision and amplified by the depth of my emotion. The sole purpose of the rod's creation had been to heal people, plants, animals, and polluted or contaminated water.

I had learned to wield great power with the rod. During times with massive projects in development in the kingdom, my mystical powers, combined with those of the other priestesses, were received and passed on through harmonious chants by trained, select groups of people. I could generate many times over the unified intent of these trained groups. Their thoughts and specific chants came purely from a desire to magnify whatever common good was already present in the hearts of those in the land. Along with physical and emotional healing, these groups could aid in sustaining positive desires of the people of the kingdom, such as compassion, brotherhood, peaceful coexistence, and most of all, a continuous flow of gratitude to the source of all. It was as though we all worked together, each as part of one mind.

The intentions of the people and these groups were further amplified by priestesses—like me—who were strategically stationed around the land. It seemed to me there were nine of us. Devotedly, we uplifted the people's will with our trained mental powers, our crystal headbands, and our power rods. Together, we all worked *our will* for the highest good of everyone.

This goal was the sacred covenant of the land.

Then the scene changed! I caught a glimpse of one of the massive projects.

A long line of large, muscular men, nearly two hundred of them, with shoulder-length hair were clad only in skirt-like garments and high-laced sandals. Wide copper bracelets inset with multiple crystals adorned their left forearms. United in every way, the men also directed their powers of strength and thought toward a single goal. In a cadence matching their own chants, their body movements were synchronized as they rhythmically heaved their weight forward. I saw that they were linked together with strong, tightly knotted rope that had been wrapped securely around a mammoth stone. The stone was to become a part of an emerging, massive structure.

Circling the men were several rows of the trained groups I had seen earlier, their bodies shrouded in long white cloths with only their faces visible. Each one held a large, precious geode of clear crystal. By surrounding the workers and chanting, they amplified their efforts into a mysterious blend of music and power, such as a shaman might summon.

Then I realized that as the presiding priestess of that particular area I held the dominating energy. Everyone was further empowered by me. They were all part of my assigned kingdom. I wielded the crystal rod with my right hand, extending it fully in their direction. With my learned powers, I intensified their positive energies to higher unification many times over.

Magically, the gigantic rocky mass was advanced up the hill, and onto the top of the last placed stone... at last united as one mind in a single great endeavor. While I remotely and emotionally witnessed this magnificent scene, I wanted to cry with joy. I felt embraced by peaceful goodwill.

But suddenly my body stiffened. Abruptly I was propelled forward in time. Something was wrong! Something dark and menacing overshadowed us. The sky was blackened in the middle of the day. Only a faint outline of the sun remained visible. I was vaguely aware of my head thrashing from side to side on the couch in Neville's office as I attempted to reject what I saw. My heart pounded in my chest. My mouth was dry, my body quivering. I felt locked in a state of helplessness.

The people of the land had wandered from our vision of the greater good. They had lost sight of the new world of harmony and peace we'd set out to build. And in its place an evil and decadent way of living was growing rampantly—a dark force was overtaking the land.

The downfall had begun when people stopped listening to their hearts. They abandoned the wisdom of their own understanding of loving righteousness to those who were greedy and power hungry, to those worshiping idols and coveting material treasures. They pillaged the crystals and precious jewels. They misused the powers of their trained will for selfish gain. Many greedily confiscated their neighbors' lands. Crowds drifted aimlessly into drinking, dancing, brawling in the streets and lustful behavior in public. No longer were they concerned for their futures or the future of the kingdom.

My feelings of helplessness intensified. I struggled to find the courage to stay within the hypnotic regression. Within this other dimension, I realized that a change had been building for some time. I knew that I had already reached into the complete depths of my own power to neutralize and heal this degenerative spirit. I had even learned the use of certain sounds to create a mood or command a gathering. Just as great music can lift the spirit, or groans of agony can accelerate despair, I had been trained to call out vibrant, restorative sounds, amplifying the energy levels of the people which could create excitement and stir their hearts back to the tranquil memory of our goals.

But my powers only worked in conjunction with the level of reception of each person's thoughts. They had to have some willingness. I struggled to magnify any trace of positive intention that remained. But their pure and decent desires were fading. My efforts were failing.

Then, another scene...down a narrow dirt road off to my left, a centurion who had served me faithfully, ran toward me. As he approached, I could see his unit's centurion banner draped across his body and over his left shoulder, his skirted garment swinging with his long strides. Swirls of dust trailed in his wake. He collapsed, kneeling at my feet.

I searched his face for any sign of good news. For anything we could work with, but I saw nothing. Instead, his steel-blue eyes telepathically implored me, begging me to help. My sinking heart knew he carried dreadful news. The news that all hope was lost.

His fear-stricken face told me that the corrupted thoughts of the people had passed the tipping point and were too powerful to reverse. He crouched at my feet, waiting for any command that would set him on a path of rescue. I glanced back and forth, frantically scanning the countryside below.

Nothing. I could think of nothing. Despite the wisdom I possessed, I was left powerless.

In the next instant, my trained mind knew this was the end of us. I foresaw that we were destined to be dragged down together. The undertow of the evil energy of darkness was consuming what was left of our lives. I knew our destiny. We would be consumed by the sea that surrounded us.

A primitive rage overcame me. I was devoured by it. Anger and disgust at the people's foolishness. Their blatant stupidity. With the fury of a primeval dragon, I rose up. Seething wrath coursed through every atom of my being. Inhaling deeply, I called forth every ounce of my strength. I summoned every power I possessed. Powers about which I had been warned that if used in excess, could precipitate confusion, disorientation, pain, and even trigger madness.

Blinded with disgust and rage, tightly clutching my crystal power rod, I climbed up to a high ledge above the land. I gripped my crystal scepter. With an icy glare, I extended my arms toward the people below me. Rabid with anger, I succumbed to my fury. I completely lost control. Drawing in a breath from the bottom of my being, I exhaled a high frequency—like the shrill, piercing note of a soprano who can shatter crystal, I exhumed a long, furious sound.

With all of my power, I accelerated the negativity and the destruction of the land. Crazed, I rode the sound for as long as my lungs could sustain the exhalation. Many died instantly. Some were struck with insanity, attacking themselves and each other.

And then...there it was in the distance! Just what I knew would be coming...a massively forming wave emerged from the sea and completely darkened the horizon. A huge cresting wall of green-black water. As the wave rose to unimaginable heights, I knew everything in its path was doomed.

With lightning speed and deafening roar, its blackness exploded onto our shores and upon the land, swallowing our kingdom. Screeching, cracking, crumbling structures in its path were ripped apart and carried along in the mad, tumbling water. Screams and wails could be heard from the people as they fled its advance. Though their efforts were in vain.

Violently, I was swept backwards and tossed into the bottomless, turbulent, green-black grave. Then, only cold, icy silence.

Why? Why had the people been so foolish? So misled? And then, immediately...oh, dear God, why had *I* added to the destruction and the suffering of my own people? Why had I betrayed myself? How could I have let my rage overcome my own goodness and reason? I was no better than the rest.

I watched my own submerged body, twisting, wrenching and helplessly struggling against the powerful force of the water. Kicking and grasping to hang on to something, I desperately sought for even the faintest glimpse of daylight.

Just then, as the water spun me out of its fierce flow into a pool of sudden calm, a narrow stream of light revealed the outline of a nearly lifeless body floating above me. For only an instant, I saw the face of my trusted centurion. In a split second I communicated to him, mind to mind. I pleaded with him to return with me in another lifetime and help me rectify the damage I'd done. Together, I declared, we must find a way to help others rebuild. As life left our bodies, I knew we had sealed a promise.

Desolate loneliness consumed me as my thoughts returned to Neville's office and the couch beneath me. I was sobbing, feeling guilt, shame and naked before the world. The person I was when I'd walked into his office had been changed. Devastating sorrow told me I had done something horrible! My first reaction was the fear that my evil deed had been exposed! Irrationally, I thought, now everyone would know that I had betrayed myself, and my people! Oh, my God, the people! I felt naked. I looked for the door. I wanted to run from the truth of what I saw; to run from my own actions.

Instead, I doubled over, wrapping my arms tightly around myself; the images still vivid. Yes, the people had been wrong to surrender their own inner wisdom and will to others; wrong to succumb to those with greedy and immoral intentions; wrong to bring us to the brink of physical destruction. But I had been wrong, too! Wrong to join in and quicken the certainty of it. To create more misery. I'd been a trusted leader for healing, yet I had accelerated and intensified their suffering. I knew better. I should have been stronger. Between sobs, in broken words, I expressed my morbid realizations to Neville. He understood my shame and guilt.

"But it's over now. That was in the past, Grace. That's the purpose for hypnotic recall of these unresolved memories—to bring them into consciousness so we can forgive ourselves and release them." He gently explained I had just experienced a *past life* memory. A memory of a time obviously concealing devastatingly deep fear. Fear still remaining in my subconscious that could only be released by lifting it into my conscious mind.

A past life! Really? I struggled to integrate what had just taken place. As though standing outside of me, I observed myself in Neville's office and remembered the shadowy images of myself in another time. It was bizarre. It was strange, yet so familiar. The power seemed completely natural, the devastation real. An instant connection with some part of me had emerged from a world that felt undeniably true. I was dumbfounded. I didn't know what to think.

Neville comforted me by assuring that in the moments this past life memory had been brought into the light of day and into my awareness, my fear had begun to dissipate. "We have a tendency to reject any part of ourselves we dislike because we unconsciously believe that once we accept it, it will be part of us forever. In reality, exactly the opposite is true. Holding onto repressed guilt is the very root of fear."

"But fear from a *past life?*"

"Yes," Neville responded. "We may be born into different bodies but hypnotists have experienced that our mind retains what went on before. It only becomes necessary to consciously remember certain events when past fears linger into our current lifetime. When we have grown to a place where, at least part of us is willing to seek deeper peace, the subconscious mind will accommodate. Any remaining blocks that hold back residual fears are weakened and the haunting memory persists in being released."

I pulled tissues from a box on the end table and wiped away tears and runny mascara in an effort to focus, as though deeper concentration might bring answers to the questions welling up inside me. This memory of *me* in *another lifetime* felt so foreign, yet really not.

I was exhausted. Neville suggested I'd had enough for that session. He offered to meet me for a half-hour during his free time the following Saturday when we could talk more.

Somehow, I drove myself home. Once inside the door, I kicked off my shoes, tossed my jewelry on the dresser, and collapsed on the bed. Fully clothed, completely undisturbed, I slept soundly through the night and into the next day.

For the next few days I gave up trying to analyze what had happened—what I had seen. I just let myself *feel,* and allowed fear to subside. I was nurtured by simple moments, like sitting motionlessly while absorbing the beauty of the impatiens lining the sidewalk outside my sliding glass door. I gratefully welcomed the respite from the turbulence I had felt for so many months.

As I drove to Neville's office that next Saturday, I became aware that part of me wanted to forget, to blank out this seemingly alien dimension of myself. Yet another part of me longed to make sense of it all.

"'Repetition compulsion' is the term Freud gave to this relentless inner drive to revisit fear," Neville began. "The subconscious mind, in its compelling need for peace, will root out any unresolved painful experiences that have occurred in this or any other lifetimes. As long as they're not resolved, they're in our memory as blocks of fear keeping us from being authentically calm and enjoying a sense of well-being. A regression experience accesses those memories. It presents the opportunity to remove these blocks of fear and the way we do that is actually quite simple. We forgive ourselves." By remembering this tragic time I could finally put it in perspective, he emphasized. Now I could understand the source of my fear, and yet in reality, it was past and there was nothing left but a memory. My memory.

His comments caused me to think of my first conversation with Dr. Ishagaki when he had talked about an *inner drive* that exists in everyone. A relentless need to recognize and synthesize subconscious parts of one's self in order to be healthy. Dr. Ishagaki had also said our subconscious wasn't limited by boundaries of logic, space, and time. I hadn't understood this at the time. I didn't realize he might be also talking about other lifetimes. Now I supposed a past life memory could be considered a submerged personality. This memory certainly had been submerged deep inside of me.

Neville told me that, by the act of remembering past lives, many of his clients had rid themselves of chronic, lifelong illnesses, panic attacks, phobias, and repetitive, destructive relationships.

So this memory, this past life, had lurked in my subconscious? It had consumed me? Had it been the cause of my recurring dream of drowning in green-black water; of my overwhelming and constant anxiety? Twenty-four hours a day, I had carried a mysterious burden of dread and fear, guilt and shame. Neville assured me that now my disturbing dreams and anxious emotions would lose their power over me. I hoped he was right. The truth was that my anxiety was waning and my nightmarish, recurring dream had not returned.

Neville continued to reveal that many of his patients had recalled lifetimes in mythical lands such as Lemuria and Atlantis, continents believed to have existed prior to modern civilizations and often ones considered to not be as advanced. But, he emphasized in direct contrast to common opinion, it was not unusual for patients of hypnosis to remember, as I had, super-human abilities and unfamiliar dynamics of nature.

He pointed out that now we have classes and philosophies that teach the power of personal change through positive thought and through a disciplined mind and goal-setting. The principle was and remains the same: controlling our choices and our thoughts helps us to achieve our goals and to attract more positivity to ourselves, not only in jobs and possessions, but in meaningful relationships and the satisfaction of deeper desires that can enhance our quality of living.

My head was still reeling with questions. I strained to bring back into perspective the mysterious pageant-like drama I'd mentally witnessed. "But, my trusted soldier was a centurion. Weren't centurions from Roman culture?"

"Perhaps," Neville reasoned. "And perhaps there were similarly organized armies in earlier lands, possibly forerunners of the Roman culture. Or, your soul might have been joined with the centurion in other prior lifetimes, and that was how you remembered him."

He said that my memory of the destruction of the continent and the advanced abilities of its civilization were similar to other accounts he'd heard regarding Atlantis. He assured me his clients were not mad or crazy, but quite competent people who led very normal lives.

Crazy! That's what I used to think of myself after my days in the mental hospital. But time had given me the confidence to trust my inner knowing.

Then Neville gave me something else to think about. He said the most important aspect of belief in reincarnation was to realize that our souls do not die when our bodies cease to function. We continue on living different lives through various personalities and those experiences help our soul's growth. Growth that eventually leads us to the heart of our authentic selves, to a deeper quality of peace, and a happier life. He had seen this positive transition occur over and over in the lives of his clients.

My soul's growth? I hadn't thought much about my soul. Ever since my childhood days of Daddy's evangelistic rule, I mostly considered my soul to be a part of me that had to be forgiven for doing something evil.

I heard Neville elaborating. Much of the world has believed in and used the wisdom of reincarnation for many centuries. He specifically noted this belief was represented in the symbols of major Eastern philosophies with examples such as the ancient religious symbol, the Egyptian Ankh, which is a representation of the regeneration of life. The Hindu symbol of the Om or Aum is a representation of the eternal process of birth, life, death, and rebirth. In Taoism, the yin and the yang symbols represent the interaction of opposites creating a continuous eternal process of becoming. And Buddhists believe the ultimate is to finally reach nirvana after many lifetimes.

Furthermore, Neville went on, some believe these lifetimes are not really in the past nor in the future. Many futuristic thinkers and even some scientists consider our experience of life to be as Einstein believed—that the concept of time, the distinction between past, present, and future, is an illusion and all time exists simultaneously.

I knew I had reached my limit when I realized I couldn't begin to grasp what he had just said. This was all too much to rationalize at once.

I was still working on...if there is no such thing as death—if we don't die when our bodies expire, what part of us lives on? And if it is true that I am healing because my own inner drive persists until I'm forced to expose this subconscious memory as a way to heal, then is this the only memory I need to recall? Or were there others?

I had so much to think about.

Over the next two months, each morning as I awakened I realized I couldn't deny the effects of my hypnotic regression. Calm was replacing my dread and anxiety and my nightmarish, recurring dream had stopped. I was able to move through my day clearly centered in the moment. But the shock for me—this mother, teacher, and business woman—actually experiencing an emerging past life, well, that would still take time. Especially when I attempted to reconcile this conflicting belief through the filters of the strict fundamentalist boundaries of my childhood. How could I ever make sense of this to my family? How could I tell anyone? It would sound crazy to anyone in the world I knew. Now I had something else to hide!

My father had always preached to us girls that his religion, his personal interpretation of Southern Baptist doctrine, and his version of the Bible, was the only way. He scolded us, warning us that we should have the fear of God in us. He threatened us with God's angry retribution as sinners. It kept us in line and Daddy made sure we knew we were sinners. What's more, he drilled it into us that not everyone would be "saved" from sin and "the wages of sin is death." Death was the ultimate punishment. As for reincarnation, he considered that to be straight from the devil. Heresy to the Bible.

Then I began to realize if there was any hope of reincarnating and living on in order to right wrongs, rather than a final death at the seeming end of our days, then his threats and the dogma of similar fundamentalist beliefs that tried to assert control through fear could hold very little power over us. Was that the purpose of such dogma? Power and control?

No matter what, I simply could not deny my own experience. I could not deny the relief that was still transforming my life. I felt a peace that my childhood religion could not give me. I especially could not forget that in the memory of *my past life,* the people's downfall had begun when they surrendered their own inner wisdom of godliness and their vision of brotherly love. The calm resulting from facing this guilt and fear from another time was compelling me to trust my own inner wisdom. I had already been shown the truth of trusting my inner wisdom. I knew I had to honor what was going on deep inside of me.

Gradually, over time, I allowed the voices and the walls of my former beliefs to fall away. Eventually, I learned to accept this expanded dimension which brought peace and greater resolve into my life than I had ever known. I opened myself to pray to a new unlimited, unrestricted higher power, for the wisdom to forgive, for forgiveness for the foolish, destructive wrath of my past life. I was confident I would learn to forgive myself. After all, here I was. I had come back into life with the memory of that lifetime. Somehow, perhaps by helping others, I could find a way to heal mistakes I'd made, although I had no idea how that might be accomplished.

As the days went by, gradually my perspective expanded while the recaptured memory faded, leaving behind the healing. The validity of my emotional reaction was undeniable. In previous weeks I had wept away the sadness and guilt that had been a part of me—its grip had been haunting in stifling my energy just as Neville had said. To my great delight, this release of repressed fear and grief *had* truly empowered me. My thinking was less clouded. I was more confident. I was happier. I had collected a lost piece of myself.

It was as though I'd awakened to find a twin sister sleeping restlessly inside of me. In the deepest recesses of my being I knew her from my past. She was me. The memory had mended a split within. I was more now. Inside of me a union had taken place. I came to recognize that a level of guilt and despair had been with me all of my life. I hadn't recognized the darkness until I was relieved of it…until it departed. I, and my world, was unfolding to an expanded view of life that was borderless, boundless.

Many questions still remained though. Like, what is the process and purpose of a soul, my soul? Is there really a past and a future? If the people in my past life had been empowered by their unifying thoughts, what would that be like?

No matter what, I couldn't deny what had happened to me. I hadn't believed in past lives and reincarnation. But now I knew I was far more than my conscious experiences…I had connected the dots to my soul.

CHAPTER 12

Dreams Come True

I returned to the harbor. It felt deeply familiar. I knew it in my bones. But my fear had gone. The high bluffs now resembled giant arms, curling around me, embracing me. The colorful boats with their sails tied to their masts, the picnic tables on grassy knolls, the tidy, small sandy beach, and the gentle curling waves of the breakwater spilling themselves upon the shore, had all been transformed into a haven of warmth and comfort. Although the memories remained, the violent energy had faded.

As fierce as the emotional storm had been within me three months ago, it was now replaced by quiet inspiration. I could no longer deny the healing effects brought by my consciously remembering terror from another lifetime. I was different. I possessed a new strength. There was a larger me. I had met another part of me that had lived long ago. She was in my consciousness now, and her memory made me more.

With a blanket and picnic basket, I routinely visited the cove in the harbor on weekends and in the evenings if I arrived home from work before dusk. Occasionally, I experienced a wave of sadness whenever I reached the curve of the bluffs where the road opened to the ocean, the spot where I'd envisioned the Indian village. But, no longer was I devastated by my emotions.

A few months after my hypnosis session, on a lovely Saturday late in January 1986, I took my usual place on the beach in the cover of the harbor to enjoy one of California's pristine, sunny winter days. On my yellow pad, my constant companion, I wrote about my transformed feelings.

Finally I have risen out of that black, mysterious sorrow and dread. That haunting dream and the fear that overcame me, the turbulent, chilling silence of the green-black, watery grave. Light has broken through. Playful images dance in my head. Here at the beautiful water's edge, I can imagine myself as a dolphin, a playful child of the sea, whole and new again. Or, I envision a clear, aquamarine ocean and, like a mermaid, I rise gracefully out of the sea. As I reach the surface, the sun's rays bathe me, and the crystal clear water purges away any traces of my old fears.

I wrote allowing my emotions to stir; inspired by the beauty of these images. A thought struck me—could my strong, lifelong desire to express my feelings through singing have arisen because I had abused my power of sound in another lifetime? For as long as I could remember, I'd had a passionate longing to sing as a way to release my bottled-up emotions. Even as a child, it was a blissful escape, and I'd been able to experience brief moments of joy.

I had a natural vibrato even when I was very small. At the age of eleven, without my father's knowledge, our neighbor, who was a voice teacher, arranged to have me sing on the radio. I sang *Lavender Blue*, a popular song in the early 1950's. She wanted to tutor me, but my father wouldn't allow it. "You're disgraceful, throwing yourself out there on display." He didn't even allow me to sing in the house. Once, when I was about thirteen, I was washing the dishes. I just couldn't hold it back any more. As softly as I could, I began to sing the song *Summertime*. A thunderous sound came from behind me as Daddy rattled through the swinging kitchen door, belt in hand. The belt stung my legs. That beating broke my spirit, leveling it to a new low.

It seemed everyone in my life sought to discourage me from singing. First, my father, then Jack, for whom my singing was never good enough. He didn't want anyone to stand in front of his piano when *he* played. I knew the suppression of my heart song had caused me to hold onto deep anger and resentment towards both of them.

Is this my destiny, or what I've heard called karma? I wondered. Does one have to continue on in another lifetime where they left off from the past? Different face, different place?

Because I'd caused destruction with the power of sound in a past life, was it my karmic path in this lifetime to discover the *healing* power of my voice? To capture the part of myself I'd lost? To be able to express my deepest feelings in melodious and beautiful sounds? Could it finally be the time to realize *that* dream?

I wondered how many other lives I might have lived. And, if there is no real death, how many more lives were ahead of me? When does it stop? Does it ever stop?

And what about my other recurring nightmare of Indians chasing me in a corn field? That hadn't emerged in my hypnosis session. Was that recurring dream, and the vague sadness I experienced while envisioning the Indian village in the harbor, symbolic of something karmic yet to take place in my future?

My recurring dream of drowning in green-black water had indeed started me on a pursuit. It had been extremely healing to remember my past life as a priestess, but even the memory of it was becoming like a dream. A dream from my past. The many unexplainable things that had happened to me prompted the question once again—was I just living in one giant dream? Was all of life one huge dream?

Ever since the '70's, when the visions I'd experienced in the mental hospital in 1960 had begun actualizing, I'd considered the absurdity of life as only a dream. Suppose that I am a dreamer...then what am I waking up to? What is the purpose? Dr. Ishagaki had said everyone has an *inner drive* to live in peace and harmony, and quoted Jung: "The mind is in an inexorable search for balance." Is the memory of my past life part of that balancing process? Where does the drive—the dream—end?

In the comfort of the harbor, I rolled onto my back and stretched, enjoying the scratchy stimulation of my terry cloth beach blanket. I gazed into the midday horizon, soaking up the beauty of the plump white clouds moving in slow motion across the pale azure winter sky. My body sank deeper into the sand as I allowed the sloshing, rhythmic sounds of the waves to caress me.

What a delicious dream come true this was. I loved my children and I loved the friends I had made in Maryland, but because of the toxic memories of my marriage, California had been the only place that really felt like home. In the charm of the beach cove, stroked by the soft breeze, my body gratefully received the warmth of the penetrating rays of the sun. Just at that moment, I realized—this really is a dream come true! The road to my present circumstances was *a dream come true.*

There it was again! That word *dream.* A dream come true...recurring dreams...dreams that bring messages...past lives seem like a dream...my dreamy visions of things to come...made life seem as one big evolving dream. Wow.

Dream is such a common word; a metaphor for lots of circumstances. Dreams are commonly thought of as experienced during periods of sleep. Yet, there are daydreams, passing time in a state of fantasy and reverie. And there are nightmares—bad dreams. Hallucinations and delusions can also be viewed as dreams. There are dreams that contain our life ambitions, such as my dream that came true in coming to California. Even the trance state I'd experienced in hypnosis is considered a dream state. Visionaries and idealists can been seen as dreamers.

We hear about dreams from the very start of our lives. Children are told fairy tales by their parents about heroes and heroines that have fallen into a deep sleep and then awakened. Like Snow White, who fell into a sleeping spell when she ate a poisonous apple, and Sleeping Beauty who, when she pricked her finger, fell into a deep sleep until her prince came to awaken her from the dream. Magical spells—a dream state. And, of course, there was Alice, who dreamed of Wonderland, and Peter Pan, who roused little Michael and John from their beds at night and away they all flew to a dreamland.

Visions possess a dream-like quality. My own visions in the mental hospital, later lived out, were like prophetic dreams—like watching a video I'd already seen about myself. When my mind slipped through a nexus-like opening, I was on a mystical magic carpet ride, dreaming of assorted scenes gliding by. Some of those scenes actually became part of my daily life—like *dreams coming true.*

Actually, returning to "normal" life when leaving the mental hospital seemed like a dream—or more of a tragic nightmare. Ordinary life appeared in surreal motion...a bog of confused, lost human beings, frenetically busying themselves at goodness knows what; milling aimlessly through crowds, acting like fools. In robotic animation, everyone and everything resembled a three-ring circus; a sleazy cabaret shrouded in disregard for others. A dream that always ends in death—a stark contrast to the divine order and beauty from which I'd returned.

Even my painting of the bare lamp and lightbulb, a symbolic message of my future, was first a vision—or a dream from my own mind that I saw before I lived out the reality. Which is the reality? The dream—or the acting out of the dream?

When my father beat me as a child, I cried for hours, hoping my mother would come in and hold me. During those sad times, my psychic pain caused me to retreat in my mind, suspended above my body so I could view myself less painfully in a dream-like state. The same dream-like escape happened to me in the hot tub at our house in Maryland the night I finally spewed out the anger and hurt I'd held back during my marriage to Jack. The moment I walked into my condo, I'd recognized it. There was that feeling I was outside of myself, watching my own life unfold. And, the images I'd experienced in the harbor; had I been the dreamer, or the observer?

I knew psychiatry often used the term "disassociation" for episodes like this—the experience of being outside of one's self. Naming it, however, doesn't explain it. It doesn't change what is happening. I remember awakening in the mental hospital—or perhaps I was still dreaming?—when I spoke the words, "Thank God, I will get my divorce." And I did. A dream come true. Or was it just one episode within a monumental dream that is my "normal" life? Only one dimension of many dimensions of the dream?

Even the state of hypnosis itself, recalling details of an apparent past life, was a truth-bearing dream from my subconscious. Is the subconscious really the *Master Dreamer?* Reincarnation asserts that we do not die when our bodies do, so does that mean that the dreamer, our subconscious mind, continues on dreaming throughout time, lifetime after lifetime? If so, what does the Master Dreamer want me to know about this lifetime? Finding and releasing an ancient cause of guilt and shame has proven to be a deep relief. But is there something else I have yet to do in this lifetime?

Time itself was beginning to feel like a trick—a form of imprisonment. Could time be the dream? Are we in a state of being housed within a dream called *time?* I sighed in surrender to my life, woven with mystery, surprise, and learning experience. I had no choice but to wait and see what all these dreams meant.

That evening, feeling mellow from the warm sun and my tranquil day, I treated myself to a luxurious, lavender scented bubble bath. I lit small, white candles in the bathroom and bedroom, and I put on a Whitney Houston tape. I felt so relaxed I nearly fell asleep in the tub.

When I climbed into bed I took time to reflect on my thoughts of the day. To live in peace and harmony is what everyone wants. I was living with greater inner calm, having released the subconscious fear and guilt of an earlier life. But what about those other symbolic visions I didn't understand—like the dream of being chased by Indians? Was that another symbolic message for something I needed to heal? And the visions of the hot tub; the mountain with the multi-lane highway straddled by a blank, white, rectangular sign. And those pink houses I'd seen on the hillside, yet there were none; my intuitive knowing about the number 52 by my condo door; my knowing that I would be fifty-two when I married. Keys to my future? "Mind and matter interacting?" I just didn't know.

What I did know at that moment was that I was happy. I felt a new kind of contentment and peace. My eyelids grew heavy. I reached up to turn out the light. Again, I caught sight of the two Asian scrolls on the wall…the woman crossing the bridge.

The next day I welcomed the chance to sleep in. I didn't have the energy to fight the traffic to go to church. Now and then, I had dinner with a friend, Kevin, whom I had gotten to know through work. He was a real estate lawyer and an instructor in real estate law at the University of California in Irvine. He periodically invited me to go with him to The Church of Religious Science in Huntington Beach.

I hadn't really formed any opinion one way or another about the church but Kevin was a very optimistic person and I liked that. He never missed an opportunity to exclaim, "There are no accidents!" A view that I could easily align with, just as I was accepting Jung's view of meaningful coincidences that he had called synchronicity. Kevin firmly believed that everything happened for a reason. He extended that philosophy to include our friendship. Then, much to my surprise, I stumbled upon a way to apply that same philosophy.

I snuggled down into the corner of my sofa which faced the sliding glass door. I was delighted as I watched a velvety, bright green and yellow hummingbird hover, sipping the sweet solution I had poured into a feeder suspended on my patio. The second it swooped into sight, I grinned with pleasure. Such amazing beauty. So delicate, yet so strong, miraculously defying gravity as it suspended itself in air.

The warmth and security of my cozy condo enveloped me more completely than ever before. This, I remembered, was how I'd felt in that moment when the realtor had first led me through the door. My condo was my cocoon. Perhaps someday there would also be a man with whom to share my life. I hoped so.

I reached for my journal and I let my feelings flow. It was good to feel safe and to write about how I was learning to greet contentment. Yet, as I sat in silent expectation of growing pleasure I noticed a dissonant, gnawing feeling that seemed to emanate from my throat, extending into my stomach. It was a desire, a longing I couldn't identify. I watched the joyous ritual of the little hummingbird as it hovered, sipped and then chirped, as if throwing kisses to everyone in earshot. Then, there it was. In my journal I wrote, *I want to sing.*

I wanted to sing as freely and as naturally as that little bird. My desire to sing had been much deeper than I had admitted. And now it was building. I *needed* to sing—as I had early in my childhood, before Daddy's beatings. I wanted to reclaim that authentic part of myself. It seemed to me the success of clearing away submerged feelings through hypnosis had started something in me. I was no longer willing to deny what I really wanted.

I tingled with anticipation. Yes, I had sung in numerous choirs, madrigal groups, and concerts over the years, and I'd even sung a lead part in a community musical. But I had suppressed my singing into a carefully controlled style that seemed safe. Now, I wanted to sing out fully, completely from my heart. I wanted to feel the joy of being myself. I knew this was one of the things that would help me to be happier. To sing *my* own natural, authentic song as freely as I had done in childhood. As freely as that beautiful little bird.

But how? Singing lessons would be great, but I couldn't afford the expense of voice lessons. Still, if I had a magic wand and could make only one wish, I would wish for some form of vocal coaching.

It was then that I remembered a practice I'd noticed which was frequently used at Kevin's church. It was called "affirmations." They taught that if one had an honest desire, it could be fulfilled by stating that desire clearly and then imagining the feeling of succeeding at that desire, even in the face of what might seem to be insurmountable obstacles. Their philosophy was that thought, or the spirit of good, or God, was first reflected into the mind and then manifested into matter. That had been the same principle in my healing from my Atlantis lifetime!

Why not try? I had nothing to lose.

Kevin had stressed the point to me that the power is in the wording of human desires, not negative but positive. So, I needed to create *my dream* in a positive form and to continue to affirm it.

I decided right then—I would do it. I wrote an affirmation to bring about the support and opportunity to sing in my own way. I did not expect that it would take so long to write one little paragraph. *I really would like to sing...* No, that's not an affirmation. That's a wish. *Dear God, please lead me to...* No, that's a request. *All my life, I have wanted to...* No, no, that's not in the affirma √√tive. What a revelation it was to me to become aware of my own thinking process.

Nearly an hour later, I finally came up with a statement in the affirmative, including a specific time, as Kevin had recommended: *By June 8th, I will find a way to sing my heart's song for loving people who support me and truly want to hear me. I will sing authentically, beautifully, and with great joy.*

I re-read it. I flinched at the date. June 8th was just one month away. Could that be possible? I caught myself. No, believe it! You must believe it or, as he said, you are canceling the order by the power of your own word. I lapsed into fantasizing about how it would feel to sing from my heart. Even about what I would wear...the blue lamé sheath dress I'd just purchased. It was so much fun. I mentally savored my own dream as it came true in my mind.

I stood up from the couch, stretching. I caught a glimpse of my face in my diamond-shaped mirror. My cheeks flushed and my eyes sparkled a bright blue. Warmth swirled in my breasts. I felt the strength of my womanhood coming alive. I turned, scanning the room. How I loved my little condo. It was my private retreat—and no one could interfere with my tranquility or hold me back. I was filled with deep gratitude.

The peaceful painting of a sailboat docked in a harbor caught my eye. Stepping over to appreciate it, my eyes wandered to the artist's signature and his chosen title, *Safe Harbor.* Indeed, it was.

By the next Sunday I couldn't wait to attend Kevin's church. I knew sharing the spirit there would encourage me to continue my affirmative thinking. This was a Religious Science community of over seven hundred people. The gathering had the energy of an exuberant rally, as well as a church. Peggy Bassett, the minister, was even more wonderful and inspiring than I'd remembered, and the morning service contained happy, rousing music. Instruments, soloists and the entire choir were joined by the congregation. The pianist possessed such a stylish flare I was sure he used every single note on the keyboard.

Later, out on the patio, we socialized with coffee and tea. Kevin introduced me to the pianist, Bill Wolfe. A tall young man clad in a tan suit with a red carnation in his lapel, his personality was as joyful as his playing. A professional musician, he had directed numerous community theatre productions in Orange County. I remarked on how much I loved his music and the singing.

"Are you a singer?" he asked.

I smiled. "I am, and I've recently decided I would like to do it more."

"Then you might be interested in a four-day workshop that my sister and I are having in two weeks. It's called *Lifesong*." He handed me a flier with the address. Like pink feathers, his words floated all around me. "It's a small group of people...an opportunity to explore and experiment with your creativity...a safe and playful environment, with personal guidance from the instructors."

Goosebumps! There it was. Just what I had asked for in my affirmation just one week ago! An opportunity to sing my own heart song in the company of loving people—a safe environment! What a blessing!

His next words brought me swiftly back into the moment. "One hundred and eighty dollars."

"Yes. I think that would be something I would like to do," I said, ignoring my unease at the idea of again dipping into my dwindling savings.

Even though I had written down my affirmation and forbid myself to doubt it, it exceeded my expectations. Coincidence? I knew it wasn't. I keenly felt the connection. And even my slightest doubt disappeared *the following week* when I received a check from my former real estate broker in Maryland for a property I'd sold that had been tied up in court. I never expected to see a penny of it. The check was for $1,500.

There were eleven of us. The practice room was large, with hardwood floors, made cozy by a semicircle of chairs arranged snuggly around the piano. I tried to brush aside a vague sense of intimidation. Besides Bill and his sister Linda, an additional volunteer staff of five people sat behind us, waiting to support our every need. The level of concern and regard for the importance of our participation in the room felt alarmingly unfamiliar to me.

The session opened with all of us singing a robust version of *Zip-a-dee-doo-dah,* a light, happy song that I'd adored as a child. I had seen the movie, *Song of the South,* and always read the cartoon strip in the funny papers. The song touched the little child in me, the child who'd yearned for happy play. I felt so emotional I wanted to cry. After a warm welcome they explained the format of the next few days. It was simple. Each person would select a song, learn it, and sing it on the final day before an audience on stage with a microphone—and wearing our best attire. Our families and friends were to be invited.

I felt trepidation at the thought of inviting my family members. All my adult singing had been done on the East Coast, and my mother and two sisters had never heard me sing in that way. Frankly, I didn't know if they would care or be interested enough to come.

Bill began by asking us to explain our reasons for attending the workshop. I wasn't sure just how much I wanted to reveal. I just wanted to sing. He then announced that they required an agreement of confidentiality. Nothing said or done was to leave the workshop. Suddenly, a part of *me* wanted to run from the room. Could I tell strangers what had kept me from singing the way I really wanted to? Could I expose the hurt and abuse by Daddy and Jack? That was my secret life. It was embarrassing. How would the others respond to my personal revelation? I felt cornered.

Some were there to learn technique; some wanted a greater level of skill; one told of a song he had always wanted to sing; and others just wanted to have fun. I simply put myself in the group that wanted to develop more skill.

Then it came time to pick a song. I hadn't really given it any thought. A long table was completely covered with sheet music and books for our selection. "Don't think too much," Bill said. "Just let yourself go to the song that calls to you." My eyes immediately fell on *Summertime* from *Porgy and Bess,* the song I had sung at the kitchen sink when Daddy had beaten me.

That was the song I would sing. I wanted to perform it again, but this time from the bottom of my heart. Bill played each of our songs on the piano as he recorded them on eight-track tapes for us to take home to use in practicing. And that ended the first session.

On Friday, after group warm-up singing, Bill's sister, Linda, a petite dynamo with a pristine, lyrical soprano voice, announced that we would each be invited to sing our song. Part of me was ready to leap up and another part of me was glued to my chair. What if they were all professionals? What if they're all better than me?

As it turned out, there were all levels of singers. Some theatrically trained, some who only sang in the shower. But, a pattern began to emerge. As Bill and Linda questioned each performer about his or her chosen song's meaning for them, and about his or her motivation for choosing the song, they requested certain segments to be sung again, and then again, sometimes asking that the lyrics be spoken or shouted. Several people were moved to tears. The emotions contained in the songs summoned unresolved issues in their lives. Some broke into sobs. Although one young man's legs quivered wildly, others supported him so that he could complete his song. I was determined that I would not lose my composure. This was my time to do it right. This was my moment. Nothing would spoil it.

When my turn came, I sang the song straight through in my soprano voice with creative expression and flair. Everyone applauded, as they had done for each person. It felt good. Then Bill asked me to sing it in a lower key. I didn't want to. I didn't feel secure there, but I refused to let on. I was there to get my full song back. As I sang my voice became unsteady and weak. I was losing control, my tone becoming thinner. It felt like someone else was singing. Deep rage was building inside of me. I realized that what I really wanted to do was to let out an angry screech. To sing shrill and off key. To make ugly sounds. A lump as big and hard as a greenplum seemed to be caught in my throat.

And then it happened. I was crying, rivulets of black mascara running down my cheeks. Repressed anger, bottled up resentment and deep hurt gushed forth. In a barely audible whisper, I confessed the truth of the abuse, repression and rejection I had lived through. My shoulders shook as I sobbed. The staff came around the table and embraced me all at once. In a moment, everyone in the room was stretching their arms around me in a group hug similar to the one I'd experienced in Al-Anon. I could not remember feeling so loved. So accepted. So safe.

It seemed that singing in the lower key was a range closer to the sound of my childhood voice. I had abandoned that place inside of myself. I sang first soprano. I never sang in a lower range. That sound, that key, that vibration in my body, churned up bitter feelings inside of me. Everyone understood. Everyone expressed love and compassion. It was then that I began to realize Bill and Linda's purpose for the workshop was beyond simply learning notes and technique to make beautiful music. They wanted to help us find the beauty inside.

A deep bond formed among us in the group. As the workshop progressed, and to the surprise of most everyone, except Bill and Linda, we all found a place within ourselves that was waiting to be healed. It seemed like the very vibrations of our songs coming through us brought forth healing. Our own sound! Like sludge moving through clogged pipes, our singing summoned our emotions, causing them to surface into the openness of the moment and then be released.

I realized a dynamic was underway that was similar to the relief I had experienced when I'd undergone hypnosis. By remembering the events and my angry, vengeful part in that tragedy, I had been able to release the guilt and shame that I still carried, and that in turn had given me courage to recognize my repression of my desire to sing again in this lifetime.

The staff passed out notebooks already bearing our names to be used for journaling. For the next hour, after a break with snacks and warm conversation, we wrote. Everyone found a corner or other comfortable space for privacy. It was a chance to reflect authentically with ourselves, allowing our feelings to flow through our pen.

Anger. That is what first spewed through my pen! My deeply buried resentment shot forth onto my paper like bullets.

Why had there always been those around me who didn't want to hear me sing? They did not want me to feel good! Why?

Sometimes, when I sing, I experience an emotional halt at the very moment I am really ready to let go! It's that old feeling—the point where Jack abruptly stopped playing the piano with that tired excuse that he didn't remember the rest of the song. He rejected me and the joy we could have shared. Often, I felt he was so close to letting go. Then, he'd clamp down. Even though he was the perennial joke teller, I know that he was deeply depressed, and I know that depression is anger held inward. His drinking numbed the anger he never faced or expressed. He rejected the joy I invited, longed for. He rejected me.

Daddy! Why had he beaten me for singing! Did the sound of singing stir feelings that he could not face or control? Feelings he had denied—repressed—in his lifelong battle between his anger, his uncontrollable temper, and his rigid religious beliefs? I know he wanted to experience the same joy—but he could not. I don't think he ever did.

When Mickey and I were little, we liked to wrestle on the floor. We laughed and tickled each other. We were in joy. Daddy always stopped us, threatening to whip us if we didn't "cut out that foolishness." He kept his feelings all bottled up. The only way he could let it all out was to explode in hurtful ways. I know that's why I would freeze up sometimes as a kid when I was asked to sing. Or there would be that one sour note in a song. I feared someone would come up behind me...that the other shoe would drop, waiting for the sting of his belt. Why couldn't he have just loved me?

I feel so rejected.

I feel so unworthy. I feel as though I am guilty of some wrongdoing.

But I was not the abuser. I'm realizing now that it is hard to accept my own innocence.

The scary, bizarre truth is that when I try to imagine myself really singing and letting out my emotions, I see myself before a group, making grotesque, grimacing, animal-like faces—exuding horror—ugliness—snarling—foaming—snapping—biting—barking—growling—while I gnash my teeth at the people who repressed my natural joy and own innocence.

Then, while writing, I had a flashback. That was just how I'd envisioned the people of the land in my past life. That was how they'd reacted when I had misused my power of sound. When I had turned on *them* in great rage. Had my ability to sing from my heart been held back by guilt from that lifetime as well?

It was time to return to the group. Darkness had come and we had an open sharing of our thoughts around a pretend campfire complete with blankets, S'mores, and light by flashlight. Just like we were kids again. It was healing medicine to be able to speak out to others, and even laugh about my hidden past and the absurdity of my thoughts, in an intimate, safe place to really be heard. It was sweet and scary all at the same time. I didn't offer a lot of detail, but I had revealed that I'd been abused. I became aware of muscles and ligaments relaxing in my back and shoulders which had been so tight they had become numb. I heard the sound of my laughter become richer, warmer. I felt compassion for others' stories. I thought of those I'd abused with sound in my past life. I was grateful to listen to others sharing and to be able to offer them empathy in response to their stories.

That night I ate voraciously. I slept like a baby. The endorphins were charging through me. I felt higher than I'd ever been from any sexual experience. I felt no panic in anticipation of my upcoming performance. Instead, I was filled with new energy, though a tiny bit scared because I had become vulnerable—but mostly excited.

On Saturday, the third day of the workshop, we began early. We all ran through our songs one at a time. At Bill's request, I sang my song in a lower key. An uncharacteristic strength was emerging, my voice gaining substance and power. My song was much lighter. My spirit was much lighter. The place inside of me where the old hurt had lived was being taken over by new, stronger energy.

The afternoon began as we learned some rousing group songs, punctuated with choreography to round out our show. We were all becoming giddy, drunk with our deeper selves emerging. We indulged in being childlike, silly. This was never a part of my personality. I had always been expected—forced—to be very serious. Such emotions had not been a part of me since childhood. I felt like a stranger, but this was a part of me I wanted to know.

When it came my turn to rehearse my song once again, I jumped up and went straight to it. No halting feeling! No caution! I knew whatever came out of my mouth would be completely accepted. Everyone held me in their loving support with their eyes. "Summertime and the livin' is easy..." I belted out lightheartedly. I could interpret the song anyway I pleased. I performed, I finished, and I virtually floated back to my seat.

We all came together in a circle for our last sharing. Their stories were different from mine, yet the same. We had let our walls down to be able to come together, and to accept each other just as we were. And, ultimately, to accept ourselves. There was just one thing we all really wanted. Love.

A thought popped into my head. I wondered if any of those present had been with me in my past life. Had we somehow come back to heal together, to be able to accept each other just as we really were? To drop our judgments and begin anew?

As the evening closed, Bill offered his perspective of our song—our *sound* as he called it. "Our sound, as it moves through us, is related to our emotional health. We are more than our bodies," he went on, "we are energy, or perhaps we might consider it spirit. And our human energy or spirit has to be expressed somehow, whether it is positive *or* negative."

His point was that our bodies retain emotional memory, and we need to release any past traumas from our body. By letting go of the stress that has held us back throughout our lifetime, and other lifetimes, I realized—our sounds, our emotions, just like electrical currents, can travel through the body. Even the emotion of love is energy. When our emotions are acknowledged by allowing their full expression, then we can be cleared of the blocks of negative, repressive energy, and we then we can be free to express our natural, positive energy. We are in balance within ourselves.

I was captivated by Bill's words because I knew how much more authentic I felt since dealing with painful, suppressed emotions from my past—from my current life *and* my past life.

I wondered. Does that inexorable inner drive for balance extend through past lives and the present? Could it be that my soul or subconscious mind has *chosen* the conditions of this life? Had the abuse of Daddy and Jack actually played a part in re-enacting, or bringing me to a level of pain resembling what I'd known in my past life, so that I could again get in touch with work to be done and find healing?

What I did know was that a steady, light hum vibrated in my body. A harmonious vibration. I knew it was affecting my song. My sound was changing for the good. I realized why we like to experience the exhilaration of singers in robust harmony with themselves. We get to vicariously feel the truth of our own power. Like the joy from simply watching a beautiful hummingbird!

Sunday came, and soon the evening of the performance. My excitement exceeded my nervousness. Although I had casually dropped the news to my mother, my sisters and niece that I would be singing, I had resolved myself to the likely probability that they would not come. But Jennifer came. Our growing connection meant so much to me, and I was so grateful for her loving support. Her presence also helped me to make a satisfying connection between my past and my present.

I dressed in my royal blue lamé sheath. The one I had envisioned myself in after writing my affirmation. It had a feminine, slightly revealing, V-neckline. I felt the fullness of my womanliness. I felt strong.

My turn came. The song sang through me. I did well. I savored every moment. I met everyone's eyes. They, in turn, met mine. Many smiled. It was food for my hungry soul. It was so good. I remembered to stay standing and soak up the applause just as Bill and Linda had directed. "Receive the love. Take it in. Feast in the beauty of who you are."

It was merely a few days less than one month since that day in my living room when I'd declared my will to sing by June 8th. Because I had made the choice to project my deep desire into an affirmation and subsequently believe in it, not just a song had been born inside of me, but a vibrant new me was born too.

That Monday morning, the spiritual garden of healthy emotions that had been planted inside of me was sprouting. My heart was light. I hurried out to the carport to start up my Volvo and head off to work.

I stopped dead in the middle of the parking lot. There it was again—my license plate which read, **2BEZ422 ... to be easy for Grace!** A line from *Summertime* rang in my ears ... "**and the livin' is easy.**" It was a moment of pure glee.

I laughed out loud, just as I had the first time I recognized this comforting symbolic message. Thank God! A spirit marker—that silent voice which expresses itself everywhere, through anything I can identify with, relays its message of assurance. It was a sign post to let me know I was on the right road. Another *dream* had come true.

CHAPTER 13

Dreams or Illusions?

I relaxed on the sofa waiting for Kevin to pick me up for an all-day trip to San Diego. Stretching my legs, I settled in resting my feet on the coffee table. Cradled in contentment, I realized that my *Safe Harbor* painting hung just above my head. *Safe Harbor,* the image of a sailboat nestled in the protective, still waters of a lovely harbor. This sturdy vessel with the capability of journeying over high seas into port after port had begun to mirror itself to me as a symbol of my own journey.

Like that sailboat, I too now found myself in a harbor town. I knew its journey so well. My mind and emotions had been tossed against the walls of blocked memories, battering my soul until I sought refuge and healing. Perhaps while docked, that boat was being restored, as was I, before setting sail once again. *Safe Harbor* was a silent, visual assurance of my security. In that instant, I saw its place in a sheltered cove as a reflection of the calm that was building within me, brought on by inner nurturing that had begun in this very room on the morning I had written my affirmation to sing.

My peace then had been bittersweet, mixed with the subtle discontent of an unfulfilled longing. In a moment of absolute stillness, I'd spied the little hummingbird, its very being symbolically charged my need. Like striking a match, its presence lit a fire inside of me. The innocent sweetness of the bird that had stimulated my natural hunger for authentic self-expression was *symbolic.*

I reached over the arm of the sofa to an end table for my paperback copy of *Man and His Symbols,* Carl Jung's book that had been by my bedside for so long in Maryland. Jung postulated that an event of *physical form can communicate to blocked information in the subconscious awareness.* I browsed over his comments... "symbols speak"... "they amplify"... "they simplify"... "wordless interaction." Through them our subconscious receives meaning... a language spoken symbolically to our subconscious mind. I had been experiencing this wordless interaction, this form of communication, for years! I also suddenly realized there was more to it than just the peace I felt in my *Safe Harbor* picture. It was mirroring a dynamic exchange of understanding between my subconscious mind and the material world.

The concept of *symbol* was crystallizing into an entirely new meaning for me. When it was least expected, some *thing* or some *event* could activate keen intuition within me, nudging into consciousness an intangible truth about myself. "Symbols *transform.*" The word *symbol* now represented to me a wordless interaction between *anything* and my own subconscious. Symbols could stimulate a powerful communication to my own healthier inner knowing. Symbols activated my own inner voice.

But why was I trying to filter everything, to mentally compartmentalize it all into little boxes? What really mattered was that it all worked in harmony.

Satisfied, I returned the book to the end table. Still waiting for Kevin, who was sometimes late, I leafed through my latest journal, stopping at my comments about the Psychosynthesis class. I was so glad I'd taken a chance and enrolled in the program. I might never have found the hypnotist or the key to my irrational fears. Many of the people in the class had become my good friends, including Dr. Ishagaki. Sadly, the class was ending. I would really miss my fellow students, but I couldn't afford to enroll for an additional year.

It had become apparent to me that all I'd learned in the class was aligned with everything I had suspected prior to the class. If I faced my fears, I would discover more about myself. If I avoided them, they caused deep discontent. The thought that there is a positive drive in the mind, soul, whatever one calls it, comforted me. Might my entire life exist solely to bring the natural wisdom of my subconscious into consciousness?

Snuggled on my couch, I smiled. *I guess there's just a darned, determined part of me that wants to be happy,* I thought.

Just for fun, I played at postulating a theory combining my experience and Jung's approach. If life *is* a dream and I—my subconscious mind (my natural state of wholeness) is the Master Dreamer, then my dream contains meaningful coincidences (synchronicity) where anything can become a *symbol,* speaking to me through wordless interaction. And so the symbol supports my mind in its relentless drive for balance and wholeness.

What if every *thing* and every *event* held the potential to lead me to my own happy, innocent nature—like the line in the Bible that says all things come together for good? Then all of life could be considered a kind of *organic interaction.* All things, both good and bad, could reflect in their own way a common meaning, and a common purpose, designed to guide me to experience my true essence...my healthy, happy self.

I'd been fascinated recently by the word, "hologram," which, I discovered, combines "whole" from the Greek word *holos* and *gram* which means "message." In a *holographically symbolic world,* everything in the dream that is life would interact for the sole purpose of helping one to discover the whole message. A symbolic world where behind everything can be found a true purpose aligned with the whole. And within every problem lies its own solution.

Wow, what a concept! I felt giddy as I contemplated my own hypothesis. It would give life a whole new meaning. Certainly more meaning than I'd previously imagined. At that moment, I wished for a guru, a wise one who could enlighten me.

Symbols and dreams. Symbols and dreams! Is all of life a dream filled with symbols helping us to become more aware of who we are? Perhaps of how powerful we are? Feeling very light hearted, I grinned at an image of me skipping through a deep forest, like Dorothy in *The Wizard of Oz,* arm in arm with the Tin Man, Scarecrow and Cowardly Lion; eyes focused solely on the yellow-brick road, chanting intently, "Life is symbols and dreams. Oh, my! Life is symbols and dreams. Oh, my!" as we made our way toward the wise wizard, who we thought would explain it all to us. I felt relief that I had reached a point where I could begin to laugh about it all.

Kevin finally arrived. His plan for our day was to drive to San Diego to attend an all-day seminar given by people connected with the writing of a book called *A Course in Miracles*. He had talked about the book for some time, and he often quoted from it. The passages reminded me of Shakespearean verse. It was from this book he quoted the cheerful line that I liked, "There are no accidents." I could relate to that concept.

I had trusted Kevin to plan a pleasant day for us, but what unfolded was monumental.

"So, is *A Course in Miracles* similar to a college extension course?" I asked, thumbing through his very big blue book on our drive to San Diego. "And, what kind of miracles?"

"It's a self-study course that guides an understanding of ourselves and of our relationship with whatever we consider God," he replied. "As for a miracle, that is the moment when one realizes what is eternally true, and recognizes the illusion blocking the truth. A miracle is simply a correction in one's mind."

The truth instead of illusion? What did he mean by "illusion?" Kevin continued, "It's been said that *A Course in Miracles* is a contemporary spirituality. It expands and connects new thoughts and themes from Eastern and Western religions."

"Is it a religion? Where does this philosophy come from?"

"No. *A Course in Miracles* is not a religion or a cult. It uses Christian terms, because that is what the Western mind is familiar with, but it addresses universal spiritual themes. In fact, the *Course* emphasizes that it is only one version of what it calls 'the universal curriculum' and states that they all lead to God in the end."

Kevin's energy picked up as he spoke. "*A Course in Miracles* came about in the mid-sixties, during a really difficult relationship between two professional people, Helen Schucman and William Thetford, who were professors of medical psychology at Columbia University's medical school in New York. And they were anything but spiritual."

Kevin suggested I open the book to the preface, which provided a brief description of how *A Course in Miracles* had begun. My eyes settled upon a paragraph in italics, written by Helen Schucman.

The relationship between her and her colleague, Bill, was competitive and strained by bickering, provoked by their drive for individualistic views and professional status.

"Then something happened that triggered a chain of events... the head of my department unexpectedly announced that he was tired of the angry and aggressive feelings our attitudes reflected, and he concluded that there must be another way," Helen wrote. *"As if on cue, I agreed to help him find it. Apparently, this Course is the other way."*

"So she wrote the Course?" I asked. Reading aloud to Kevin, *"During the following three months, Helen began to have highly symbolic dreams—"*

"Yes," he interrupted. "And the last of them included her vision of entering a cave in a rocky hillside on a seacoast. In her dream, she found a very old parchment scroll. When she opened the scroll, on the center panel two words were written. They were, GOD IS."

Then, Kevin's voice became intense. "A few years later, when Helen went to Israel at the request of Ken Wapnick—the man we are going to hear at the seminar today—she actually saw that same cave! They were on the seacoast at Qumran, where the Dead Sea Scrolls were discovered. His account of their visit says she burst into tears when she saw the cave."

My whole body had goose bumps. I told Kevin I *knew* that phenomenon. I knew what it was like to envision something and then to discover it in the light of day. Kevin was already aware of all the mystical experiences I'd experienced.

"I'm not surprised you feel that way," he said. "I think there may be other similar moments in store for you today."

Really. Well, hopefully it would complement our plans for a fun day. Returning to my original question, I asked, "So, what happened then? How did *A Course in Miracles* actually come about?"

"Helen said that after the dreams subsided, for the first time she heard a 'voice.' She was quite surprised when she wrote the words, *'This is a course in miracles.'* So then it began, and for seven years, she recorded in shorthand what this voice said. She didn't understand it and thought it was craziness, but when she read it to Bill, her colleague, he heard something valuable and began to type it out. She said it seemed to be a special assignment she had somehow agreed to complete. Being an atheist, she was uncomfortable, but she never considered stopping. Helen and Bill kept it to themselves, knowing no one would understand—there was no telling what might happen to their professional lives."

I instantly bonded with her. I knew what it was like to have something mysterious and inexplicable happen, along with the sense that somehow there was a deeper meaning that couldn't be understood with ordinary logic. And, that it couldn't be talked about for fear of being viewed as irrational.

I noticed that the names of the recorders of the *Course* didn't appear on the book's cover. *"Its only purpose is to provide a way in which some people will be able to find their own Internal Teacher"* the preface said. I respected the absence of ego and a sincere attempt to simply deliver a message. What dedication that must have required—seven years!

I rifled through the book, as he commented, "It's actually three books in one; a text which is theoretical, and presents the concepts on which the *Course's* thought system is based; and a workbook which contains the ideas of the text and provides lessons for practical application to bring about the *experience* of the concepts. He added, the *Course* emphasizes *experience* through *doing,* rather than simply through learning a theory. As Ken Wapnick often quotes about the workbook, it is a beginning, not an end. From then on, when you have found the 'Voice for God' it will direct your efforts."

A personal inner voice? This dynamic I knew. I also liked the idea of an intimate, connection to God rather than another interceding, or having to feel somehow obliged to believe in guilt-laden edicts passed along by religious leaders and doctrines. Certainly that had been my past experience. "And the third book?" I asked.

"In the back there is a section called the Manual for Teachers, written in question and answer form and it addresses some of the more likely questions one might ask. The *Course* uses many of the same terms found in Christian literature, but the way they are expressed is quite different. Early on, Helen came to believe that the voice she was hearing was that of Jesus."

Jesus? I wasn't sure how I felt about that. My past association with Jesus had left me with deeply mixed emotions. While the name did stir thoughts of love, kindness, and peace towards others, at the same time my perspective had been weighted down with feelings of guilt, the certainty I was a sinner, and admonishing fear. Including the fear of an eventual judgment day if I didn't keep myself in line—in line with what, I'd never been clear about.

I didn't have much time to deliberate as Kevin parked the car and opened my door. He led me into a large meeting room inside a community building where, I guessed, close to one hundred people gathered. We found seats in good view of the speaker, Ken Wapnick, who was at a table with his wife, Gloria. "So, Kevin, what does Dr. Wapnick have to do with the *Course?*"

Answering softly as everyone took their seats, he explained that Dr. Wapnick, who was also a psychologist, had been introduced to Helen and Bill in 1972 by a friend, a Catholic priest. Dr. Wapnick, who'd been raised in the Jewish faith, had gone to Israel and spent almost six months in a monastery in Galilee. He thought that would be his final destination, until he was allowed to read Helen's manuscript. He knew he was to be connected in some way with the material. He began working with Helen and Bill, and for a vacation, they accompanied him back to Israel to tie up loose ends. That was when Helen actually saw the same cave she'd seen in her dream.

The dream! There it was again. That word, "dream." And her dream actually revealed itself in physical form, as had my visions.

Kevin concluded by saying that in 1973 Ken began meeting daily with Helen and Bill to assist in editing the material. Whenever they couldn't agree, they sat silently and listened for guidance and then their answers always coincided.

I respected what appeared to be a strong determination by Dr. Wapnick to find the truth for them and their joined willingness to merely listen for guidance. Now, I wanted to know more. More about this woman who had a dream that actually happened and messages she heard for seven years that she couldn't tell anyone about or they might think she was crazy. Our experiences were so similar. I opened my yellow pad, prepared to take notes as Dr. Wapnick began.

Dr. Ken Wapnick, slight in stature, had dark hair and a spontaneous smile. He spoke with purpose and obvious, keen intelligence. He began with the wisdom of early philosophers.

"A great, ongoing debate that started with Socrates and Aristotle asks the question, is the world we see actually within the mind, or outside of the mind as has been presumed?" Dr. Wapnick's tone became more forceful. "Although the *Course* is over 1,200 pages in length, its message is quite simple. It answers that question. First, it says that everyone in this world is part of *One Mind.* Second, that the entire world we see is actually within that *One Mind,* not without. What we consider to be our reality, we have first projected from our own mind."

This was a sweeping concept to take in all at once! Everyone being of one mind was an idea I understood, since it was the basis of Jung's theory of collective consciousness. But my experience being the result of my own thought? That sounded like a lot of responsibility. I wasn't sure what I thought about this.

Dr. Wapnick continued, "The *Course* tells us that, like Adam in the Bible, we went to sleep. But nowhere in the Bible is there a reference to him waking up. We, the *One Mind,* went to sleep, and we are still asleep. We are projecting what we see from our own minds into our dream of life. We are dreaming." Reading from the *Course,* he said, "You are safe at home in God, dreaming of exile but perfectly capable of awakening." His eyes scanned the audience. "We think that we have separated ourselves from God. Yet, we are only in a dream, and like a child, we are gradually awakening..."

The hand that held my pen froze. Everything stopped; blood rushed to my head. My ears rang. I could no longer hear his words as he spoke. My mind struggled to grasp what he had just said. Was he telling us that this new twentieth century document says we are living in a *dream?* That was *my* theory! That was what I'd been secretly wondering, postulating, but I dared not talk about it to anyone or they would surely think I was crazy. And I had not been able to fathom the how of it, or the why.

I don't know how long I sat utterly stupefied before his voice floated back into my consciousness. "The purpose of this *Course* is to help awaken us from the dream. And furthermore, just as God is perfect love, we, the *One Mind,* are also love—*only love.* We were created by God and, like God, what we really are is pure love. Everything else is not real."

Nothing else is real? *Only* love. I'd never thought of the dream in that way, although that was a good description of my sensation during my kaleidoscopic visions. And at times I had considered that, if I looked hard enough, love could be found deep down inside of everyone. But what did he mean by "everything else?"

"The *Course* is a beginning, not an end. It is to help us begin to hear our own internal voice."

The *voice of love,* he called it. The timeless calling of an *inner voice* that guides us back to the memory of the love we've forgotten that we are—that guides us to inner calm and quiet, no matter the circumstances. A voice that helps us see that *everything else in the dream that is not love is only a part of the illusion.* A voice that guides us to awaken from the dream. Dr. Wapnick said, "the *Course* calls it The Voice for God."

The Voice for God? Your own internal voice? A reliable inner voice that leads to love, to wellbeing? Almost in a state of disbelief, I wondered if Dr. Wapnick was addressing the same constant inner knowing I'd learn to follow over many years…my growing acceptance—almost a haunting quest—to find a unified purpose in my symbolic visions and dreams. And whether the events in my life, as well as the visions and dreams, all held a specific purpose and guidance that was leading me toward inner peace and calm. Toward love. Had my visions awakened an inner wisdom, a Voice from God?

As Dr. Wapnick continued I was no longer aware of being in a room full of people. He was talking only to me. I could not believe what I was hearing. He was addressing all the confusing, conflicting questions and thoughts I had had for so many years.

Dr. Wapnick offered the *Course's* explanation of how *the dream* had begun. "In that instant when we were created by God, we—the *One Mind*—had one tiny, mad idea…the idea that we could separate ourselves from God. In that moment, the thought became a serious idea, and that idea became the dream we now call life. It is a joke to think that a dream can intrude upon eternity. The only mistake we made was we forgot to remember to *laugh* at the idea."

Laugh? Laugh! That had been my reaction right after I'd had my first glimpse of what seemed another dimension. Laughing was all I *could* do twenty-six years ago when I'd surrendered to the force pulling me into the beautiful, divinely peaceful, kaleidoscopic light. I'd laughed and laughed, even as I was being driven to a mental hospital. I was in a sweet place of serenity outside of this world—somewhere beyond our known thought system. Back then, I'd believed *that* experience was the dream!

No matter, I had found something true. I hadn't wanted to return to the world that, in contrast, seemed like a bizarre three-ring circus. Could the real dream actually be the real world, as I had suspected?

Dr. Wapnick continued, "Because at a subconscious level we think we have separated from God in our dream world of illusion, we expect to be punished for such an unthinkable act. We are in denial about it, but we subconsciously feel guilt for our imagined deed. And yet there is no reason for guilt. The world we see is not real. Guilt is not real. It was a mistaken idea. There *was no* separation from God. We are only dreaming it. The world never happened."

The world never happened? We are only *dreaming* of separation from God?

"Still," he went on, "we unconsciously carry guilt until we begin to wake up and realize that the dream is an illusion...that we are what we have always been, and always will be—we are one with God, and we are only love. Guilt makes us think we have sinned and keeps us in the illusion. Yet there is no sin. What we see as sin is simply the absence of love."

Guilt! It's part of the foundation of the doctrines in all of the churches I'd ever attended. In some form or another, there was either a direct or indirect message that everyone needed to be saved from sin; to pay some form of penance. Certainly it was the driving message in the various fundamentalist churches I'd been required to attend in my childhood and teenage years. Guilt had been at the core of my father's beliefs and the motivation he used in his tyrannical rule in our home. In one way or another he reminded us daily of our sinful natures. Yet, even though he got down on his knees every morning to pray to his god, it didn't stop his abusive and hateful behavior.

Later, after my children were born, I'd found a church that suited my lifestyle a little better. For over fifteen years I'd raised my children in the Methodist church, taught Sunday school, directed vacation Bible school and worked as a teacher and director of their weekday school. The Methodist doctrine was far more liberal than the one I grew up with, yet its message still focused around original sin and the need for redemption. The closest to a guiltless philosophy

I'd ever been exposed to was near the end of my time in Frederick when, for a short while I went with my friends, Jane and Mona, to a Unitarian church. There the emphasis was more on personal responsibility rather than on sin and guilt.

Actually, I realized, wasn't that what hypnotically dredging up my memory of a past life in Atlantis had been all about? To release guilt? By simply being able to remember the mistakes I'd made, I found I could forgive myself and release the guilt I had carried in my subconscious. I didn't need to dwell on it and create more guilt by obsessing over it. The healing came when I forgave myself, when I recognized that what happens in the present is all that matters.

Dr. Wapnick added that guilt also fuels a collective subconscious fear we will be "found out" for this seemingly preposterous thought that we could dare separate ourselves from God—that is the root of the fear. Guilt creates fear in the one mind that we are. In our guilty, fearful, dream of life, we've collectively created a world of chaos and separation—a smoke screen to create distraction from our own guilt; to keep the illusion of the dream going because we can't face what we thought we did. We can't face the sinners we think we are.

I remembered my fantasy in my living room that very morning...a smokescreen...like the wizard in the *Wizard of Oz*. He created blusterous images with fire, loud roaring, and scary faces. He frightened everyone, and that's how he controlled them. But, in the end, Dorothy discovered the image he portrayed wasn't real. He was a fake. He had created an illusion. Finally they saw who he really was. A harmless, little, old man. Then he had to admit to Dorothy that she had had the power all along.

Grinning impishly, Dr. Wapnick said, "But not to worry, this entire thing we call life, the dream, our illusionary universe, is only an instant in time, and, *time* exists only in the dream!"

Time is an illusion? I remembered Neville had referred to time after my hypnosis session, saying that, like Einstein, some scientists consider the concept of time, the distinction between past, present and future, to be an illusion. I thought of something else Einstein had said. He said the only reason time existed was so everything didn't seem to happen all at once. He believed that all time exists simultaneously, a concept I never could wrap my head around. Now I was hearing it again.

At that point, an obviously frustrated, middle-aged man asked, "So what does the *Course* tell us we can do about it? How can we wake up? And what do miracles have to do with it? It is a course in miracles, is it not?"

Dr. Wapnick thanked him, saying, "You ask the perfect questions. What do we do about it?" His answer was one word! "Forgiveness." We must see love. Not guilt and fear. We need to see love in ourselves, and see it in everyone else. "Don't make guilt real," Dr. Wapnick counseled. We did nothing wrong. We are not separated from each other, or from God. We can let go of our imaginary guilt by forgiving.

I remembered how it was after I forgave myself for the mistakes I'd made in my Atlantis lifetime—how fresh and new the world seemed. I'd been inspired to improve my life by singing from a deeper place in my heart in the Lifesong Workshop. Without guilt, a new beginning opened up for me.

Moving on to the rest of the man's question about what is a miracle, Dr. Wapnick explained that a *miracle* is the replacement in our mind of fear with love. What occurs then is a change in our perception from the illusion to truth; the truth that love *is all* that is real. When we see each other as the same image of God, we recognize our oneness in God. When we shift our perception to only love, responding with forgiveness, this is the moment of the miracle. It is a journey without distance from our head to our heart. And we are continually removing the blocks to know love's everlasting peace, one miracle at a time.

As Dr. Wapnick dismissed us for lunch, he cautioned that as we approached the *Course,* it would never be understood by theory alone. He quoted, "A universal *theology* is impossible, but a universal *experience* is not only possible but necessary." While we may think we understand theory, we will only come to love by living it. Don't get hung up in the theology.

My head was reeling. This new spiritual psychology addressed so many things I'd been longing to understand. Yes, it seemed to begin to make sense of my own revelations, but it was such a leap from everyday life. And all this coming through a woman who thought what she was hearing was *crazy*!

Yet, I couldn't deny a feeling of destiny. As I strolled through the large room, I had very little awareness of my body's movements.

I wandered through the milling crowd as if making my way through a busy train station. I didn't feel lost. I simply felt it didn't matter which way I decided to turn. The journey would lead me to my destination. At the same time that my head was struggling to resolve what I'd heard, my heart leapt with a sense that I was being led to the real me.

Seeing my dazed condition, Kevin offered to get some sandwiches for us from a deli across the street. I strolled outside and sat down on the gray steps of the building, allowing the midday sun to embrace me in its warmth. My vision blurred as my eyes welled with grateful tears. I wasn't exactly sure why. I didn't even notice Kevin's return until he placed a tuna and tomato on rye sandwich in my lap.

I knew he realized how overwhelmed I was. He didn't seem surprised. Setting aside the paper plate, I reached out and gave him a long, wordless hug. We ate in silence.

"You knew I would be blown away about the *Course's* message that we're all in a *dream,* didn't you?" I gave him a playful nudge with my shoulder. He just grinned, put his arm around me, and gave me a little squeeze. Then I confessed to him that I had so many questions and that I had discovered something I wanted to know more about.

The rest of the afternoon passed in a blur. My mind had reached its saturation point. That is, until I heard Dr. Wapnick say in reply to a woman's question, *"Everything* in this illusory dream of time that we call life is a symbol."

Symbol?

I had stopped taking notes, but that word *symbol* prompted me to retrieve my tablet from under my chair.

Dr. Wapnick opened the *Course* with the familiarity of a handbook and read his answer to her. "You live by symbols. You have made up names for everything you see."

Signs and symbols! I sat there once again mesmerized.

Still puzzled, the woman responded, "Everything? Everything is a symbol?"

"Yes." Dr. Wapnick quickly flipped backwards to another page in the book. He read, "You could, in fact, gain vision from just that table, if you would withdraw all of your own ideas from it, and look upon it with a completely open mind. It has something to show you; something beautiful and clean and of infinite value, full of happiness and hope. Hidden under all of your ideas about it is its real purpose, the purpose it shares with the entire universe."

Vision from a table? Like my painting...the abstract painting of a lightbulb. It had held a message for me; an omen that had gently prophesied a path of many trials, but in the end one that brought comfort and hope.

Oh, my God. Dr. Wapnick was actually saying that this modern document, *A Course in Miracles,* revealed that all of life is a *dream*—and everything in the dream is *symbolic* of something. On that very day, earlier that morning, I'd been philosophizing that this concept could be a possibility.

I sat motionless in my chair, hugging my stomach, trying to calm waves of churning emotions. In conclusion, Dr. Wapnick asked us to close our eyes while he read brief selections from the *Course,* and then to remain silent for a minute or so. I welcomed the comfort of simple darkness.

"Heaven waits silently, and your creations are holding out their hands to help you cross and welcome them...across the bridge is your completion, for you will be wholly in God, willing for nothing special, but only to be wholly like to Him, completing him by your completion." After a few moments, Dr. Wapnick dismissed us with these words, "You have not lost your innocence. It is for this you yearn. This is your heart's desire. This is the voice you hear, and this is the call which cannot be denied."

Innocence. That was exactly what I'd known so many years earlier when I'd surrendered to the euphoric kaleidoscopic light. Innocence had been the feeling that had enraptured me and sent me into gales of laughter...I had been rejoicing in my innocence.

As Kevin and I walked to the parking lot I couldn't believe we had only been there for a few hours. Time had stopped in its tracks. Here was a spiritual philosophy that claimed aspects of what I had been put away for envisioning twenty years earlier! All this time I dared not talk about it in public as I had just witnessed Ken Wapnick do that day.

Yes, I had come to trust an inner knowing through symbols— an inner voice. Dr. Wapnick talked about it being a voice for God. Really? Where specifically were they leading me? The voice? The symbols? And just as I had been reasoning, Dr. Wapnick said that life is a dream, but furthermore he said I am responsible for my own thoughts! Could it be like my hypothesis? That I am the master of the dream. I had been led to my theory through symbols, most of them from my visions. Now, as in my own theory, I heard Dr. Wapnick say *everything* in the dream is a symbol. Not only that he said that, in the dream, only love is real. Really? Not when I looked around me. Then he added something completely confounding. He said that the dream is already over! Now that does sound crazy!

I was caught in the sensation of riding on a merry-go-round that was going too fast. I needed to get off. I needed time out!

My life was changing so rapidly. What was happening to that mother, that teacher I used to be? That woman who managed to exhume herself from a life of oppression? All I had wanted was a chance to live a "normal" life! But no. First I discover I've lived at least one past life, and now it's as if I'm being led by the Pied Piper through a land where I see symbols at every turn. Led to where? To what?

My emotions were splattered all over the inner walls of my mind. Yet, I was grateful and comforted to hear another's confirmation of my secret beliefs though I was dumbfounded and confused by some of Dr. Wapnick's claims. Claims that all that is real is love and the dream is over. Heck, I was dumbfounded by the very presence of that inner voice. Where was it taking me? I longed for peace of mind. When would it be time to laugh? I shuddered. No more! No more questions now.

Kevin and I drove home in silence. The sun setting in red and gold streaks above the ocean painted a fiery backdrop on the horizon as Kevin's car cruised along the beautiful Pacific Coast Highway. I angled my seat and rested into a partial recline. In my state of mixed emotions I slowly rolled my head in confusion, and in wondrous amazement.

I felt Kevin watching me, assessing my mood. Finally, he said, "I told you there were no accidents."

CHAPTER 14

And the Dream Goes On

The sun and the beach always made me feel vibrant and alive,
but this day I felt electric. Instead of my usual spot for nesting
on the beach by the still water of the harbor, I needed to find
a place as alive as I felt. In the outside flap of my overstuffed beach
bag was my copy of *A Course in Miracles*. I was poised to thoroughly
scrutinize my new find. Like a pilgrim stumbling upon ancient scrolls
lost for centuries, I needed to retreat to a secluded place in order to
explore my newly found treasure.

With high anticipation, I parked the car at the end of the bluff
where the road opened to the ocean, as ten foot waves from lunar tides
collided with the shore, and a new moon due that night. I removed
my flip-flops and made my way down the cement block stairs to the
damp sand, settling for a dry spot at the foot of the high bluff. It was
not yet noon. I would have at least until four o'clock before the tide
would spill its way onto my blanket.

I opened the book. After the table of contents was a page
with only two paragraphs. As I quickly scanned, a few lines jumped
out at me:

*"This is a course in miracles. It is a required course. Only the
time you take it is voluntary. Free will does not mean that you can
establish the curriculum. It means only that you can elect what you
want to take at a given time…"*

Skipping a few lines, I read:

*"It does aim, however, at removing the blocks to the awareness
of love's presence, which is your natural inheritance."*

The second paragraph ended with:
"Herein lies the peace of God."

My thinking faltered as I struggled to decipher the message. Yet, stillness had reached into my heart. This was unlike anything I had ever read. It spoke to something inside me. It spoke with an ancient voice, softly beckoning me to come along, to remember. I wanted to read and thoroughly digest the message contained in this book. I didn't notice the tide rolling ever nearer until it floated away with my flip-flops.

And so it was. Over seven months during every stolen moment I could find, I made my way to my lair at the foot of the bluff until the winter chill drove me inside. Releasing emotions into the crashing waves, I often wept with gratitude and relief to find such a beautifully written document that declared all of life to be a dream.

There were moments I found myself laughing with a degree of light-heartedness that had caused me to break into laughter during those few memorable days after Jennifer was born, when seeing the kaleidoscopic light that had overcome me, even as I was being taken to a mental hospital. I was both delighted and amused that the voice which had dictated this message of miracles was saying that the *illusions* we call life are *insanity,* and too ridiculous for anything but to be laughed away.

That had been my own revised view of the world after leaving the mental hospital—ridiculously crazy. I had rejoined earth from another dimension, and what I witnessed as life on earth was absurdity. A preposterous game wherein there was too little love, where people had their own agendas, selfish interests, and separate ideas about what was right, and fought to their death over them.

From then on, *A Course in Miracles* became my constant source of inspiration. I often carried it in my car to read if I dined alone or while waiting for professional appointments or to meet someone. I read it while doing laundry and sunning by the pool. When it wasn't with me, it rested on the nightstand by my bed. Most mornings and evenings, I made a point to read at least a page or two before starting or ending my day.

The *Course* seemed to echo its same message, expressed in many different ways. Beneath every situation and within every person there is always an opportunity to see love. In verse and in metaphor,

I started to see how relentlessly everyone's ego—my ego—was convinced of its importance. As the *Course* instructed, I attempted to see my daily worries as dramas. Things that seemed so important started to lose a little of their grip. The text challenged me to think about what it might be like to have more compassion for myself, and to truly connect with others; to think of everyone, no matter how unlikeable, as part of me...without anyone being guilty. Not them, and not me. That proved to be a real challenge. Most of the time, the best I could hope for was to catch myself in the act.

Then it became more real to me when I began doing the lessons in the second part of the *Course* book. The workbook contained 365 lessons, one for each day for a year, that helped to alert me to when I was actually judging and projecting guilt onto others, my family, and especially on myself. Although I certainly couldn't always do it, I discovered when I did manage to keep it simple and give my best effort to forgive, I felt lighter. It brought me peace when I released my own judgmental and attacking thoughts. After all, the thoughts were in my own mind. It was me who was making me unhappy. Whoever I had a grievance with wasn't even aware of it, and probably wouldn't care anyway.

But even with this inspiring new way of seeing myself and my life's situations, there were many questions I still needed answered. I had found enormous relief and liberation in my discovery of a written spiritual theme that made my view of life as a dream sound almost rational. But there was much within the dream itself that I wasn't sure about.

What were the purposes of the "light bulb" moments I had experienced in this dream of life? Where specifically were they taking me? Why had I seen the visions of places in the mental hospital? Why did I see things I was sure were going to happen? How did my past life fit into the big dream of life? Where were these symbols/signposts/spirit markers leading me? I still couldn't explain it. Were they all a series of random events?

The *Course* presented a radical spiritual theme, literally teaching that all that ever really matters is love. But how did love resolve my questions?

Written in an archaic Shakespearean style, the *Course* read so beautifully, but its message of over 1,200 pages did not come easily.

Eventually, I grew restless. I yearned for companionship. I needed a timeout. Although I was deeply inspired to continue my study of the *Course* and felt strengthened by it, I wanted to put the serious considerations I had been absorbed in for so long into the background for awhile. I needed to lighten up. I wanted to have some fun.

But, fun was not exactly what I found. It was more like distraction. I decided to start going out with friends for drinks and appetizers after work and began to date once in awhile. I had learned so much about myself, especially during the years of counseling while divorcing Jack—I had learned what qualities I would never again tolerate in a man. But I soon realized that I didn't know a whole lot about the kind of man with whom I *would* be happy.

The two men I knew the most about were my father and Jack. I had spent my early years avoiding my father whenever possible. Later, during my marriage, I had forced myself to believe in a version of Jack who didn't exist, often pretending affection to suit a situation in order to lessen tension and possible violence.

I was distressed to find the kind of men I was drawn to. At first, they seemed different from my past experiences; they gave an appearance of being thoughtful and considerate. But with time, under the cautious eye I had developed, I could detect there was more to be discovered.

For example, I eventually realized that one man, Larry, whom I had dated for several months, was looking for someone to soothe his damaged ego after he had gone through a stressful separation. It was probably no accident that I was attracted to him; he was six feet five inches tall, like Jack, and had blue eyes, blond hair, and a timbre in his voice like Jack's. I think I liked that the sex was rather casual and I wasn't required to express a lot of emotion, quite a contrast to the stormy, forced sex of my marriage. But Larry couched unpleasantness in the guise of a joke, using humor to manipulate me—just like Jack. Even my family saw his resemblance to Jack.

After I stopped seeing him, I couldn't help but wonder if I'd been drawn to someone with such astounding similarities to Jack as part of my process of becoming healthier, like a re-staging of my past situation and the opportunity to consciously reject it. Now that some time had elapsed, perhaps I could bear to look more consciously at my painful past and missed judgments. A chance to let go even more deeply.

A few months later, I found myself involved with a man who had never learned to love women, even though he worked hard to give the impression that he was a consummate gentleman. I enjoyed his company in the beginning, particularly when treated like I thought a lady should be, but his suppressed anger for women eventually revealed itself. It grew obvious his intentions were more about him and less about me and our relationship. It was like I was being shown a mini-series of my past.

When I did recognize the truth, it didn't take me long at all to walk away. But, it was getting harder and harder to trust men. The greatest heartaches in my life had been brought on by men. I had known deep-seated rage disguised as love that became emotional and physical abuse. But, I didn't give up. I knew there were healthy relationships. And I knew I deserved to be in one. Somewhere, there was someone trustworthy enough for me to open my heart to, regardless of what I had been through. I felt certain of it.

Late that summer, in August of 1986, my sister Mickey and I went to an art auction. Since I had never been to one, I was curious, and thought it sounded like fun. She was still the director of a fine arts gallery at the Fashion Island shopping mall in Newport Beach. I had absolutely no money to spare and certainly no intention of purchasing anything. We stopped for cocktails and appetizers on the way, arriving a little late. The only seats left were near the back of the ballroom at the Sheraton Hotel, which made it difficult to discern the details of the artwork—a beautiful variety of period paintings, sculptures, and signed and numbered prints by contemporary artists such as Peter Max and Aldo Luongo.

Near the end of the evening, a Leroy Neiman print in a lightly stained wood frame, about forty by thirty inches, caught my attention. Leroy Neiman created brilliantly colored screen prints of athletes, musicians, and sporting events. This one was a tennis match with four players—a mixed doubles game.

I had played a great deal of doubles tennis during the last five years of my marriage, mostly with girlfriends, but Jack and I had been members of a mixed doubles group. I had dreaded playing with him. His aggression and critical wisecracks under his breath, either toward me or our opposing team, made my game painfully tense. But the players in this picture were not like that. An action shot was being taken by the girl at the net, and her partner was dramatically poised in a ready position behind her, loyally guarding her back.

I don't know what came over me—but I felt compelled to have that painting. Up went my hand, without any difficulty at all, and for two hundred and seventy-five dollars, the image was mine. When it fully came to me what I had just done, I realized I hadn't even been able to see the detail of the print I'd just bought.

As I approached the front to collect my purchase, I blinked to be certain of what I was seeing. The girl was wearing a tennis dress exactly like one I still owned. It was white, trimmed in red rickrack around the square neck and the bottom of the flared skirt. I didn't really know why I'd had an uncontrollable impulse to buy it, but as I drew closer, I felt confident that it was rightfully mine.

As I hung the painting over my TV-bookshelf in the living room, I wondered if it might possess some symbolic importance for my future. I also felt little pangs of regret when I recalled the cost. Was my impetuous moment a foolish one? Had I gotten carried away? Had I read meaning into things that weren't really there? Wishful thinking?

But it did truly warm my heart as I took in the girl in perfect playing form all set for the winning shot, and all the while this lovely man was hunched in total readiness to protect her success. A real team.

Christmastime came along with parties and events to celebrate the season. Jennifer had met a young man who seemed quite nice, and she had enrolled in a class to become a travel guide. She was quite busy which limited our time together. I was trying to be merry, but I had grown a little sour on the dating scene. This was Orange County's fashionable Newport Beach, so of course everyone was fashionable. Many of the women wore false eyelashes and hair extensions, and were not bashful about showing considerable cleavage—very much on the cutting edge for the eighties. High heels were a staple in their wardrobes. Lots of the men wore dark, three-piece suits with starched cuffs and collars, and they drove luxury cars or colorful sports models. It was a red carpet moment when one of them pulled up to the valet in front of a restaurant or a hotel for the evening, especially if they had a beautiful girl whose long legs appeared as the valet opened the door—then the swish of long blond hair as she unfolded herself into full view of other arriving guests who pretended not to notice.

The men carried business cards obviously worded to convey high-end professions, because that's what the girls wanted. Under the shallowness, I hoped for something real. I admit I had always enjoyed dressing well, and, since coming to California, I had stepped it up a level or two. But I never thought I would yearn for the solid and stimulating straight talk I'd shared at academic parties on the East Coast.

In the ladies' rooms the conversations always led to the same questions. Like giddy teenagers, they gossiped about their heartthrob of the moment. The question inevitably came, "So what does he do, and what does he drive?" To close friends, I started referring to such scenes as "plastic," lamenting that the town and many of its people seemed so artificial.

One Friday evening, a little weary after the work week, I joined my girlfriend, Loretta, at a wine tasting, and the opening of a swank and dramatically decorated southern style restaurant called Remiks. Trying to work through a divorce after a marriage of several decades, she was showing me pictures of her children.

Suddenly a wine glass was plopped down on the table between us and a voice said, "Hi, I'm Aaron Cavilar." I thought he was probably feeling his chardonnay and I tried to ignore him. But Loretta, new on the dating scene, was taken in. They began to chat, and I moved to the bar for a pinot noir, even though I had already had one.

When I turned around, Aaron was standing there. I couldn't avoid him. So, taking a big sip of wine, I heard myself say, "So. What do you do and what do you drive?"

He burst into hearty laughter and said, "I sell plastic and I drive a Chevrolet."

Too funny! What an ironic answer in a *plastic* town packed with *Mercedes*. I found his honesty and obvious naiveté regarding the ways of Newport Beach endearing. Perhaps he just didn't care. Either way, I decided to talk to him.

He wore a neat, navy blue sports jacket with khaki-colored slacks—rather preppy—with well-polished cordovan oxfords. He was fairly handsome with dimples, trim, blond, and blue-eyed, like me, and was probably nearly six feet tall. He was forty-four years old, four years younger than me. In sales and originally from Ohio, he had come to California a few years earlier to join a Fortune 500 company. He marketed raw materials used to make plastic products, and drove a company car. A Chevy. With a bit of humor, he admitted that his career was inspired by the movie *The Graduate*.

We spent much of the evening together. When Loretta ran into some old friends who invited her to dinner, we left and went to a nearby area known locally as "Devil's Triangle." We ate and danced until the restaurants closed.

There wasn't a lot of animalistic attraction as I had usually felt when drawn to a man, but Aaron made me feel lighthearted. He smiled a lot and had a way of looking at the positive side of things. I liked the sound of our laughter together. In fact, I hadn't laughed so much all year.

However, as the evening unfolded I learned that he had been separated for only two weeks from his wife of more than twenty years, and had two college-age children. I had been there. I knew how long it really takes to get over a transition like that, no matter how we think everything has been resolved. I was interested in getting to know someone who was in a more settled place. I certainly didn't want to be the girl on the rebound. So I chose not to answer his calls. And there were calls.

Aaron traveled a great deal and many evenings a week when I got home there were lengthy, colorful message—addressed not to me but to my recorder. He was funny. He asked the recorder how it was doing and left all kinds of information to the recorder to give to me; where he was, what he was doing, thinking, and good wishes for me. This went on intermittently for three months. Finally, one day he left a message for me at work. I didn't feel comfortable with that. So, that evening, when he called I picked up the phone. There was a brief silence, and then he said, "Oh, I didn't really want to talk to you. I was calling to talk to your recorder."

Well, I laughed in spite of myself. I decided to accept his invitation for a simple, harmless lunch. We met at a Chinese fusion style restaurant near my office. He was already there when I arrived, and had secured a table in a cozily lit corner with a decorative lamp on the wall beside the table. His smile and cheerful demeanor gave me an instant lift. As we talked, I felt my usual distrust and defensiveness fall away. He was complimentary, but not too much. His inquiries seemed genuine and respectful.

Suddenly, I had the urge to be very frank. I said, "Well, you *say* all the right things," as I tilted my head.

He reached across the table, took my hand, and said charmingly, "Oh, does the lady not trust?"

Well, not only did he hit the nail on the head, but in that split second something very profound happened. As he spoke, he also tilted his head. The light caught one side of his face. It was then that I knew. In that split second, I flashed back to Atlantis. To my recurring dream, to drowning under the green-black water, to the face above me. *That face. It was him!* Aaron was my centurion!

Steam from the shower had always managed to clear my head. Hot beads of water pelted my tense shoulders. I stood there with my eyes closed, motionless, gratefully accepting relief. In a few hours I would be on my first real date with a man I was certain I had known in my past life. The centurion. The one who had served me faithfully in Atlantis. There wasn't a doubt in my mind that this was the same soul, or spirit energy, I had known before. He was now Aaron Cavilar. How astounding to think that he had reincarnated! But then, so had I. We had crossed paths once again.

Since our luncheon that week, I had not been able to think of much of anything else. It had lasted for over two hours. I found myself opening up to him, though not because of the feeling of familiarity from our past life connection. I was too stunned at that moment to really take that aspect in. I shared honestly because he was making sincere inquiries about me. It was easy to be forthright with him, because he really listened. I told him about my children, my teaching career, some details of my marriage, and even about the divorce.

I'd summed it up by telling him what Denise, my first counselor, had said that had given me great clarity about my relationship with Jack. "Jack always gives you a rose with a barb," she said. Meaning that there was usually a cloaked, hurtful intent in any seemingly positive gesture from Jack. I liked it that Aaron appeared to really "get" that.

As my shoulders relaxed, and my warm body melded back into one piece again, I turned the shower knob to cooler water. My head was clearer. I decided I would just see where this would go. I certainly didn't want to jump to any conclusions about Aaron because of our startling connection. For all I knew he could have come to me from my past life to be another lesson about the kind of man I did not want in my life.

Although, I had to admit he was making a pretty good impression. He insisted on coming to Dana Point to pick me up, even though he lived twenty-five minutes away. Socializing as I did in such a large county, many of the men I met in Newport Beach would have considered me GUD, a "geographically undesirable date." Most of them requested that we meet somewhere halfway between our homes.

For my date with Aaron, I didn't feel the need to dress up in the stylish way I had become accustomed to, but it occurred to me that I wanted to. I pulled out my favorite little black dress and black, patent leather sandals with rhinestone florets, and the most glamorous, dangling earrings I could find. I felt quite feminine when I answered the door.

There he was, standing under the porch light outside my front door. In a flash my mind darted back to that day I had been watering my geraniums and noticed the number "52" on my door, certain that someone would come to that door to whom I would be married when I was fifty-two. That was practically four years away. In that same millisecond I shook off the image, cautioning myself not to get carried away.

He held one half-dozen lightly tipped, multicolored roses. "Here," he said, "I cut off all the barbs."

I was stunned. I really didn't know what to say. "You did what?"

"These are roses I grew at home, and I cut off all the barbs for you so you wouldn't get hurt."

I made some jumbled sounds of gratitude and quickly invited him in for a drink and appetizers I had prepared. I was torn between being moved by this sweet, symbolic gesture and feeling everything was moving too fast.

I poured vodka and grapefruit juice into a tumbler for myself, sipping as I mixed, and served a glass of chardonnay to Aaron. I placed the Maryland crab dip, toast points, and vegetables on the coffee table as we sat down together.

"I grew those roses in my backyard," Aaron began.

Wow! Indeed, I was surprised. Although he admitted he wasn't much of a gardener, he explained he had learned to grow and tend roses during his recuperation six years earlier after he had undergone open-heart surgery. Open-heart surgery! He had been only thirty-eight years old then. It wasn't the usual heart attack procedure, but a much less common problem in a mitral valve of one of the chambers of his heart, a relatively new corrective procedure at the time.

I was truly shocked. He looked so healthy. I felt a deep concern for him. In my forty-eight years I had never known anyone who had experienced such a life-threatening operation, especially when he was so young. Impulsively, I asked to see his scar and was surprised that I actually became a little teary-eyed when he showed me. But he laughed lightly, assured me the surgery was successful, and he said he was perfectly fine.

"I have a little something else I thought a former teacher like you might appreciate." From a small plastic bag he had placed on the sofa, he pulled out a book with a gold ribbon tied around it. "I'll bet you know this one from your years of teaching." But, I didn't. Although he assured me it was a classic, I had never heard of *The Little Prince* by Antoine de Saint-Exupéry. Originally written in French, it was first published in 1943. Its pages were filled with several animated drawings like a children's book

"Thank you," I said, obviously puzzled at his choice.

"I wanted you to have this because it's about a little prince from another planet who falls in love with a rose with only four thorns."

"Oh, that's so sweet. I will read it."

"Ah, but there's more," he went on. "The story asks you to decide whether love is truly a matter of consequence," and he touched my cheek. "And, there is a fox who offers wise words of wisdom to the little prince. Pay attention when you come to that part."

"Oh, now you have come this far, you have to tell me what they are," I prodded.

"Oh, okay. You look so pretty tonight, how can I possibly refuse you? The words of wisdom are, 'It is only with the heart that one can see rightly.'"

Well, whether he knew it or not, he certainly seemed to be breaking down that cautionary wall about men I had built around myself.

Aaron had made reservations at a charming and well-known Mexican restaurant in a town that turned out to be only three miles north of my condo. I hadn't paid attention to the fact that I lived so close to the legendary San Juan Capistrano. I had become completely regimented in my daily work routine and any exploration I could make time for always drew me southward to the beach. We drove by the mission to which the swallows mysteriously returned every year. As if the evening had not already been extraordinary, seeing the old mission gave me goose bumps. More than once when I'd lived in Maryland, I had watched news reports of the swallows returning every March to the mission in San Juan Capistrano. When the camera shots of the mission came on, they stopped me in my tracks. I could never explain it to myself, but the mission held a deep fascination for me. Something tugged at my heart, luring me toward the television set.

The restaurant, El Adobe, was only two blocks from the mission. It had gained notoriety from being a favorite dining place of President Nixon when he had established what became known as the Western White House in the neighboring town of San Clemente.

Aaron and I ate and talked for nearly three hours. I learned that Aaron had been raised in a strict, Catholic, Midwestern home, had been an altar boy, and had attended Catholic schools right into high school—all-boys parochial schools. He claimed this had prompted the breakup of his marriage. He was undergoing a change in how he saw all of his past religious rearing, and wasn't quite sure where he was headed spiritually. He seemed a little confused about it all. I knew that the Catholic Church did not condone divorce.

I began to wonder what he might think of me if I told him that I remembered him. That we had been together in a past life. That I had seen him before. I was pretty sure that past lives weren't a part of Catholic doctrine. As we talked I began to concentrate on his slightly thick glasses. I wondered what his eyes looked like without them.

As the evening wore on we heard hard country rock from a live band wafting its way into our restaurant from across the street. Even though I wasn't a fan of country music, they were pretty good and I noticed my toes rhythmically tapping under the table. "What is that place?" I asked rather playfully.

"Oh, that's the old Swallows Inn. A boot-scootin' cowboy country bar. It's a landmark in San Juan. Someone usually gets thrown out of there every night."

Suddenly, I felt daring. I wanted to see just who Aaron was. "I bet you would never go in a place like that," I goaded.

"Oh, you think so?"

Without missing a beat, he called the waiter over, paid the bill, and took me by the hand.

I giggled all the way across the street as he playfully pulled me along. I couldn't believe I was walking into a real live cowboy saloon. There was sawdust on the wooden-planked floor and a crowded room full of people in cowboy hats and boots. The dudes next to the door practically elbowed us well-dressed city folk onto the dance floor.

Well, we danced until we could hardly breathe, and we stayed until they closed the bar at one o'clock in the morning. I discovered a lot about Aaron that night, and a lot about myself.

Within a few months we were drawn together in an exclusive relationship. Aaron spent several nights a week at my condo. The sexual part of our relationship began the night we had danced in the saloon. It wasn't like anything I'd ever experienced. It was non-demanding, tender, light and sweet, and uncomplicated. I never went to his home since his divorce proceedings were still ongoing, even though his wife no longer lived there. The nature of our relationship was hard for me to define. Rather than the usual romantic attraction, the most prominent interaction was more of a child-like playfulness. An exchange of innocence. The first time I really got it was that night he teasingly pulled me by the hand across the street to an actual saloon.

Eventually, over the course of numerous evenings, I decided to share with him the other part of my life. Those remarkable occurrences that also had been part of my past. I told him about my time in the mental hospital when I was twenty-two; the visions that came, and then later actually took place in my life. I also shared some of my mystical experiences since coming to California, like seeing the pink houses on the hillside that were not there, the déjà vu experience of finding my condo, my two recurring dreams—the one of Atlantis and the one of Indians chasing me—and the terrible scenes and sadness I saw and felt in the harbor. All of which led up to revealing to him my hypnotic regression with Neville, and then consequently—the moment. That moment when I remembered my past life in Atlantis. Our past life!

He didn't even flinch. He seemed to be taking it all in and was very compassionate. He expressed concern about the hard times, and the hurt and sadness I had been through. However, without his raising an eyebrow or confronting me in any way, I could tell he wasn't really relating to most of what I told him. When I got to the part about knowing him in a past life, he appeared flattered and responded with a big hug, and a much too forced grin.

I pushed it. I asked him directly if he believed me. He said he believed in me, but he couldn't really say that he believed in past lives. I could see that more talking wasn't going to convince him. So, with a sinking feeling of emptiness that quickly turned to genuine disappointment, I let it drop.

The warm-heartedness of his manner, his attentive personality, the familiar feeling when we were together—I knew it all so keenly from my past life. A deep desire was building for him to know me as he had in Atlantis. I wanted to share a bond with him spawned by our remembering together our ancient connection. I wanted us to acknowledge each other in the reunion that I was feeling so deeply.

"But," he said, trying to cheer me up and further our connection, "I do like to think of myself as a little bit of an idiot savant!

Well, maybe not an idiot, but I believe there are rather unusual events of good fortune that have consistently happened to me, and I don't understand how or why, even when it involves others. I seem to have a more than average knack for being in the right place at the right time."

He gave an example of a situation of his standing in a mile-long line for tickets to a U2 concert for his kids. When he got to the window there were exactly two tickets left. Then he added that if he was shopping for something specific and there was only one left, he would be the one to get it. And, at work, he had been known to wander in just in time for a meeting that he didn't even know had been planned.

"I've also always known that the number 'four' brings me good luck," he told me. "When I was admitted into the hospital for open-heart surgery, I was pretty scared until they told me I would be on the fourth floor. Then, I knew everything would be all right. And, tucking me under the chin, "I am forty-four years old now, and I've met you, haven't I?"

I allowed his sweet manner to console a gloomy heart that longed for him to know all of me.

Most weekends Aaron and I spent attending events along the coast and sampling Orange County's bevy of gourmet restaurants, sometimes combining dinner with entertaining his customers. Aaron usually went home on Sunday evenings to be close to his office by the airport for Monday morning business.

On one such Sunday evening we had each driven our cars to a Laguna Beach restaurant so he could go to his home from there. By that time I had sold my Volvo, due to a serious repair I couldn't afford, and bought a 1982 white Chrysler Limited Edition convertible with a beige top and custom, caramel-colored leather seats. Even though it was five years old, I loved it. It was the first convertible I'd ever owned. But it wasn't as reliable as my Volvo had been, mostly because I couldn't afford to take it in for regular full service.

After dinner in Laguna Beach, Aaron and I said goodbye, and I headed toward Dana Point. I had driven less than ten miles when my car completely quit, leaving me stranded on the Pacific Coast Highway. I walked to a nearby gas station and called a tow truck. My heart sank. Now how was I going to get to work the next morning? I didn't want to call and ask Aaron to take me. I didn't want to rely on him. I was determined to take care of myself.

I was riding in the cab of the tow truck as it pulled into the circular parking lot of my condo development to drop me off, my car chained securely on the lift in back. Just as I got out and was walking to the back of the truck, another car pulled in, its lights blinding my eyes. It was Aaron. He rushed over to me. I was shocked, though I was relieved to see him. There was deep concern on his face.

"How did you know?" I asked.

"I didn't…I don't know. I just knew I had to come back here. Something told me you needed me."

There was no way he possibly could have known that I needed his help. I didn't know how he knew, but after that night I never questioned his claim to having a touch of being a savant. What's more, I found myself thinking that, just like the faithful centurion he had been to me in Atlantis, here he was watching out for me once again.

The innocent, playful nature of our relationship often served to strengthen a bond between us through rough moments. There were challenges, as in any relationship. I felt part of it might have been caused by the emotional upheaval created by his ongoing divorce process. Sometimes he could be distant and emotionally unavailable. In spite of myself, on occasion I let that translate into feeling rejected, and I gave in to suppressed resentment born from the "little girl" part of me that had been emotionally neglected most of my life. Our stormy moments were almost always quelled by him. He was quick to understand and to try to lift the mood.

One lovely Saturday morning in July, just before his birthday on the eighteenth, he challenged me to a game of tennis. I had playfully bragged about my game in the past, even though I was only a "B" player. It was just a way of having some fun with him. He told me he had played a little tennis in high school.

We dressed and walked to some courts in a neighboring subdivision. As we warmed up, I felt pretty good about my strokes. I was hitting the ball every time. I really wanted to look good, and I knew I was playing beyond my usual ability. After about a fifteen minute rally, I suddenly realized why—the ball was always coming right to me, right where I could take my best shot! Aaron had complete control of the ball! And he was returning them to my forehand so that I could hit every shot. I caught the ball in my hand and stopped the rally. "I thought you said you played a little tennis," I shouted to him across the court as I walked to the net to meet him.

"Well, I did. I played on the tennis team in high school, played in some state championships, and then I played in college."

"That's more than a little," I shot back. "Did you win very often?"

"I won a few trophies."

"How many?"

"Oh, I don't know. Haven't really counted them. Maybe twenty, twenty-five.

I had a pretty good coach. He was the brother of Vic Braden."

I practically tumbled myself over the net, playfully punching him in the belly for putting me on as he laughed all the while.

After two sets where he mercifully kept me in the game, I was exhausted. We went back to my condo, and I fixed iced tea with lemon and a sprig of mint. As we sat down, I swung my aching legs up on the coffee table and rested my head on the back of the sofa. In the midst of a roaming gaze, my eyes suddenly settled upon the Leroy Neiman picture directly across the room. The one that I had compulsively bought that night at the auction I attended with my sister, Mickey.

There I was. Looking at my print of the doubles game where the woman was taking the shot coming right from the sweet spot of her racket, and the man, her partner, was behind her backing her up in perfect ready position. There it was! A pictorial depiction of the overwhelming feeling I was having about Aaron. I had just played the best game of my life, because he'd fed me returns I could hit. His primary interest was to support me in my game.

Staring fixedly, I realized that his support was also the pattern our relationship was taking. It seemed that regardless of how conflicted we could become, he would inevitably put my well being or our relationship first. He would most often be the one to apologize or come up with something humorous to start the process of lifting our moods.

An enormous rush of gratefulness came over me. Here he was—my centurion—and my devoted tennis partner. Without looking down at myself, it suddenly came to me. I was wearing my favorite tennis dress with the red rickrack around the neck and skirt, just like the dress in the picture.

I did not tell Aaron what I was thinking, nor did I mention the significance of the painting. I didn't want it to affect our relationship, whatever that was going to be. And I didn't want to jump to conclusions. For the same reason, I also did not tell him about my vision of my condo address, number 52, as being the age I knew I would be when I married again. I was forty-eight.

CHAPTER 15

Another Dream Comes True

It had happened again! The tennis doubles game print I had bought on impulse, and in which I had sensed the warmth of a supportive partnership, now seemed to be mirroring my relationship with Aaron. I recognized it as a symbol. I felt tapped on the shoulder. I was being guided. I wondered what I should make of the coincidence of the feeling generated by the painting and my having known Aaron in a past life. Were we to be together, partners in this lifetime? Did we have a higher, mutual purpose to accomplish as in our past lives? Or something else?

On Sunday evening, when Aaron had gone home after our tennis weekend, I spent some time snuggled in bed, reading the *Course,* a routine I had continued as often as possible since finding the *Course.* On this night I searched for more understanding of the meaning of all the visions, dreams, signs, and symbols that seemed to carry messages to me.

But then, if we live in a dream there is *no real physical reality.* That means that even the symbols themselves are not real! The *Course* said the part of everyone that is real is our *mind,* not our body. Funny, it was my mind that held the beautiful visions when I returned to "reality" after leaving the mental hospital. I had seen the *world* as unreal.

Then I found a section of the *Course* that was actually directly about symbols! It said to use all of the symbols that delineate the world of darkness, but don't accept them as reality. Just what I'd thought. The symbols are merely guides! Furthermore, it said the Holy Spirit, which the *Course* also refers to as the voice for God, uses all of them—and "creation" has one meaning and a "single source" that unifies all things.

One meaning, a single source that unifies all things? How? That was my big question.

Although my reading did not define the specific function of the symbols, my image of God was changing from the angry, vengeful one of my fundamentalist upbringing, to a loving God with no ledger of sin, a God accepting of joy and rapture. This God must have been there during the beautiful visions I'd experienced when I was twenty-two. In those kaleidoscopic scenes, I was happy, loved, and innocent. I was not a sinner. There was no need for anxiety in this God's world. The dark impression I'd had of a crumbling, decaying world that left me in such a state of fear, according to the *Course,* should be used in understanding the one *meaning* of creation, but not accepted as my personal reality.

If the world I see is not real, then what—in this insane world— could be the true purpose of symbols? The *Course* said the Holy Spirit uses *all of them.* Anything and everything…art, night dreams, objects, numbers, license plates, familiar scenes, events, chance encounters, even premonitions. Whatever works.

But, works for *what?* One symbol, the lightbulb picture I'd drawn, gave me comfort when my life had been turned upside down. Another, my license plate, helped me to laugh at myself. A recurring dream led me to relinquish fear and guilt from a past life in Atlantis. From a print of tennis players I found assurance about my relationship with Aaron. But what was that *one meaning*—that *single source* that unifies all things?

How does it work? How does it all come together…love, guilt, symbols, signs, visions and dreams, miracles, one mind, illusions, past lives? Is it all a mistake? Is it all a big joke? What kind of a joke would that be?

At the very least, I knew I was going to need much more study. But it was after eleven o'clock. I placed the *Course* on the night table. As I reached to turn off the light, I caught sight of the familiar scrolls on the wall across from the foot of my bed. Ah, yes. Another symbol. I was sure of it. My old companions from my life—or my dream of my life—in Maryland. They still held a luminescence, a silent lure. I continued to see in them a message. There was a bridge I was to cross.

Aaron traveled a lot on business throughout the weeks but always returned for weekends. His being away during the week made the weekends seem that much more special. But certain frustrating patterns were emerging.

As our relationship grew, I was inspired to plan romantic surprises, picnics, or intimate evenings in my condo with music, something special to eat and to wear, and I expected sometimes they would naturally culminate in physical intimacy. My past physical relationship with Jack had been obligatory sex. But I was now becoming more comfortable, more willing to be open, to explore the fullness of myself, of my sexuality.

Yet it also grew apparent that Aaron was not comfortable with situations allowing for deeper physical expression and intimacy. It was beginning to look like he was more at ease with arranging public dinner dates together, or with other couples, and letting sex be something that could happen briefly at the end of an evening. There was limited pleasure in that for me. I'd finally found someone with whom I felt safe enough to begin to let my guard down, both emotionally and sexually, however now he was the one who was guarded. I was becoming frustrated and irritable.

Also, I began to notice that Aaron was a rigid planner. He had every minute of our evenings, and sometimes our entire weekends, planned. He seemed driven. He was preoccupied with urging me to take care of myself. Get lots of rest. Get my teeth checked. Start walking or exercising. I wondered if being overly concerned was a way for him to feel in control. But if so, was his control just related to me, or was he trying to get control of his life in general?

I tried to understand it. I attributed some of his habitual behavior to the fact he was going through changes in his family life brought on by the divorce. I knew that situation caused him a lot of stress. As for the disappointing times at the end of our evenings, I eventually brought it up. That began the first of many discussions about our separate expectations.

He didn't readily admit it, but I could see he had a lot of guilt about his divorce, perhaps due to his rigid religious upbringing. I questioned what he really wanted. Did he want to have a physical relationship with me? He quickly assured me he did. He promised to work on being more relaxed and open. He said he was ready to let go of the blind loyalty he'd held sacrosanct all of his life to past religious training, parochial schooling, and his parents. He just wanted some time to sort out what he did believe.

The truth was, if it had not been for that strong and unyielding presence of our ancient past life connection, and the most recent symbol, the tennis picture, I might have broken off our relationship at that stage. But, I was willing to be patient and trust all of the symbols' messages until I understood in what way our relationship was important.

However, after one particularly volatile weekend where it seemed we argued and bickered about nothing, and whenever a good opportunity for sex became obvious yet nothing happened, in exasperation I declared to Aaron that we shouldn't see each other again. He left my condo and drove home. I think he agreed. My original reluctance to become involved in a relationship with someone who had just come out of a long marriage was proving to be justified. At times, he was unpredictably sad or withdrawn. At other times he would overcompensate with gifts or glitzy dinner plans to make up. It felt like a roller coaster ride. Even though I could appreciate his position, the truth was I wasn't willing to put my life on hold for any man. I had begun to feel trapped, caged—I was losing the space I had worked so hard to create.

Then one early morning the week after he had left, he called me. His voice was much more emotional than usual. In a halting manner, he told me he'd had a dream. It was about a fire on a hill, and the fire was threatening me. He had to come back to help me put it out. He was convinced we should get back together.

This was so unlike him. Earlier he had told me he didn't believe he had dreams at all. But I had learned for myself that dream images carried important meaning, especially vivid dreams. I was surprised he had considered his dream to be so important.

Perhaps, I thought, it was possible he could learn to be more open. We made a date to have dinner together the following Saturday. It became obvious to both of us that our feelings of attraction, both emotionally and sexually, had surely deepened during our brief separation. We agreed to get back together. Again, he promised to ease up on his preoccupation about my health, and to make a concerted effort to allow more time for us and for our physical relationship to grow. Although Aaron did try, he often fell back into his old ways. At the same time, another dynamic within me began building. I was shocked to find myself meeting his rigidity with an equally strong defiance.

My response was to vent my emotions in frank and assertive confrontations over whatever bothered me. Not my usual behavior. I began to get it, though as I let out pent-up emotions, I was making a contract with myself. I was no longer willing to hold anything back. I would not allow myself to be suppressed as I had in all the major relationships in my life. I had learned not to talk back to Daddy. I did argue with Jack, but I guarded my words, fearing the violence that could follow. Now I was going to give priority to my authentic feelings with Aaron, even if it meant the end of our relationship. My feelings counted.

Paradoxically, as I was learning to move beyond the restraint of my previous life, the innocent, sweet, simple friendship between us that I had valued in the beginning of our relationship not only continued, but strengthened. I started to believe that Aaron's concerns for my welfare were genuine. I was surprised at his willingness to rise above our situation. He was tolerant of my outbursts, and had the patience to talk me down when necessary. But I did wonder if his attention to my newly expressed self was because he was more comfortable talking about me than himself.

He chose demonstrative ways to reach out to me, such as rubbing my feet after I'd spent a long day at work in high heels. He bought me a radio alarm clock to replace my old fashioned one that sounded like a fire alarm—he even playfully surprised me by taping paper footsteps on the carpet to guide me to this gift when I came home. My favorite, after a tiring day, was when he would talk me to sleep by describing a magic carpet that carried us cozily and swiftly to wherever we fancied, our arms around each other. In those days, we laughed a lot on our dinner dates. A mutual respect between us was deepening. This was such a good thing. A friendship like this had been missing in any past relationship I'd had with a man.

But, simultaneously, something very irrational was building inside me; an uneasiness with this new type of budding friendship. My feelings grew unpredictable, often edgy without provocation. Why? I had never experienced a relationship this genuine or unguarded with a man. I knew that part of my edginess came from my desire for a closer physical intimacy, and at the same time I couldn't seem to allow myself to trust our friendship. The closer we became, the more vulnerable I felt. I overreacted without understanding it.

I had to admit that the simple presence of this masculine person who stood at my door every weekend caused me to feel anxious. Irrationally, I wanted to either have sex with him or ignore him. Being in between was making me uneasy. Many times I wanted to give in to a strong urge; to ask him to hold me tight and make my anxiety go away. But I didn't. I couldn't justify my feelings, and I didn't want to appear needy.

It was about that time when I began "borrowing" my friend Barbara's dog. I had met Barbara through the church Kevin had introduced me to, and it turned out we lived within a few miles of each other. We got together on occasion. She had a sweet, twelve-year-old golden retriever named MacArthur. I shared with her that for most of my life I had owned a dog, and lately I had an insatiable desire for the unconditional love that animals give so freely. Barbara immediately offered rights to MacArthur whenever I desired.

Lying on the floor of my condo with MacArthur made me feel safe. With his head resting on my hip, I could stroke him and be totally calm. He loved me, and he required nothing of me. In those moments, my apprehension was quelled. Funny, I thought, if that calm was a musical note it would be within the key of C Major; a nearly imperceptive, inner hum that gently vibrated, lulling me, consoling me. But it lasted only for those moments.

After several weeks in the quiet company of MacArthur, I decided I would not fight whatever lay at the root of my anxiety. Resisting it was not helping. Anxiety such as this had in the past led me to a better place. I was not going to stop trusting my inner wisdom now. I would let me feelings come; I'd observe them without judgment.

It was late spring of 1987. Aaron and I had been in a relationship for over four months. I wondered where it was going. I had to admit I was looking for some level of commitment, at least emotionally. He had never told me he loved me. I wasn't sure I loved him. Aaron's divorce proceedings were moving at a slow pace. His two children were home from college, and he saw them regularly. It was not unusual for him to meet with his estranged wife to, as he said, "work out the details of the divorce." He was often vague, and he consoled me when I became uncomfortable by him telling me that she was depressed and he simply wanted to help her through the closing stages of their marriage.

I fought with myself not to be a little envious of the attention and consideration he was giving to his family. There had never been any cooperation, and especially not concern, from Jack during our extremely stormy divorce. Quite the opposite. Nevertheless, I realized I had to be patient and supportive of Aaron and what he was going through. I did my very best to be fair and understanding, but sometimes I did not feel that I, or our relationship, were high priorities to him.

I was beginning to feel like the other woman, a little cheap and disrespected. I wondered if, after all, we had become a rebound relationship between his marriage and divorce, the very thing I had wanted to avoid. We never traveled together, not even on his business trips. I didn't feel I deserved to be kept at arm's-length. It brought back whispers of feelings I'd had while divorcing Jack, when he'd cold-heartedly attempted to destroy my reputation as a good wife, mother, and professional. I deserved to be appreciated and cherished for the respectable being I knew I was.

One Friday evening after drinks and appetizers at my condo, Aaron reached into his brief case which he always carried with him, and unfolded a page from an old newspaper. It was a full-page article about a charming, small town on the central coast of California called Cambria. He said that when he had read about it more than two years earlier he made a decision to go there whenever the time was right.

"Now might be a good time," he said with a wide grin. "What would you think about the two of us going there?" I sensed there had been a shift in him. He looked very pleased with himself in a way I had never seen before.

I brought up concerns he might have regarding his divorce proceedings. He said that he and his wife had come to a firm agreement on paper and it was finally in the last stages of the process. It surprised me to realize how much the finality of his divorce meant to me. Maybe now the distance between us would be dispelled.

We had a playful evening planning the trip. I was excited to go away with him for a long weekend to focus just on us, just for fun. I couldn't remember ever taking a trip planned purely for pleasure. Any excursions we had taken when I was married had been mostly in the nature of visiting grandparents or my family in California or going to Jack's parent's cabin.

The scenery heading north along the shoreline of the Pacific Coast Highway was beyond beautiful. I sat motionless in the car, taking it all in, wishing I could remember it forever. When we arrived in Cambria just before dusk on Friday evening, I was in high spirits to find that only a small by-road lay between our little white hillside bungalow and the gently rolling ocean. The view of the water was spectacular. As we rounded the curve of the coast, the setting sun projected finger-like streaks of light, transitioning into luminous hues of chalky purple that cast a glow upon the white-stoned, sandy carpet of Moonstone Beach. I had never experienced such a stunningly serene landscape. Aaron and I exchanged wordless glances as we drank in the exquisiteness of the moment.

The next day, Saturday, was the Fourth of July, and there was a parade in the little town; it was like we could have been in any charming, Midwestern community. Coming from Ohio, Aaron especially loved it. As we strolled to find our viewing place along the street, one of the quirky antique convertibles in the parade pulled alongside of us and three men from the Lion's Club invited me to sit atop the back seat and ride with them. Aaron insisted I should. I felt like I was eighteen again, beautiful, young, and vibrant—riding in a homecoming parade!

A few minutes after we'd returned to our bungalow that afternoon there was a knock on the door. It was the owner of our lodgings with tray in hand, prepared to serve us high tea. Every piece of the service was sterling silver and the cups and saucers were bone china. We sipped fresh mint tea and ate little *petit fours,* savory cheeses and grapes. Then Aaron and I walked along the beach as the sun began to set. I was the most content I could ever remember. In those moments, I forgot about the growing apprehensiveness of weeks past.

Returning to our room, we opened the door to another surprise. On an ornate, marble-topped stand beside the bed sat a silver ice bucket with the tip of a bottle of Dom Perignon protruding through a burgundy linen cloth, alongside which stood two exquisitely cut crystal flutes. Aaron had arranged it. I was being treated like a princess.

As we prepared to share our first glass, Aaron's demeanor turned somewhat formal. I could tell he was about to say something, something he had planned. In a very measured tone, he apologized and admitted that he realized he had been holding back emotionally. He explained that he needed his affairs and settlement with his wife to be cleared up before he could feel free to express his feelings for me.

With that he opened his briefcase and pulled out seven greeting cards! "One," he said, "for every day of the week." He had carefully selected each card over a period of several months. He placed them all out on the bed, fanning them out like a deck of cards. He raised his glass of champagne. "To you," he toasted, with a playful, shy grin.

One by one I opened the cards as joyous tears slipped down my cheeks. The cards were elegantly romantic, they were poetic, some were funny—and all of them declared his love for me. I could only weep. I was speechless.

He reached out to hold me. At that moment I felt a rush of pent-up exasperation. Even though I knew and understood he needed to be cautious because he was in the midst of a divorce, I felt a little manipulated by his sudden unveiling of his true feelings. Yet, I had to consider that it had been hard for him to be honest with himself until his responsibilities had been handled. Still, I had waited so long...and he was obviously aware of it.

But, he was saying what I had wanted to hear. Releasing my frustration, I turned on him. I playfully expressed my exasperation by pounding on his chest, throwing fake punches at his belly. I messed up his hair. I shouted, "How could you! You rat! You kept me hanging out there all this time!" He roared with laughter, and we both collapsed on the bed rolling around together like two kittens. We made passionate love. Although somewhat intense, his ardent manner made me feel as if there was nothing he wouldn't do for me.

His declaration gave me permission for the first time to be honest with myself about my own feelings. I realized I had grown to deeply love him. I, too, confessed my feelings that afternoon.

That evening was magical. He took me to the little town's most popular restaurant, and I wore my favorite strapless, red jumpsuit. Nearly every five minutes he told me how beautiful I was. We ate, we laughed, and several times my eyes welled up with tears of joy. I, too, had built a wall around myself and it was finally crumbling.

But the evening's surprises weren't over yet. When we got back to our room, he said mischievously, "Put on your swimsuit. I want to show you something." I thought we might be going down to the beach. However, once outside he led me to an area a little beyond our cottage. We had been so busy since arriving that I hadn't paid much attention to the grounds. He then led me onto a platform in the middle of which was a large, steaming hot tub, radiantly glowing with underwater lighting. It looked out onto a calm ocean as it mirrored the glow of the setting sun.

I was taken back. The sight of a hot tub instantly drew me to the memory of the spa Jack and I had in our house in Maryland. A haunting, depressing image of that fateful night flashed through my mind. The night when I could no longer bear my resentful anger and I had finally exploded at Jack, screaming, letting fly those decades of biter hostility. I didn't want to remember anything about that part of my life. Not that night.

It took an effort to bring myself back to the moment and to Aaron. As I slipped down into the water, I noticed that he'd brought with him what looked like a portable radio. I hoped dreamy music might pull me out of my unpleasant reverie. He pushed a button and dropped in a tape. He slipped into the water across from me as it began, watching me intently. Aaron and I both loved music, and we were currently caught up in the trendy new modern country rock. I expected that was what I would hear.

Instead, the strains of *She's Too Good to Be True* by Exile floated around us in our watery nest. Aaron grinned, and he was still grinning at the end of the song. I was puzzled. Another group, Foster and Lloyd, began to sing *Crazy Over You*...then, *Small Town Girl* by Steve Wariner. This was no ordinary tape. As I looked at Aaron out of the corner of my eye, he was still staring at me with his big grin. Babbling the obvious, I said, "These are different artists. Where did you get this tape?"

He shrugged, slid closer to me, dropped his voice to a croon and said, "Why don't we just listen?" Then came The Judds with *I Know Where I'm Going, Stand by Me,* and on and on. It was rigged. He had put that tape together himself!

So many emotions encompassed me. I wanted to laugh and cry at the same time. How had he done it? I had never heard of a mixed tape. How long had it taken him to put this tape together? And the cards? How long must he have been planning and preparing to show me his real feelings? Many weeks? Months? All the while he had kept his distance from me. He kept his feelings from me. He kept me waiting and wondering.

Aaron was obviously relieved and grateful the time had come when he felt he could give himself permission to expose his real feelings. He watched me intently with a look on his face of a little boy waiting for approval. "I hope you like the tape," his voice turned cautious.

I couldn't help but appreciate how loving his intentions were, and how eager he was to please me. This whole weekend had been planned for me. No one had *ever* done anything like this for me before. The whole day, the whole trip, had been beyond astonishing. And now this. Whatever his reasons had been that compelled him to keep his feelings bottled up, he was opening his heart to me now. I realized that all I wanted to do was receive them. To accept his love. To return his love. To be with him.

"So, how does my queen feel now?" Aaron inquired. I knew he was humoring me by calling me "queen," referring to the relationship I believed we shared in Atlantis as the centurion and the priestess.

"I feel like a queen," I purred. "You make me feel so appreci-ated, so loved." I hugged him tightly. I nestled under his arm, resting my head on his shoulder. For the first time in my life I thought I was actually getting to know what it was like to be at ease in a relation-ship with a man. I was grateful for a budding contentment gently urging me to open up.

I almost forgot the odd, bewildering discontent that had stubbornly persisted for some time. Dreamily, I gazed out over the expanse of ocean. The nearly full moon cast a glaze on the water as the rolling waves crashed, spawning families of smaller waves, all glowing brilliantly in the night with luminous, phosphorescent tips.

As I lifted my face to the brilliant starry sky, I couldn't help but compare this night to the night in the hot tub in Maryland with Jack. That night, also, I had looked up to the stars and screamed at the top of my lungs, releasing the toxic pain inside of me. This night was so much an antithesis of that dark memory and the misery of that life so long ago.

Then, the moment came. Another one of those lightbulb moments. A moment of remembering something I had seen as a vision in the mental hospital twenty-six years ago. A happy vision of a hot tub somewhere in the west, near the ocean. Even at the time of that vision, I'd thought it was telling me about my future.

This was it! It had happened! So many of my visions occurred at difficult and horrible times in my life, but they had offered me hope and encouragement. This one was simply a gift. This one had become a dream come true! *Another* dream come true.

Within a few weeks Aaron and I were off again on a long weekend trip to New Orleans. It was exciting to be traveling together again so soon. And to The Big Easy! I had heard so much about the Cajun food, the down-home hospitality of the people and their fondness for partying. Aaron flew there often as this wonderful city was near his company's headquarters.

Our hotel was right in the middle of the French Quarter. We walked everywhere, wandering in and out of boutiques and following the lowdown wail of jazz into neighborhood bars. In Jackson Square we enjoyed butterscotch glazed beignets straight from the oven.

In the afternoon we stood in a long line at Pat O'Brien's bar and were seated at the very first table right next to the foot of a slightly elevated platform where two people sat at dueling pianos and played and sang. What fun! We ordered the signature house drink, a Hurricane, which was large, pink, and strong. Together, we drank it with two straws, and we sang our hearts out to every song along with the crowd. On the hardwood stage floor in-between the pianos was an inlaid circle with a starburst in the center. Aaron said, "I think we should dance on that star." I laughed, recoiling at the very idea.

But then, before I knew it, sometime during the second Hurricane, Aaron was on the stage pulling me up with him. Well, now that I was up there was only one thing to do! I had to dance! In less than a minute we were escorted off by two men. The crowd went wild, cheering us and enjoying our exuberant display.

When we finished our second Hurricane and started to leave, I gasped as I caught sight of the doorway. Half the people in the room had formed a double line for us to walk through, making a tunnel with their arms held up. Just as if it were planned, we didn't miss a beat and we danced our way down the line and out the door. Once outside we hugged and laughed with the friendly crowd. We practically skipped all the way back to our room.

That evening Aaron took me to one of New Orleans' finest restaurants, Galatoire's, and the next night we went to another of equal reputation, Arnaud's. On Sunday, before returning to California, we enjoyed an outrageously grand brunch at the Commander's Palace in the Garden District, where I ordered a bread pudding soufflé with Kentucky bourbon sauce. My mother made great bread pudding, but it was nothing like this!

This was another world for me. A whole new way. I had never known life to be as exciting, or as rich. Or that a relationship could be like this. I was in completely uncharted territory.

Most of me was fully on board. Yet, no matter how hard I tried to shake it, some part of me felt subtly haunted by a ghost-like emptiness. A gnawing unidentifiable fear.

CHAPTER 16

The Dream Becomes Lucid

The Cambria weekend and New Orleans were the first of many trips Aaron and I took together. Most of them were arranged around his business travels. At those times it was challenging for me to work through the week, be gone over a long weekend, and be back to work on Monday. Still, I loved the excitement of planning and shopping for them, and I looked forward to each of our getaways. Aaron loved planning surprise evenings for me, and he was always taking my picture—as if everything I did was important. I felt special.

On the one hand, our friendship was continuing to develop and grow stronger. It seemed that no matter what our challenges, we always turned out to be there for each other. And there were challenges. Although Aaron appeared to be sincere about being more relaxed, he remained prone to over-planning, often becoming too spent to devote himself to private time for the two of us. I tried to be considerate of his time-consuming job and the ongoing stress of his divorce which, thankfully, was moving along. However, I couldn't help but express frustration now and then.

Likewise, he tried to guard his strong penchant to act as a protector. But even without his saying anything, his watchfulness was obvious. I had to admit I liked feeling treasured. When he grew particularly anxious about my welfare, I was reminded of his dream of a fire on a hill that was endangering me. Even in his dreams he felt a need to guard me.

But I was having mixed feelings. Ironically, the closer we became the more I felt myself internally recoiling. There was an indefinable discontent welling up inside. Moments of feeling exposed, unsafe, like something was closing in around me. Something dark was catching up with me.

But why! Why, when I had found a loving relationship that was filled with good times and laughter, and when for the first time I felt truly appreciated? Why, when I had every reason to feel safe, to trust Aaron? To be content? Hadn't I recently concluded that through my relationship with Aaron the life I was living was a dream come true? I wondered where and when, if ever, I would reach contentment. In this lifetime would I ever find any of the peace I had found so briefly in the kaleidoscopic light so many years ago?

One day when I dropped MacArthur off at his home with Barbara, I was feeling particularly tense. Barbara noticed, and I shared with her a little bit about my undefined anxiety. I dismissed it by telling her I must be trying too hard. Being the caring person that she was, Barbara gave me the name of a friend who owned horses and taught riding. She was sure Joanne was someone I would like. Since I enjoyed MacArthur, she thought being around horses might also be relaxing for me.

Joanne and I finally met for the first time over a cup of clam chowder at a restaurant in the harbor. We stumbled a little awkwardly, looking for things in common to talk about. Then, she asked me how I had come to live in Dana Point. Barbara had shared that she'd known Joanne for a long time, and described her as a deeply sensitive and understanding person. So, calmed by that reassurance and the familiar, embracing energy of the harbor, I swallowed hard and took a chance on revealing myself to this stranger. I told her all about the mystical events of the day I found my condo, my vision of the pink houses, my overwhelming experience of emotion in that very harbor, and even about my immediate reaction to my condo's number, fifty-two.

We sat side by side at the counter, her head cocked sideways toward me, her gaze fixed directly on me as I talked. Then, this once beautiful but now deeply suntanned, rugged appearing lady said, "Oh, hell, now I know why we were supposed to meet! I believe in such things, you know. You need to get on a horse and ride. It would be good for you. Help you figure things out."

I loved the idea, but my immediate response was about my financial situation: a little tight. I knew that horseback riding and all the accompanying gear could really add up.

"What I can do for you is let you ride old Rusty for ten dollars an hour if you're willing to clean him and rub him down when you're finished." I hadn't a clue how to do that, but I was instantly enthusiastic at the prospect.

Rusty was a magnificent animal. He was a reddish-golden palomino with a thick flowing white mane and white socks. In the past he had earned countless ribbons and championships in shows as a jumper. "My friend Rusty here is a real thoroughbred, but he's twenty-two years old. Now all he wants is a gentle walk every day, some fresh oats and an apple. That's what you can do for him. Later, I'll teach you a little bit about riding."

When I looked into his big, serious, brown eyes, I was surprised to feel an instant, spontaneous, hot rush of raw emotion. I had the urge to cry my heart out to this creature. His eyes were accepting and serene. Almost as if they knew me. "For a while, you can get used to each other by taking him for a stroll around the corral." I had ridden a few times before but only as a tourist, so I had very few skills.

Joanne pushed my back end up and over, and with little effort I mounted him. As I opened my legs to rest on either side of him, a tidal wave of emotion consumed me. My hips had never opened that wide. Panic and passion—all at once! With a mere flick of my wrist he started walking, his giant, muscular hind quarters undulating, rolling me steadily from one side to the other.

The curves of his rounded belly were soft and warm between my thighs. Right, left, right, left, his huge body rocked me. His gait lifted and dropped under me, thrusting me up and down, up and down again, into the hard saddle.

It felt bittersweet. I was overwhelmed with the fervor of a deep passionate longing. But at the same time, a deep sadness—something between overwhelm and heartbreak.

A part of my anatomy that had forgotten to feel, or that had never felt that way, was beginning to live. I surrendered to the obsession. My cheeks were flaming. Big hot tears welled up from some dark, emotionally estranged part of me, and spilled down my face.

Along with this new, raw sexual flood of passion—came panic; panic locked inside of me demanding to be released. I was losing all resistance, as though something that had died in me a long time ago was letting me know it would no longer be suppressed.

Dear Rusty was safe. On his back it was alright to feel. He was a precious creature of creation. Simple, gentle. I looked around to see if Joanne had noticed my tears. She had gone.

With blurry eyes, I lifted my gaze up to the sapphire blue sky, dotted by fluffy, white clouds. For a split second, in between the clouds I saw a mirage. A prism, sparkling and spinning like a multifaceted pinwheel. I was drawn into its tiny, glistening center point. I knew there was something here for me to learn. Embracing the bitter sweetness I knew its meaning would begin to open—but only as I would allow it. It would be at my own pace. Like Rusty, I knew I was very slowly, but steadily, plodding forward.

As if on cue, my subconscious had permission to be heard once again through a dream. It was Saturday morning. I had awakened at 4:15 a.m. I was short of breath and soaking wet with perspiration, still tormented with very real images of the frantic dream racing through my head. Not the recurring dream about drowning in greenish-black water. This was the return of the other recurring dream I'd had in my teenage years when I'd been an Indian maiden, and I was running for my life, racing through a tall corn field chased by a band of Indian warriors with bows and arrows. The dream always ended before they caught me. But I knew I would be caught.

I jumped up for a glass of water and grabbed my journal. Then I collapsed back into bed. I had been journaling a lot lately. When I put my feelings on paper, I could be free of them. At least for a while.

What was causing me to dream about Indians? Although I had not had any significant association in my life with American Indians, it was true I was part Cherokee. My great grandmother on my mother's side, Mama said, was a full-blooded Cherokee. I had never met her. She lived in the Blue Grass Mountains in the late 1800's. My mother had kept a tintype picture of her. Her face looked strong and rugged. I journaled a description of my dream hoping that writing about it would lessen my fear.

I startled myself, realizing my chin had dropped suddenly to my chest. I scooted my body back down under the covers and surrendered to welcome slumber. But I wasn't to sleep soundly. Short brown snakes were everywhere in my dreams. I was moving from room to room in an endless big old wooden house. As I stepped into a room with bare feet, I put my foot down to empty floors. But before they touched the ground, the floor was teeming with writhing, slimy snakes. I darted from room to room, looking for clear ground, but the snakes always reappeared. Finally, I found a door to the outside. But as I stepped onto the lush lawn, I realized to my horror it was not really a lawn but a massive bed of greenish-black woolly spiders. I was gripped by terror. The same haunting terror that had consumed me in my earlier recurring dream of Indians chasing me.

Instantly I awoke. My knees were drawn up to my chest, my head jerking from side to side. I knew then I was not going to be able to escape whatever was inside of me. I threw off the comforter. No sense in trying to get back to sleep again. I was awake. Besides, it was nearly eight o'clock. Taking off my gown, damp with perspiration, I jumped into the shower, then slipped on a pair of jeans and a soft knit sweater to ride Rusty. The warmth and comfort of his big friendly body would calm me, I was sure.

And it did. Even the ritual of rubbing him down was soothing, stroking him rhythmically, brush in one hand, the other hand sliding along his body, communicating the position of my presence...like finalizing the bond between us after my ride. I looked forward to my hour with Rusty. I had been riding him whenever I could, which was about once a week.

One day while finishing up with Rusty and treating him to his fresh apple, Joanne came over to talk. I was surprised in our conversation to discover that she knew about the book, *A Course in Miracles*. "I found it at the Healix Center," she said. "If you have a little time, let's have some breakfast. I'll take you over there." Breakfast. Hearing the word made me realize I was hungry.

But what I couldn't possibly have realized was that something was waiting there to stoke the raging fire within me, and change my life forever.

The Healix Center turned out to be a "New Age" bookstore and gathering place fifteen minutes away from Rusty's coral in San Juan Capistrano. The term "New Age" was becoming rather common. Joanne volunteered that New Age referred to the exploration of spiritual matters without constraints of any set religious doctrines. The center was a large, attractive space with a sizable bookstore and many meeting rooms. As a non-profit business, Joanne said they offered lectures and workshops on health and healing, addressing a spectrum of areas from stress management to herbal wellness to acupuncture, self-help, and spirituality. "Sort of a healing place for mind, body, and spirit." I could relate to that. Its purpose was similar to the Psychosynthesis classes I had taken.

We wandered into the bookstore to browse. It was cozy, even smelled good. Soft harp music played. Fat white candles glowed. So this was a New Age bookstore. Strange, I had heard the words "New Age" thrown around, usually with a little tongue-in-cheek tone. Sometimes the attitude was outright ridicule. Funny, I thought. What's wrong with a new age? Given the situation of the world, why wouldn't we want a new age?

I scanned the spines of their self-help books, some by bestselling authors I'd heard of. Their collection included customs of ancient cultures, mythology, and early American Indian folklore, along with inspirational and mystical writings.

Joanne made a purchase while I waited. I felt drawn to stay. It was as though I was standing in the presence of centuries of knowledge. In a fleeting moment I wished there was a way for me to know everything in those books. Surely, the answers to the mysteries of my own life would be there.

A delicate alabaster goddess figure attracted me, and I wandered over to examine it. My eye caught sight of the front cover of a small blue book featured on the shelf behind the goddess, bearing the title *Medicine Woman*. I remembered my dream that morning about Indians. A surge of emotion momentarily connected me to my Cherokee heritage.

On the back cover of the book, a review read:

There is much wisdom here... What sometimes appears as madness may contain its own wisdom; and what may sometimes sound like wisdom may be madness. It is precisely this intricate balance that the medicine woman must learn to keep.

Madness containing wisdom. That's just what it had been like for me as I sorted out what I'd seen and felt during and since my visions, along with the challenge to know how to regard the accompanying symbols.

Medicine Woman was an account of a journey by a Beverly Hills professional collector of African and Native American art named Lynn Andrews, who had followed a Heyoka medicine woman, Agnes Whistling Elk, into the wilderness of Manitoba for seven years. Agnes had taught Lynn to celebrate her power as a woman.

Intrigued, I randomly opened the book to a passage near the middle. Agnes was telling Lynn about an evil sorcerer called Red Dog, and a young maiden, named July. Agnes used a metaphor to describe how the sorcerer had taken woman's power away from July in the same way a spider kills a butterfly.

Have you ever seen a spider kill a butterfly?... The spider played games with her. He didn't kill her off quick with a merciful sting. He [Red Dog] danced around her with his flute, torturing her with his music, just like he's doing to you. And like the spider with the butterfly, he slowly sucked her insides out. She became his lover. He carried off her spirit and her power along with it, put it in a gourd, and hung it up in his cabin. It's a big joke to that bastard.

A sharp, icy cramp knotted my stomach as I read the part about Red Dog carrying off her spirit and her power. Like it was yesterday, those words brought back a lightning bolt of fear-filled memories; how trapped and powerless I'd felt in my former life with Jack. Although it had been four years since I'd left him, in that moment it was like yesterday, and I had been like that butterfly with my insides sucked out.

It had taken me so long to see what was happening to me. Jack had used sex to toy with me. It was always on his mind. He used sex to keep me at the cabin, to induce the premature birth of our son, to maintain his power over me, and to destroy the relationship I'd had with his mother. Right after we had sex, even multiple times, he would complain it was too bad I wasn't more interested in sex—as though we had not just been immersed in it. I felt I would go mad. I think that is what he wanted.

Jack had toyed with me in so many ways. Like when he'd left that book for me on the kitchen table—the autobiography of the actress committed to a mental institution. He had been trying to break me. I think he actually wanted to drive me back to the mental hospital.

My stomach flinched again as the flashbacks persisted...I felt a pang of the cruelty of the night Jack had locked me out of our house when I'd come home from an Al-Anon meeting. I had pounded on the window and could see him, calmly drinking his scotch, knowing I was there, but ignoring me; playing my favorite songs on the piano that he would not play for me to sing, and then time he gave me the sheet of music, "Face it Girl, It's Over"—clearly his wish for our marriage to end. But he wanted to force me to leave placing all the blame for our marriage's failure on me, and allow him to stay in the house. He wanted it all. Like Red Dog, he toyed with me.

Even when it was known that Jack was involved with other women, he stalked me and tried to brand me as a whore for leaving him. He wanted to keep me powerless by refusing to give me a divorce—just for spite. He put me through hell keeping me in financial stress and allowing our home to deteriorate to lower my part of the settlement. He played with me mercilessly like the spider in Agnes' story.

I realized I had died inside while living with Jack; especially after that night he tried to strangle me. Yet he was sexually aggressive and continued to use my body. I had given myself away to Jack. He had taken my spirit voice. My heart song. My power.

Just as the spider sucked the power from the butterfly, so Jack had tried to suck the life out of me. I had to escape his devouring hate to find my power... to fly away. In a flash this simple metaphor brought it all together as I'd never seen it before. I did find power—and I did get my divorce.

Although it had been four years since I'd left my marriage, I was amazed to realize I was still learning about myself. Unlike the butterfly, I had gotten away. I had started a new life. My mind gratefully returned to the cozy bookstore.

So why then was I still so fearful—sensing some sort of danger, feeling vulnerable? I wanted to know more of what the medicine woman said about a woman's power. My power.

I paid for the book, said goodbye to Joanne, and went straight home to read it.

Changing out of my jeans, I tossed a can of fruit cocktail onto some cottage cheese and carried it on a tray, along with the book, to the bedroom. I created a snug nest with the bedding and pillows surrounding me. I couldn't wait to read this book.

Medicine Woman was unlike anything I had ever come across. Lynn's story was set in the rich detail of Indian customs and in a world seen through the folklore of the Cree tribe. It touched something in me, connecting me to my recent recurring dreams as an Indian maiden. It was told in a mystical style that was multi-dimensional. It pulled me into a near-hypnotic trance right from the beginning.

Lynn Andrews, the author and art collector, had been obsessed with finding something called a "marriage basket," an object she'd briefly glimpsed in a painting. Shortly after seeing the painting she began to have recurring dreams about the basket. Like me! I related to Lynn immediately. She was entranced by a symbol and haunted by her dreams. She was pulled to it. Obsessed by it. She had to learn what it was all about. She had an understanding that there was something for her to discover.

I, too, learned from symbols. Symbols I saw in my visions and images in my dream of drowning under greenish-black water. My dream had become a driving force that led me to hypnotherapy, and to remembering a past life. Out of it had come welcome relief from guilt I didn't even realize I was carrying. Yet there was still something unsettled in me. I knew I wasn't where I wanted to be.

As the story unfolded, Lynn's mentor, Agnes, the medicine woman, described herself and all medicine people as travelers of the dimensions. I was astonished that Agnes referred to Lynn as one who is the dreamer. The *dreamer*! I must have read that paragraph five times. When Lynn asked what a dreamer was, Agnes said that dreamers are those who see the dream of themselves and others. She referred to life as the dream. Now, I was really interested. It was as if I had stepped into the book.

Lynn's journey appeared to be both physical and mystical. Agnes told Lynn that unconsciously she had made a bid for power when she succumbed to her vision; to her passionate desire for the marriage basket. Lynn learned that such a basket is considered a very sacred symbol in the world of dreamers. But even though Lynn had dreamed about it, she couldn't fully describe the marriage basket. She only knew that it was exquisitely luminous.

According to Agnes, the basket was woven by dreamers and was the representation of an unspeakable void—the womb in a woman. All things are born from the womb of woman. The male was created to balance that. But instead, men have claimed the void as theirs and, as a result, our Mother Earth is in great imbalance.

Men have claimed the void…the womb in woman as theirs! That had surely been my experience sexually. But I knew there was a deeper wisdom signified by this elusive symbol of the marriage basket.

Agnes told Lynn it was her quest—her duty as a woman—to find her power, to fight to get it back. It's how she could manifest herself. The marriage basket became symbolic to Lynn of coming into real womanhood. Agnes warned her that to take the marriage basket she would have to be relentless. "In your world, womanhood is lost," she told her.

Was that true? What and where was my sense of womanhood? As a nineteen-year-old teenager, I married Jack in large part to get away from my tyrannical father. I didn't really have an inkling of who I was. I allowed Jack to rule my life the way my father had done. I hadn't trusted in myself to make a different choice. I'd even given up my dream of going to college.

Although I'd become more aware of myself since then, a persistent whisper told me there was more to learn. Meeting Aaron, who was truly different than Daddy or Jack, was opening up a place in me. We had a mutual respect for each other. Our relationship had a childlike element to it. Playful and innocent. Sometimes he seemed like the loving, gentle big brother I'd never had. He often gave me greeting cards with children's pictures on them. I was getting a little taste of the childhood I had missed. But on the other hand, there was still some hesitancy on his part to connect with my feminine sensuality. It felt like another form of control; a rejection of my feminine power.

For seven years Agnes counseled Lynn in the ways of her culture, and helped other females to find their power. Agnes hounded her, testing Lynn's strength of character and will in many ways, including sending her out into the wild Canadian forests on solitary, sacred journeys; sometimes spending nights alone under a full moon surrounded by predators—coyotes, wolves, and snakes. But by facing her fears she would have a spiritual awakening. Agnes told her, "You must first have a courageous heart," but the real secret is that power is gained primarily from visions and dreams.

Visions and dreams! For two decades I had been having visions and dreams. And I was learning what it meant to have a courageous heart and to trust in what I was being shown. At that moment, I was caught in a stark realization that the same voice I had heard in so many ways, as well as the symbols, was once again leading me as I read.

The image of my dream as an Indian maiden fleeing for my life was vivid as I journeyed with Lynn, engrossed in Indian customs, yielding, relating to her driving obsession to know, no matter how much time and effort it would take.

Agnes told Lynn that to get the marriage basket she would need to "ripen her void" so that the energy of what she wanted would flow magnetically toward her belly. "Start thinking with your stomach...use your intuition...you must intuitively rise *above* the problem to *find* the problem."

Oh, yes. That had been true for me. Certainly I knew what it was like to use my intuition—to trust my stomach, my gut-level reactions. And I'd been thinking that way a lot lately.

When Lynn asked Agnes how she would know when she'd ripened her void, Agnes replied, "You will know. You will simply become aware of your power." I wondered what that would feel like.

According to Heyoka legend, Lynn would need to wrestle her power away from the forces of evil that held it. In the book, the forces of evil were embodied by the male sorcerer Red Dog. As it turned out, the evil Red Dog was the possessor of the marriage basket. He had great strength, and the power to shape-shift, appearing in many different forms, but usually as a gruff, husky man with red hair and a tangled red beard. Red Dog used sex to steal a woman's power.

Shape-shift...uses sex to take a woman's power...Jack had kept me in an emotional prison, a psychological straitjacket, by his shifting, his unpredictable Jekyll and Hyde behavior. He could be charming and attractive one moment, controlling and violent in another. And sex...sex was his primary way of dominating me. Even Aaron's way of sometimes being sexually unavailable felt to me like an act of domination. In a different way, I was still not feeling in control.

Had I ever known what it was like not to be dominated? Even as a child I'd endured the abusive tyranny of my father. Were his beatings related to some sort of sexual energy? Then it came back to me—the creepy night as a teenager when I had come home and my father pulled me down in a chair with him and started kissing me.

The story told of July, the young maiden with beautiful jet black hair who had been Agnes' apprentice before Lynn. She had walked into Red Dog's trap...he had her in his power; eyes vacant, in a trance, she had no will—her body rigid as stone. Although she'd been warned of his power, she let him lure her with the music from his flute.

And then I came to the same page I'd randomly read in the bookstore; the page on which Agnes had compared Red Dog and July to a spider killing a butterfly. It went on metaphorically to tell how Red Dog toyed with her; grasping her spirit and her power, and sealing it in a hanging gourd, leaving her empty shell on the porch with the flute. Possessed by its monotonous music, she could only play the same maddening notes—only the song that Red Dog wanted her to play.

All my past victimizations were coming up. My father had not allowed me to sing in our home. He beat me for singing and I never knew why. Jack in his domination tried to silence me. He never wanted to hear me, to play for me, to give me attention. Eventually, my spirit had been sucked out. I had learned to sing only the tune I was expected to sing in the voice I was allowed. I sang guardedly, carefully...with very little emotion. There was none of me, or my authenticity in the song. Just as July's flute had played itself without her heart, my song had shrunk to a diminished sound. That is until I'd found my own authentic voice in the Life Song workshop through the healing of unconditional love and acceptance.

And the gourd! The image captured perfectly how small women can feel when robbed of their power. So small their spirit can be hung by a string and buffeted about by the breeze. While married to Jack I had lived in an emotional box locked with his key, one he could kick tumbling down the road on a whim.

But, unlike July, I'd found my own voice. I was beginning to see how important that step had been. However, the nagging discomfort still haunting me told me that only part of my spirit had escaped from the gourd. I wasn't sure what. I only knew there was more. I knew I couldn't stop now.

As the story advanced, Agnes warned Lynn that she, too, faced July's fate. Time after time Red Dog lured Lynn and she barely escaped losing her spirit. She told Agnes that she struggled to control her desires for him. I couldn't help but think about my desire for more physical expression of my femininity in my relationship with Aaron. Was I giving away my power? I felt so confused, so conflicted.

The early afternoon sun streamed through the window in my bedroom, inspiring me to spend a few hours by the pool. I went into the bathroom to change into my bathing suit. As I entered, my eyes locked on the piece of art I'd hung there two years ago because the print was feminine, rectangular in shape, and contained the colors I'd wanted for the room.

I stared in disbelief. It was the print of an *Indian maiden* with long dark hair—and a flute held to her lips. The one I had been drawn to because of her beautiful, mystical grayish-blue eyes.

I shook my head to be certain of what I was seeing. Was I a character in the book? I saw myself in July, and there she was in my bathroom. I'd chosen her from four hundred prints nearly two years earlier. The woman in the print met the same description of July. I stood looking, absolutely motionless. She seemed to be looking at me too. In that instant, life was mirrored back to me...her life story reflecting mine. At that moment, all of my life became an illusion.

This coincidence was startling, even though I'd experienced some pretty surprising coincidences before.

Unlike earlier years in my life, I wasn't about to rationalize this away as mere happenstance. Indeed, I intended to remain open to whatever this lovely symbol would impart. I knew from my recent discoveries there were no accidents. I could learn in many ways—through all kinds of symbols. Like Lynn and her marriage basket, I must have seen something in that painting when I'd selected it, as I had in the tennis painting.

No longer interested in going to the pool, I prepared a light lunch and settled myself back on the bed. I was determined to finish the book that evening, especially now with the synchronicity of the Indian maiden picture in my bathroom. Perhaps it would guide me to a deeper understanding of the persistent restlessness inside me.

As Agnes tutored Lynn, she told her there were many teachings revealed to Lynn in her lifetime, but that she hadn't been awake enough to see them. The "awake ones" can wander beyond "even the far-away." Then Agnes told Lynn something I immediately understood; that most teachings are too heavy to bring back, but how glad we are if we can return through that door once it has been opened. Then the dream can never own us again.

Just like my experiences in the mental hospital, I'd been on the other side of the universe. Instead of losing my ability to cope, as it appeared at the time, what I saw forced me to release old ways of thinking, and guided me to self empowerment. Taken to another dimension, I did come back. I saw with new eyes and became more like an observer of myself, in a dream-like life. My visions were being projected through the world of substance...the evergreen trees, the highway sign, a hot tub, perhaps even a number on my door, a mountain by a highway, missing pink houses, or Asian scrolls. Substance that represented significant learning. This book spoke to me in a language I understood.

Lynn was worried about July, the maiden who'd lost her spirit to Red Dog...July's likeness was in my bathroom. July was losing strength and was looking half-dead.

"She has lost her *smoke spirit*," Agnes told Lynn. Red Dog had imprisoned it in a gourd.

Agnes told Lynn that July needed to reclaim her smoke spirit if she wanted to live.

In rapt fascination, I read as Agnes and her blind friend, Ruby, finally, cleverly, retrieved July's spirit. They stole Red Dog's gourd that held July's spirit.

Lynn's multi-dimensional account told how Agnes, standing behind July, lifted the gourd directly over July's head. Ruby pushed on July's stomach. As Agnes twisted her hands on the gourd, Lynn heard a sharp crack, like a pistol shot. A plume of smoke swirled around the top of July's head and was jerked down inside her by a silver thread.

July's eyes cleared, and she started to smile. She declared she'd tried desperately, but just couldn't get back. Agnes informed her that she had at last walked across in return to her own power.

And finally Lynn too pushed through her own fears and her struggle between her blind obsession to find the marriage basket, and her uncontrollable desire for Red Dog. She confronted him, raiding his cabin and, in the midst of a treacherous struggle, she captured the marriage basket armed with only a knife. In a mystically symbolic scene, Lynn cut away luminous fibers that shot out from the marriage basket representing her captivity. Red Dog began to shrivel up, diminishing into a powerless and ancient white-haired man. Lynn finally seized the marriage basket she had dreamt about. By pushing through her fear and following her inner knowing, she'd discovered that Red Dog was not powerful at all. She had only *thought* he possessed power.

The same thing happened to me that night in Maryland…the night with Jack in the hot tub when I'd screamed at him, finally dumping all of my imprisoned resentment, no matter the possible dangerous consequences of his rage. But instead of employing his usual dominating tactics, he just watched me. He had never seen me take such control. I pushed through my fear because the truth demanded to be heard. That one moment of blind courage had set me on a healing path to a better life.

Soon after claiming the marriage basket, Lynn experienced a symbolic dream. She saw a vision of a male with whom she was mating—but she was mating with herself. By finally moving through fear to possess what she had wanted most, she had mated with the warrior—the male—within herself.

I knew about the left brain and right brain hemispheres within everyone—the masculine and feminine—but the concept of mating with one's self?

Confused, Lynn asked Agnes what her dream had to do with the marriage basket.

"You have become aware that the marriage basket was conceived by the dreamers to symbolize the union between the high warrior and high warrioress within your own being," Agnes replied.

"Every woman seeks after that high warrior, that most magnificent of men, within her. We seek him all our lives. If we're lucky, we conjure him in our dreams, mate with him, and become whole…Its symbol is big medicine."

"A sorcerer is simply one who holds power," Agnes added. "A sorcerer can be a man or a woman, good or evil. Somewhere on Mother Earth great men like Buddha, Jesus, and Crazy Horse also found their power. But you must first have a courageous heart before you can take power."

I sat there, hardly breathing. Hot energy welled up in my belly, ascending through my chest to the back of my head. In slow motion it exploded behind my eyes and, like raining fireworks, it trickled gently down to the base of my spine and to my genitals. I knew, like Lynn, that I had an intangible deep desire. Or was it emptiness? I hungered for something. Yet, I also feared it.

By possessing what she feared, Lynn had merged into a whole being. She'd faced down her fear. Agnes called it a union of the male and the female within her. I knew I had no choice but to come face to face with whatever was causing fear inside of me.

I don't know how long I sat locked in that trance-like review of myself. Something old and familiar in me was stirring. Was it a part of me I barely knew before the first time Daddy had whipped me? Before the first time Mama told me she wished I was dead? Was it the strength I had been struggling to find when I attempted to go to college before I felt compelled to leave home? Or before I met Jack? Before Jack had shamed me into feeling like a whore because I enjoyed sex that night right after we were married? Before he began to suck out my will? And was I now giving my power away again to Aaron?

I closed the book.

What a suspenseful, transcendent, symbolic journey. I was glad I had "accidentally" come upon this book at a time when I felt so conflicted. I yearned to be whole and peaceful in the ways I had glimpsed in this book.

Like July, had I lost my own smoke spirit? Perhaps I'd never really found it yet.

Overcome with simple wonder and humility that something inside of me had led me to select an art piece that fit the exact description of July, I slid down off my bed to study her once again. There she was with her long dark hair, starry, vacant eyes, and a flute held to her lips.

But wait!

In the next moment, time crashed down around me in a screeching halt. In the right hand corner just above July's head and over her left shoulder, was a round, blue-grey, ball of smoke.

I stared in utter disbelief. Why hadn't I noticed it before? It was July—with her *smoke spirit* suspended just above her left shoulder! And there she had been the whole time—in my bathroom.

Life itself was mirroring my truth back to me! In my heart, I knew I would yet learn what I needed to know. I profoundly trusted that there is an inter-relatedness between all life and things. There is a connection, a communication, a voice, between the substance of my world and my being. Symbolically, within the dance of my consciousness and the world of form, an orchestrated symphony played a grand composition—my life—my dream.

CHAPTER 17

The Morphing of Day Dreams and Night Dreams

A lthough an indefinable weightiness remained in my belly, my trust was renewed by the startling coincidences around the symbol of the Indian maiden with her *smoke spirit*. Wherever this symbol guided me, I would follow. The image of the Indian maiden who'd lost her *smoke spirit* was dramatically displayed on the screen of my mind. I knew it was a guiding symbol I could trust. I knew I was moving toward an understanding of the source of my nagging anxiety.

Seeking tranquility a few days after discovering the *smoke spirit* in my picture of the Indian maiden, I drove down to my familiar harbor. But the comfort of the high bluffs that had recently curled peacefully around me like gigantic, embracing arms was gone. Their energy had transformed!

Once again the bluffs loomed darkly over me as my car crept below them. The pristine boats with their sails and my favorite tidy little beach had lost their appeal. Impending peril, underlain with deep, empty sadness enveloped me. This time I was not overtaken with wrenching sobs as I had been before. This time I felt consumed with despair. Hopeless despair.

Again I envisioned the small Indian village perched on the edge of the cliff, but I saw no danger of overwhelming water as before. All was quiet. All was dark except for a low campfire encircled by eight or so teepees. No one stirred. There was an eerie silence. Something was about to happen.

I couldn't make myself push the accelerator for the final quarter of a mile to where the road arched and ended at the ocean. Time halted as I helplessly passed through this no-man's land. After the car seemed to pass the distance on its own, I found myself at the end of the road by the shoreline where, in that space, the crush of sadness and the images of the village faded as they had at other times in the past. I parked the car, facing the steel-gray ocean.

It was an unseasonably warm Friday night in early February of 1988. With the top open on my convertible, I sipped on an iced coffee as a brilliant orange sunset was about to fade away. Heaving a deep sigh, I dropped my head onto the headrest, drawing in cleansing breaths; the salt air filling my lungs. I tried to relax.

Eyes closed, I succumbed to that now familiar feeling. An underlying sense that the overwhelming emotions I'd been experiencing, and the images that had just passed through my mind in the harbor, were connected in some way to the many other visions and symbols I'd known—the specific art pieces, finding my condo, even the mountain and the pink houses. All of it. They resembled old, familiar tales. There was some common purpose to them...some important, unifying message for me, for my future.

Ever since I had stumbled upon the book *Medicine Woman* and realized I had a picture in my condo exactly like the character July in that book, each morning in my bathroom my Indian maiden illuminated herself to me. She reminded me to have courage, just as July had bravely recovered her spirit.

To have courage to find, and to take back one's inner power, was the message I received from the book. I thought about how each day as I looked at her, the same question kept arising. What power did I need to reclaim? When had I lost it? I was functioning well, and my relationship with Aaron was going smoothly enough. Why would I want to stir things up?

I knew these thoughts would not cease by taking the picture down. I knew something else would occur. I completely trusted the inner guidance spawned by the symbols.

I took a sip of my coffee inviting clarity. Why was I not content? What was this haunting reoccurrence of seeing the Indian village steeped in doom? It was distressing. Was the image of the Indian maiden in my symbolic world coaxing this former vision from the harbor back to me? And then there had been that first morning while riding on Rusty. Something frightening had stirred inside of me. In varying degrees, the bittersweet, passionate panic was still present as I continued to ride him most every week.

Pushing the car seat back to stretch out my legs, I tried to wipe everything out of my mind except the rolling, rhythmic sounds of the surf crashing against the rock wall below.

In that moment, as if I didn't already have enough to think about, the memory of an old and forgotten vision from my childhood intruded my thoughts. More visions! What was prompting this? Was it because of what had just happened as I passed the cliff? Was my subconscious trying to vomit everything? However, this was a vision I recognized.

On the whole, I never could remember very much of my childhood. Only a few incidents stood out in my mind, mostly the painful ones. But ever since I was a little girl certain images had come to me on occasion. Strangely enough, they weren't scary. They just were. Coming mostly in the mornings when I was not quite awake, they continued from about age seven to the stressful pre-teen years, a time when my father became especially violent. But each time I had quickly forgotten them. Thinking back, I realized there had always been a little corner of my mind trying to communicate to me through visions and dreams.

This flashback was that time when I first entered this world. But it was *before* my birth. I was without a body. I was suspended in a space/consciousness above the earth. I could see the curvature of the globe. I descended, hovering above a geographical area that I now know as the southeastern region of the United States. As some part of me neared the earth, I could make out a large, oblong-shaped, gray stone protruding out from the ground.

This first part of my vision was always accompanied by an overwhelming dread. I knew that I was to be born, and I was very frightened. It was a fear similar to jumping into an ice cold lake and not knowing how to swim.

In the moments following that image I always sensed something else had happened, but I'd not been able to remember it. An instant later, I saw myself in an infant's body lying in a warm bed next to my mother. I was aware of feeling deeply grateful to be there. Actually, though, it was more like an extraordinary sense of relief. I knew more had happened during those moments around my birth, but I never could summon a clear image of it.

Then the vision skipped ahead in time. I was nearly two years old and in a large black baby buggy being pushed by my mother. With my head turned to the right, motionless, I stared out a small isinglass window in the collapsible top. In the vision, I was aware I was deciding whether or not I wanted to live.

And that was how it ended.

Oh, my God! Only two years old...thinking of life versus death! Where had that sorrow come from? With the memory of the vision returning now, I recalled how deeply disturbing it had been in the past. And now how it was again.

Ironically, each occurrence of this fragmented vision also brought a feeling of reunion as if connecting me to another part of myself. It left me now, as it had in the past, with a surge of energy that actually reaffirmed my will to live. I had had a very real moment of linkage to something. But I could only relate it to being from that nebulous somewhere, where everything originated.

I'll always remember the shock I felt much later when, as an adult in my early thirties, I actually saw a monolithic stone like the one in my childhood visions. It was in the movie *2001: A Space Odyssey*. I didn't even know what I had seen in my vision was called a monolith. I sat pinned to my theater seat. Something about that startling recall from my childhood caused a shift in me, right there in the theater. It was then that I first got any inkling there was more of me than I knew.

The sun had set beyond the horizon of the water. In dusk's dim light, I watched the phosphorescing waves as they rolled onto shore. The winter air growing damp, I pushed the button raising the top on my convertible and headed home.

Strange I should remember flashbacks from my childhood again in my late forties. I wondered if other people had moments like that. Could anyone else remember before they were born? Maybe they did but they just didn't talk about it.

To pick up my spirits, back in my condo I pampered myself with my favorite meal of steak and fresh asparagus spears. After a hot shower, I decided I would rest in bed and read.

As I toweled off, my eyes once again found their way to the Indian maiden. She had come to feel like a sister. Was I like her? Was she hanging there to tell me that my discontent, my recent visions and dreams, were guiding me to find my own spirit? My lost spirit?

Then I realized there was another question regarding my childhood flashback that evening which I hadn't stopped to ask myself. Why in those images did I remember a time as a distraught baby when I might not have wanted to live? Why hadn't I questioned that before? Why did it not seem important until now? I had no answers.

Heating up some cocoa to warm me inside, I picked up a book by Robin Norwood, *Women Who Love Too Much*. I tried to quell my racing thoughts by reading. Like many women, I had bought the book with the desire to protect myself; to be as realistic about my relationship as possible. But after a few minutes, my mind wandered. I had to admit my thoughts were becoming scattered.

I couldn't forget that July's spirit, in the *Medicine Woman* book, had been taken from her when she'd allowed herself to be completely possessed by the alluring sexuality of Red Dog. Like her, I didn't want to be totally possessed, but I deeply craved to be loved and desired. Was that so unusual? Unlike Red Dog's seductive ways, Aaron's only potential rule over me seemed to come from his sporadic withdrawal.

I also had to ask myself, was it me? Was I the one afraid to surrender, to trust in our relationship? Was I fearful of letting my guard down? Would that be losing my power? My father took my power away. Jack took my power away. But why did I think Aaron would do that?

Furthermore, I wondered if the safety I had found with Aaron was providing a sort of hot house for buried feelings to sprout. Like the feelings that had rushed in when I'd ridden Rusty? Could the returning gloomy vision of the Indian village and childhood memories be precursors to some new understanding or to some new sense of freedom in the same way that my visions and dreams of an Atlantis lifetime had helped me to release overwhelming anxiety I held at the time?

I knew I had become preoccupied with the image of the Indian maiden, her separated spirit. So I picked up my copy of *A Course in Miracles* from the bedside table and opened it to a page I had marked, wanting to re-read a passage that said God's messages are not limited to those who see only with the body's eyes. They can arrive in many forms—as an object, a dream, an image, a brief feeling. And then the form's meaning is understood through our inner voice.

Yes, that was what it was like. Each time I re-experienced a dream, a picture, a vision, it was as if I was being coaxed by an inner voice. Something was tugging me deeper into myself.

I looked up, as I always did before retiring, to take in the familiar Asian scrolls on the wall across from my bed. They were more unresolved images that kept calling. It had been three years since I'd been unable to ignore their silent bidding. They were the last thing I saw as I went to bed every night. Now there were two symbols distracting me—the Indian maiden and the scrolls.

As my gaze fixed on the two scrolls, I succumbed to the weariness of my very unusual day. Laying the *Course* aside, I repositioned the pillows, pulled up the comforter, and reached to turn off the light. When my eyes accommodated to the darkness, the image of the footbridge in the scrolls floated luminously in my mind. There was a bridge I must cross. I knew it!

And then another dimension? Another time? Another world? Another past life? It seemed so real! Yet it was a dream. A night dream.

...I am there in the Indian village that I had seen on and off by the harbor for over two years. But this is new. I am sleeping on a bed of warm blankets on a dirt floor inside a large wigwam. In the center is a cooking fire that had burned down to embers. I'm an Indian maiden.

Someone has entered. I turn to look. As in my earlier dream of drowning in Atlantis, I see a face in front of mine. With great joy I realize it is the face of an Indian brave for whom I feel a deep passion.

Wait. Although we are both in American Indian bodies, I see the spirit of Aaron in this brave—in his eyes, in his voice. He has come to my bed in the night for the first time. I become lost in the rapture of making love with him. It is innocent, sweet, gentle, real. Just like the first time Aaron and I had sex in this lifetime. But in my dream I know it is forbidden love...I know that I belong to another man.

Abruptly, I hear rawhide slapped heavily against the side of the tent as the door flap is thrown open. Two warriors with painted faces, bows and arrows drawn, glare angrily down at us. They drag us both from the tent.

Somehow, we wrench free of their hold and attempt an escape, racing into the corn fields that surround the village. This part was the same recurring dream I had dreamt countless times throughout my life...running through cornfields. I am the fleeing Indian maiden. This time, the dream continues. I am crippled with fear. My legs won't move fast enough. We are caught.

Then I am brought back to the outskirts of the camp. I am shoved down on the ground to lie flat on my back. Aaron and I are being tied with rawhide to wooden stakes pounded into the dirt—our legs and arms bound tightly to separate stakes; my body stretched wide to nearly breaking. Then one of the warriors who held a round straw basket with a lid opens it. He tosses a coiled snake onto the ground near us.

Bitten, I am left in the hot sun to be nature's prey, to dehydrate and bake. To be covered by flies, infected with the venom of insects and the snake. My body swells with the poison and dehydration. After two nights the warriors return. I fear the worst. Searing pain burns between my ribs. I look down to see an arrow in my chest. The warriors unfasten axes from their belts and they chop me into quarters. They cut off my legs and arms. Somehow I do not die. They place my body parts on a rawhide stretcher and carry me to the top of a small mountain nearby. The village people follow, chanting and dancing. They lift the stretcher, lash it to high wooden stilts, beckoning The Great Spirit to take me. I sense the presence of another body on a similar stretcher not far away.

From the platform, I see blue sky, wispy clouds. I smell salt air, feel a damp ocean breeze. I know the mountain is near the shore. My dehydrated, swollen body aches for the comfort of the water. The part of me that is still alive fades in and out of consciousness, in and out of all-consuming pain. I can't understand how I still live. A sense of desolation permeates my fragmented being, but then gradually disperses as I am embraced in a velvety, silent, presence. I am lifted into the grandeur of all life. An embracing lightness commences to consume me. I pray—I plead—for the Great Spirit to take me; for my body to die ...

And then I woke up.

Saturday morning. I don't know how long I lay there immobilized. Sweating, exhausted, and completely overcome by emotions from my dream, I tried to push away the violent images. My mind darted back and forth, reviewing the scenes, realizing I was now in possession of the entire dream which had been coming to me in piecemeal as visions of a village by the harbor and of me running through corn fields. A dream in which I knew the maiden was me, and I was fighting for my life.

This dream was the most painful emotional roller-coaster I'd ever ridden. It moved from the ecstasy of sharing love with someone I was sure was the spirit of Aaron, to a desperate, futile attempt at escape. And then to a brutal mutilation after which I had been left to die.

On one hand I felt exhausted, yet within the dream there had been fleeting moments of pure, sweet calm. It had been a frightful, gory dream, yet the serenity of its ending stayed with me. The ending was a sensation of joining with an all-consuming, silent presence. Once again, this felt familiar. As I stared at my bedroom ceiling, I was able to recall at one time earlier in my life when I'd had that same feeling.

It was over twenty-five years ago now, the night I saw the kaleidoscopic light before going into the mental hospital. That night, the light and the accompanying blissful exhilaration had made me want to forget everything horrible in my life and do nothing but laugh. How strange that this horrendous dream had also taken me back to similar moments of blissful peace. I realized in that moment how much my heart longed for this peace.

But the serenity from the dream was short-lived. As I faced the day, I began to ruminate about the disturbing events of the dream. I had envisioned my own brutal murder. And for what? What had I done wrong? I was sure the reason I had only been able to dream fragments of it, the chase in the cornfield in my recurring dream, was that the rest of the story was too horrifying. Why had it suddenly come time for me to see it all? What had changed in me?

Suddenly I wanted to get out of the house. I needed a change of scenery, anything. I decided to finally carry out my promise to myself to drive the two miles north from my condo to San Juan Capistrano for a little sightseeing. I'd wanted to go there for some time, ever since my first real date with Aaron. This would be a good weekend to do it since Aaron was moving into his new condo in Irvine. He wanted to make that transition on his own, and I understood. He and his former wife had sold their home, and they were finally settling the last details of their divorce.

The town of San Juan Capistrano is small. I poked in and out of the shops on the main street, and passed by the legendary Swallows Inn saloon where Aaron and I had danced on our first date until they'd closed the doors. I couldn't help but grin as I remembered the fun we'd shared.

Something made me feel I needed to be in San Juan Capistrano. Having wandered through it and not wanting to leave, I walked into a plaza called The Mercado, and sat down at a table in a lovely outdoor patio near a water fountain. It was mid-afternoon, and the winter sun was still warm. Birds chirped, flittering around me in the fountain and hopping on the red brick flooring. I ordered a glass of pinot noir and a slice of New York cheesecake.

I took a deep breath, settling back in the wrought iron chair. I was enjoying the afternoon, but my mind kept returning to last night's vivid dream of torture for sexual betrayal. But who had I betrayed? Even though I had sensed in the dream I belonged to another, it hadn't been revealed to me who that person was, or why my love of the Indian brave was a crime.

And Aaron was once again with me in another lifetime! Although this time the memory was coming from a dream, not through hypnosis. Just thinking about it, I could still feel the innocence of the love we had made vibrating through my body. In fact, in the present there was still an innocence between us in all aspects of our relationship. I liked that part of us. That childlike openness. We could laugh at ourselves. It was only when he was distant that it became hard for me to remain calm.

I thought about how, for years when living in Maryland, I'd been drawn to the TV whenever the evening news covered the annual return of the swallows to the Mission San Juan Capistrano each March. Even then, I couldn't explain my attraction. I'd felt a connection to this town for so long, but now my feelings were tied in with even more emotion.

I'd been led to live near this town. I belonged here. Moving to a place near San Juan Capistrano and the Dana Point Harbor was a quest, a destined journey for me. Everything was speeding up; even erupting from my childhood...the memory of the vision of before and after I was born...yesterday's vision in the harbor, about the Indian Village...my vivid dream as an Indian maiden. They were important. They were leading me somewhere.

I also trusted deep in my heart that these day dreams and night dreams, as disturbing as they were, were leading me to that peace I'd once tasted years earlier, just before being committed to the mental hospital.

I paid my bill. I knew what I had to do next. I had to come to back to San Juan Capistrano on March 19th for the celebration of the return of the swallows to the mission.

One month later, on the morning of March 19th, 1987, I felt anxiety as I awoke. I had been on an unexplainable high the day before. It reminded me of the restless, almost super-human surge of energy that had come the day before each of my children had been born. That previous day I had obsessively cleaned out bathroom cupboards, my desk, and I'd put away a lot of clutter and old mementos. This day, I felt both apprehension and a sense of urgency. San Juan was calling to me.

I had been very insistent with Aaron about spending our day there. He just shrugged his shoulders, acquiescing with an amused grin. The day was really warm, and we found a good spot along the curb where we could watch the town's Swallows Day parade. There were finely-groomed horses with riders in colorful Spanish regalia, Mariachi bands, a few local marching bands, and adults and children dressed in what looked to be deerskin clothing and tunics. The town did not permit any motorized vehicles in the parade so it was sweet, simple, and festive. However, the blazing sun was giving me a headache. I began to question why I was so drawn to this event. My daughter, Jennifer, had told me about a beautiful prayer room at the mission two blocks away. Since the heat and the congestion of the crowd had intensified, I suggested to Aaron that we check it out.

We entered the Mission San Juan Capistrano through its side door, near the prayer chapel. As we moved along the arcade of the open courtyard and approached the tiny chapel, I heard the sounds of instruments playing a few yards away in the center of the courtyard. There were drums beating with a loud, heavy pulse, tambourines shaking, sticks rattling, and horns, oh my God, the horns. Their piercing wail went right through me. I felt myself moving toward them.

People sat and stood on chairs, and some occupied the ground in the open plaza, all gathered around a group of fully-costumed American Indians, some with musical instruments. In the very center was a large pit containing a roaring fire. The music abruptly stopped, except for the drums which continued to beat: thudding, thumping, steadily pulsing.

An Indian brave with long, ink-black hair pulled tightly back, and his face and body painted all over, began to tell the story of the ancient ritual Aztec dance they were about to perform. This dance had been performed by tribes of the Aztec people for eight hundred years. It existed in their culture as a reminder to those who did not obey their laws. I cringed as I realized he was holding what looked like a live black snake, extending it toward the audience, and passing it back and forth from one hand to another.

I stumbled and clung to a pillar behind the crowd, in the arcade that surrounded the open outdoor plaza. That was as close as I wanted to get. I realized I felt weak and fearful of what was about to happen, as though it was about me. As he went on with the tale I could barely hear it. My ears rejected the words. His voice grew farther and farther away.

"In the dance," he continued, "we will circle around a woman, wife of the tribal chief, who has betrayed her husband with another man. The chief will then confront her lover, and order him to put the woman to death. At the moment of the kill, the snake will be thrown into the fire. Then her lover will be killed by the warriors."

I couldn't believe what I was hearing. This was so much like my dream. I too had been murdered for betrayal.

The ear-piercing horns began wailing again. I was vividly aware that their sound was directly penetrating my groin, deep into my pelvic area. I stiffened, lifting myself up on tiptoes, clutching the pillar. Charged through and through, I was electrified, muscles spasming. I wanted to run, but I couldn't. I feared the kill.

A group of painted Indian warriors with dramatic, feathered headdresses leaned down and began to dance, bouncing, lifting their knees high, chanting in a circle. The instruments were loud—so loud. The chief, dressed in an elaborate mask of an eagle's head that extended over his nose, with feathers trailing down his back onto the ground, moved to stand before the lover and pointed at the woman. The reluctant lover walked in front of the woman and stopped. He lifted his bow and obediently simulated the shot of an arrow into her heart. Then the completely unfurled snake was immediately thrown into the fire by him.

In that moment, a wild, raging burn ignited inside me and ran throughout my body. Strong, deep passionate emotion took charge. I didn't understand what was happening to me. Remotely viewing it all, I took in the mounting realization that the pageant I was witnessing was mirroring back to me a story similar to the lifelike dream I had been having since I was a teenager, and similar to my dream only a month earlier that had fully revealed the story.

Hypnotized, in passion and pain, I watched. A little voice in my head began to whisper. "I am alive, now. Yes, I'm alive. I came through this. I do not need to feel fear or guilt anymore for anything I might have done in that lifetime."

Words cannot describe the tumultuous, obsessive feelings that overtook me. The drums, the horns, the story, the fire, the snake, the ruthless execution of this kind of justice, were directed solely to me. The sounds projected bittersweet waves that purged, purified, and pulsed through me, waking my weary soul. It was cleansing, yet it was so disturbing. Something I could not identify was being stirred within my being.

As the music grew louder, I breathed short breaths in and out to the rhythm of the throbbing drums. It was as though I was dancing with them, panting as if I was giving birth. I inhaled courage. With each exhale, I intentionally pushed out old, fear-packed emotions and ancient feelings of guilt. *I want to be done with that!* Tears streamed down my face.

Aaron had been standing behind me. He moved closer and put his hand on the back of my waist. He didn't question me. He knew me well enough to realize something very important was happening.

Finally, the lover was attacked by several warriors. He, too, was symbolically killed. He disappeared as the warriors swooped in to hover over him, waving their hunting knives over their heads.

At that point something remarkable happened that must have been staged somehow. A coiled snake appeared at the foot of the Indian announcer. The announcer said that the snake always came back that way. It was believed by the tribe that the snake, perhaps a symbol of human fallibility, had been cleansed and purified.

By then I was completely drained. I could hardly walk. With his arm around me, Aaron led me back the way we had come.

As we passed the little chapel Jennifer had told me about, its peaceful stillness called out to me. I leaned in to see a very tiny adobe-bricked room with maybe four rows of pews on each side, each only a few yards long. The small prayer room was warm and glowed from the dozens of candles on the altar directly opposite the door.

I asked Aaron to wait. I stepped through the door of the chapel and paused, feeling a deep reverence. I made my way the few short steps to the altar. Never having worshipped at a Catholic church, I felt like an intruder. At the same time, I felt grateful for its sanctuary. I approached the altar and my knees buckled. I surrendered myself onto the prayer rail.

My prayer was simple. "Oh, God, please help me to find peace in my soul." Then came the welcome release of hot tears. I'd lost all sense of time.

There was a tap on my shoulder. Aaron asked if I was ready to go. "We have dinner reservations."

Of course. He had no way of knowing what I'd just been through.

As we drove home, I was exhausted. I also knew I was in a mild state of shock.

CHAPTER 18

Chasing Dreams

I was mystified by the similarity of my dream to the Indian ceremony at the Mission San Juan Capistrano... actually by how closely
the events matched. I tried to explain it rationally, but couldn't. I'd
had the dream of a terrified maiden running for her life since I was
a teen. The part of the dream where I saw myself murdered for a
crime of betrayal had happened only a month before the ceremony.
The coincidence was too incredible to have a logical explanation.

As I thought more about it, I became certain that the dreams
were flashbacks of an earlier lifetime. I was amazed that Aaron
seemed to be part of two past lives—as my centurion in Atlantis, and
as my Indian lover, especially since just a few years ago I hadn't even
believed in past lives.

I shared all the details of my Indian dream with Aaron and
tried to describe the emotion I felt while watching the ceremony. He
listened authentically, but he seemed unable to relate to my amazement about finding another past life. I did understand how his
Catholic upbringing would affect his receptivity in that Catholicism
denies any belief in past lives.

On the evening of the ceremony I had been unable to accompany Aaron to dinner as I was exhausted. Still, I had to write down
every detail I could remember of the day. In the past I'd learned that
re-living the details on paper could help me to release emotional
trauma—the dream and ceremony had definitely been traumatic. The
writing process did bring some relief. However, I became more agitated and anxious, which was not what I'd expected.

Searching for perspective, I reasoned that witnessing the ceremony had been good for me. It enabled me to get in touch with, and to release fearful emotions I had connected with my recurring Indian dream. As well as those I had suffered in the dark vision of the Indian village—a catharsis had occurred as the result of being able to watch this violent episode as a bystander; re-living the scenes and the emotions from a distance, in broad daylight. It had helped to dispel my fright and my preoccupying sense of despair. It brought me into the present realization that I was a good person, just as I had realized following the session with Neville regarding my Atlantis lifetime. When I had been able to bring it into consciousness, and look at the subliminally suppressed fear and guilt haunting me in dreams and visions, they gradually lost their hold over me.

This time, the healing came without hypnotic regression. Led by my own inner voice, the old, repressed fears from that lifetime were being left behind. They were becoming emotionally benign.

Yet, I couldn't shake a feeling of instability, a deep need to cry or scream. The disturbing feelings that enveloped me while riding Rusty, and the emotional tug of the Indian maiden picture were only intensifying. It perplexed me that her image still caused me unease at the same time I was learning to be at peace with my own violent past life as an Indian. She became more daunting; a marker of something still not yet divulged. It haunted me that she had lost her power, her spirit. How did that apply to my current life?

As one level of healing took place, an old fury moved in. I had opened one door and was stumbling head-on into an emotional hornet's nest. The walls were caving in around me. I couldn't concentrate at work. My inbox piled higher and higher. The simplest task of filing became daunting. I missed exits on the freeway, and stared at the shelves in the market for hours, leaving without buying anything. Bank deposits never got done. I made a thousand dollar error on some tax forms at work.

Most disturbing were the visions from childhood that had come back to haunt me. Accompanied by overwhelming dread, my visions of the moments before my birth, then as the confused infant beside my mother, and as a toddler in the baby carriage thinking of life and death, struck me at random times. I'd be overcome with fear and lethargy. I felt desperate…sinking in quicksand. I wanted this to end. I needed help.

For financial reasons, I had not signed up for the second year of psychosynthesis classes, but I had stayed in touch with Anita, the friend and social worker from class who had first referred me to Neville. I called her, hoping she could help. It was comforting to talk unguardedly, and she referred me to someone she knew of through the county's human services department.

Her name was Elizabeth. A woman once diagnosed with breast cancer, she'd made the decision to quit her job doing cancer research at the University of Irvine to concentrate on healing, not sickness. Being of American Indian heritage, she became drawn to native ways of healing. When she researched various approaches to good health, and changed her lifestyle, including eating more natural foods, her body began to heal itself. But what Elizabeth considered the most helpful in her recovery, Anita had said, was taught to her by a medicine man. She'd learned to use sound for healing.

Healing with sound! That's what had happened in my Atlantis lifetime! We healed with sound and crystals. I knew I had to meet this woman—this woman of *Indian heritage*—even if I did nothing else.

Elizabeth invited me into her home in Newport Beach, with a big smile and gracious manner. Perhaps in her mid-forties, her long black hair moved freely as did her ankle-length, dark blue jersey dress that swayed widely on her lanky body. Barefooted, she led me into a small, cozy inner room. Placed around the candle-lit room were softly illuminated geode clusters and varying sizes of crystals; rose quartzes, citrines and amethysts. The walls were lined with framed snapshots from her many trips to western Canada, home of her ancestors. Elizabeth was in several of the snapshots, dressed in native Indian garb with a feather in her hair, and dancing with other Indians. She was half-Indian from a little-known tribe of the Cree Nation, and she'd learned their ways.

Warmed by the presence of the crystals, I started to relax, but immediately caught myself in a reality check. This was no longer the time of Atlantis, it was April, 1988. Was I really standing in a room filled with crystals? Did I really want to be here? In this lifetime I was taught that this sort of thing reeked of witchcraft. My memory of using crystals in Atlantis and the scorning of "the ways of the devil" by my father stirred a conflicting pang of resistance.

Distracting myself, I moved away from the pictures. Elizabeth invited me to sit on a small chintz loveseat while she told me of her illness, and her healing. Then, she became very expressive. The biggest surprise, and the point when her healing had accelerated, was when she was working with a medicine man who had made her scream.

"Scream?" I would have expected chants or songs.

"Yes. It helped me to bring up held-back traumas that I had unknowingly suppressed…resentment, failure, abandonment, family betrayal, even abuse—you name it! Our bodies hold onto the memories and feelings until we make a conscious decision to let go. Suppressing them makes us sick. But we don't realize they are there until they have come up. For example, we usually don't know we are depressed until we no longer are. "Screaming helps a release to happen. Volatile, poisonous memories can erupt, leaving our spirit freer, lighter."

Elizabeth didn't have to convince *me* of the value of recognizing feelings and letting them go. But screaming?

Many, including her former research colleagues, had been inspired by her healing, which led her to open a studio to work with people with various health and emotional problems, not just cancer. She and a business partner gave presentations on their approach to healing for interested groups and organizations. Elizabeth's partner, Susan, a locally recognized artist, used art to stimulate healing. The pair's recommended procedure was to begin by working with Elizabeth.

I wanted to know more about Elizabeth's method to promote healing through screaming. She gently placed her hand on my shoulder and told me, "There really isn't much more I can say. The understanding comes in the doing." She suggested I try one session and then decide if I wanted to continue: "At that point, I recommend a commitment to six sessions."

Her fees were fifty dollars per session. A nagging voice in my head taunted, charlatan, while on the other hand I felt I had to take a chance, as I had with Neville. But Neville didn't seem like the right choice for help now. Something deeply primitive inside me ached to be known and I had a hunch about Elizabeth. I didn't have much money to spend, but I didn't care. I couldn't go on feeling like I couldn't breathe. Otherwise, my heart would stop.

I pulled my day timer from my bag and picked the following Wednesday evening.

After each of the first two sessions I drove home exhausted, my head spinning. With Elizabeth, I found I could indeed scream, loud and long. As she suggested, when I got home I soaked for nearly an hour in a hot bath. I barely recovered emotionally and physically before it was time for the next session. I walked around feeling that if my head had been my living room, all of the furniture would have been upended and rearranged. Yet each week I returned, hoping that I would learn the secret underlying my constantly growing discontent. It was becoming a feeling that something worse than death was about to befall me.

Elizabeth's sessions were simple. She had me select crystals that attracted me, and directed me to sit in the center of the room on the carpeted floor. Then, she placed the crystals in a circle and she sat down inside the circle with me. With her legs crossed Indian-fashion, she directed me to do the same. It wasn't easy for me to do that. I didn't understand why, but my hips had always resisted opening in that manner. When I was a little girl, my friends could do it, but I couldn't.

She took my hands in hers and said, "Now let's rock together a little." While that sounded simple enough, it was disturbing. The rocking motion she created with me made me want to cry like a baby. Continuing on in a soft but firm voice, she coached me to start making low, gentle growls and then let them become whatever sounds they wanted to become. It was embarrassing. I didn't want to sound like an animal. I liked to make harmonious sounds, like when I was singing. Groaning wasn't lady-like.

"No one else will hear you, Grace." She started a soft, deep growl and tugged on my arms, signaling me to join her. Shyly, I felt myself making a sound that resembled a moan. Very quickly, tears began to come. I didn't know why I was crying. The more tears that came, the louder my voice grew, and the more I heard Elizabeth encourage, "More, more, don't resist, let it go. Stay with it."

During the fourth session with Elizabeth, something uncanny happened. As it was each time, I began with a sense of irritation and resistance to opening up in such an uncivilized way. I started with my head down, focusing on one of the large amethyst crystals beside her. This time, I felt the vibration of my own voice, low in my body. In this space of free thinking, I was momentarily taken to my memory of Atlantis...how my thoughts and my own vocal vibrations were amplified by crystals for healing and for the power of good. In an impulsive moment of surrender, I let my head roll freely around, catching the various crystals in my peripheral vision.

Suddenly, I was looking into a mirror. But it wasn't my own image that I saw. I saw the face of a giant tiger with blazing amber-yellow eyes, just as I had seen in my bathroom mirror in our barracks apartment in 1960, the day before I'd been taken to the mental hospital. The tiger roared. I roared back. Louder and louder. As I roared, Elizabeth roared, encouraging me on.

I rocked back and forth, faster and faster, squeezing Elizabeth's hands tightly. The pitch of my voice rose to a sharp squeal and ballooned into a full scream. Then, as had happened before, the image of the tiger suddenly transformed into the regal head of a large, yellow lion. With the reflexes of a cat, in my mind I watched myself pounce toward the mirror. I began growling deeply, and with a vengeance. I was absorbing the strength of that kingly lion. Years before when I'd envisioned that lion, its image had faded in and out...tiger to lion, lion to tiger. But this time, as I bellowed and roared, loud and long, the image of the lion prevailed and persisted. I growled masterfully, in full recognition of my emotional victory. I knew then that it was crucial for me to summon up that ferocious courage.

When I arrived at home that evening after the fourth session, I was totally depleted. I lit candles around my bathtub and sprinkled drops of lavender into the steaming hot water from a vial that

Elizabeth had given me, along with small crystals to place near the candles. I lost all track of time as I soaked, and listened to the soft strains of recorded harp music.

The anxiety and distress that drove me to Elizabeth, a sense that my body wanted to explode...the presence of an unknown malevolent force, was clearly leading me somewhere. Where? To relive the bizarre image of the tiger and lion I'd seen in my bathroom mirror at age twenty-two was uncanny. I thought I had put it out of my mind long ago. Something was taking over, ruling me. Something wanted to be heard—a magnifying feeling that something horrible was about to happen—something was going to fall on me.

I didn't know why the screaming with Elizabeth was so necessary or where it would lead me, but I knew it was the right direction. Once again, I accepted that I would surrender to whatever my spirit wanted me to know. I was getting to something. It was clear I'd reached another juncture. Another phase in my life of dreams and images was having its way with me.

During each of the last two sessions with Elizabeth, I'd felt a new power rising up in me; power birthed by the lion. As if I was growing a true backbone. Simultaneously, unpredictable rages were rising to the surface. In the sessions, Elizabeth prodded me with open-ended questions about my childhood, my family relationships, and my marriage. She didn't require me to answer; I just had to think about them. I growled. I groaned. I shrieked. I screamed. I howled—primitive jungle sounds erupted from me like a volcano.

Then I recalled when I had finally sung my own heart song in the Lifesong workshop the year before. The process was also one that had allowed me to let go of repressed feelings by using my own voice. Crying through the notes and lyrics, I'd expressed anger at my father, at Jack, and at others in my life who'd discouraged me from expressing my natural song. However, this screaming process was so much deeper than singing. My emotions were primitive; much more overwhelming. I didn't know where to direct my fury.

In Elizabeth's studio, as the image of the lion in the mirror continued to stay with me, a line from A Course in Miracles kept coming back..."Look into the glass and understand the loveliness you look upon is your own." This became my mantra. That thought inspired me to push on. It gave me hope.

In the last session with Elizabeth I didn't hold anything back. I cried more than usual. The rages that were building were powerful, but still no peace. That night, the same dream came back to me again that I'd had right after riding Rusty for the first time. The dream about being in a house where skinny, brown snakes were everywhere around me, and there was no place to set my foot. I couldn't escape. When I awoke, I was shocked to find I literally had wet the bed. A heavy sense of shame overtook me, an old familiar feeling. I had wet the bed as a child until I was nine. Daddy had whipped me many times because of it.

After all that had taken place in my sessions with Elizabeth, I was still distressed, but, I couldn't stop now. I had to move on to work with Susan, and whatever her art therapy might provide.

At first I was disappointed to learn that Susan's part in their team work was merely a slide presentation before a group. I had expected her to do something similar to the therapy I was familiar with as a teacher, where a child drew an illustration of whatever subject we felt would help them to clarify a situation, and that would help us pick up clues about how best to work with them.

Susan's presentation came only a few weeks after my last session with Elizabeth. It was on a Friday after work in a small room of a community center on Balboa Island. There were perhaps ten people present when I arrived, and I chose a seat in the middle. Susan, a petite woman with long, brown hair, spoke softly and firmly. She had studied art as a career but that was not the motivation for her slide presentation. The art we were about to see, she explained, had come out of her experience of severe sexual and emotional abuse by her own mother.

After hearing that, from that point on I can remember only fragments of the evening. A tiny high hum switched on in my ears as Susan began to tell of some of the horrendous acts her mother had perpetrated on her...laying her in the sink and doing things to her...tying her naked in a chair and opening her legs...using objects...forcing her to lay flat on her belly on a bed until her mother was through with her...shaving off all of her hair...demanding she go naked for days at a time. Susan chose her words with care, but the picture was vivid. I was stunned.

She then gave us a glimpse into her long journey of healing. From a state of near-complete withdrawal, she was rescued by a family member just before her teen years and brought into therapy. She was still shy and frightened and had difficulty relating to and trusting people until she found art. Art provided a way of expressing the unspeakable. Later, studying art in college brought her a sense of power, allowed a deep healing, and provided a way for her to communicate with the world.

I had to strain to focus on what Susan was saying because I was swimming in the emotions provoked by her story. Additionally, the image of the Indian maiden picture was fighting for my attention.

Susan turned out the lights and began her slide presentation. She narrated a series of illustrations done exclusively with depictions of scissors. It was through her creation of various situations and positions of the scissors that she finally was able to get in touch with the feelings at the very bottom of her emotional well, and with her profound feelings of powerlessness.

In the first group of slides, the scissors were placed in various circumstances—all with the blades closed, expressions of her sense of helplessness. There were scissors wrapped tightly in wire, on a large, bare mattress, abandoned on the sidewalk, buried half-way into the ground, blades tied tightly with string, hanging upside-down, and dangling from a tree.

In the second part, Susan showed a group of illustrations in which she began to allow the scissors to open. At first, only millimeters wide. To her, the degree of the opening expressed her own willingness to open herself to life.

Immediately, I was uncomfortably alert; frozen, fighting to remain in my chair. I realized I did not want to see the scissors open. I didn't know why. I felt threatened, vulnerable. The slides continued. In one the wire around the scissors had been cut. In another, lying on a table, a pencil was wedged between the blades. In another, BandAids held the blades open on a chair seat. In another, the scissors straddled a garden hose draped over a hedge, gushing water onto the sidewalk. I wanted to bolt for the door, but my legs wouldn't move. I couldn't watch any more of the illustrations. I looked away.

Finally, Susan came to the end of her presentation. I looked back to see the last slide. The scissors had opened full range and a single rose lay between the blades.

By then I had disengaged from the room, distracted by a sobering memory I'd worked hard to suppress—those times while growing up when I'd witnessed my mother in grand mal epileptic seizures. She would fall to the floor with a loud scream, writhing helplessly in her own form of what I thought was craziness. I was deeply disturbed by her powerlessness.

I sat limply in my chair in that little building on Balboa Island, overcome by the images and by this returning terror from my childhood. Instead of being uplifted by Susan's sharing of illustrations that empowered her, my reaction was the opposite. For me the opened scissors triggered feelings of extreme danger and disempowerment.

I don't remember the drive home from Balboa. Once home, I rummaged through my desk to find my old address book and searched frantically for Neville's phone number, resolving to call him the next morning. I had to have some answers. I had to find some peace.

It was now the spring of 1988, almost two and a half years after I'd first found Neville. When I called him I was surprised he remembered me. We talked for quite awhile as I tried to relay what was taking place in my mind, my dreams, with the childhood flashbacks and anxiety. He felt that hypnotic regression could indeed be helpful and said he would be glad to work with me again. However, this time he thought it would be a good idea for me to see Andrea first, the family therapist who worked in his office with him.

When I asked Neville why, he stated that given the obvious level of my disturbance he believed the regression would go better if I were in a more receptive frame of mind. I was concerned about the cost, having just paid for sessions with Elizabeth and Susan, but Neville said that Andrea would arrange for payments on a sliding scale, and for a schedule that would work for me.

I remembered Andrea, the lovely young woman with long blonde hair who, that time before my first visit with Neville, had offered me tea. Our conversation had flowed so effortlessly, it had quelled some of my apprehension about the hypnosis session. It turned out Andrea remembered me too and the warmth between us was still there. Because of our conflicting schedules, we agreed to meet in her home near where I worked.

It took most of the first two sessions to fill her in on what I had been going through. It was hard to explain, because nothing really external had happened to me. The only physical manifestation was wetting the bed. The rest was all internal. Andrea asked about my marriage and specifics about the abuse of that time. She worked back in time to my childhood and my mother. Then, she wanted to talk about my father. I didn't. I said I had tolerated him. I avoided him whenever possible. I was relieved I didn't have to live with him any longer after I left home. When he died in 1973, I didn't attend his funeral, and I never looked back.

Andrea's questions became more specific. What was he like? How often did he beat you? Why did he beat you?

The walls of her living room began to close in around me. Just the effort to answer exhausted me. I asked Andrea if I could lie down on the couch. "Certainly." She assured me we could come back to those questions about Daddy later, asking instead about my relationship with Aaron.

Was he anything like my father? Of course not. I felt so safe with Aaron, but I admitted I had noticed his physical resemblance to my father in certain photos. I shared my frustration regarding Aaron's tendency to become withdrawn in intimate situations. Andrea suggested a joint session with her, Aaron and me in order to discern the dynamic of our relationship and perhaps relieve some of my stress.

Fortunately, Aaron was open to the idea. I think he felt it was something I needed rather than something we needed as a couple. I had not revealed my inner conflict to him, but I knew he recognized we both struggled to cope with my anxiety and irritability. Aaron's gentleness with me brought back the centurion who'd served me faithfully in my lifetime in Atlantis. He did not try to force anything on me, but instead simply showed concern for my welfare. At times, I felt his main focus was to offer me support. And I welcomed it. I'd come to depend on it, and on him. He was always optimistic. He knew how to cheer me up. In our session with Andrea, I became more aware of how Aaron's rigid orthodox background conflicted with his ability to be open both emotionally and physically. Andrea had offered a metaphor for Aaron's consideration; that he might be similar to the briefcase she had noticed that he always carries, keeping everything he values locked inside of it, never letting it out of his sight. The truth of her comment startled me. I realized that no matter where we went or when he came over, his briefcase was always with him or in his car, even when he arrived dressed in warm-ups to play tennis. One time I actually teased him, telling him that my image of him with his briefcase brought to mind the character in the movie, *Mr. Smith Goes to Washington.*

After our session with Andrea, she had commented that this time in Aaron's life represented a turning point for him, coming out of a marriage of two decades, and she suggested he attend separate sessions with her. I strongly encouraged him. To my surprise, he consented. I hoped it might help to bring us closer.

It was inevitable that Andrea would return to the topic of my father. Somewhere around my fourth session, she began probing again about my childhood and my relationship with my father. The term relationship felt absurd. As a child, whenever I thought of my father, it was with fear and trepidation. That was no "relationship." I struggled to answer Andrea's questions, because I couldn't remember much of my childhood. I soon realized that I was actually afraid to remember.

Again she asked me why he beat me. I couldn't give her a rational answer, because none existed. It had happened often. Whenever he felt like it. Whenever things didn't go his way. If I slipped, said or did something he didn't like, my eyes immediately darted to his hands to see if they were moving toward his belt. Beating was all he knew.

Did I bring my friends home to visit, she asked, and if so, how did I feel? Well, I tried not to. I tried to visit my girlfriends at their homes, because I never knew what rude things my father might say to them or whether he might yell at them. Andrea questioned his treatment of my mother and sisters. The same. He treated all of us alike. We were there to take his orders and endure his punishments.

Going back to the past made me so uncomfortable. Remembering it, I wanted to collapse. I found myself leaning to the side, actually sliding down on the couch. But Andrea persisted with her questions, turning to the reasons for my anxieties, my dreams, childhood flashbacks, and my sense of doom. She asked me to describe my childhood flashbacks in detail.

At that point, I was coiled into a fetal position, cupping my hands tightly over my lower belly, shaking my head from side to side, gesturing rejection. I started to weep. My childhood vision was coming to life, and there was so much fear within it. I tried to avoid it again.

"This is what you must look at, Grace," she said firmly. "I think this is what Neville can help you with. Do you think you can do that?"

I knew she was right. But I couldn't. I just wasn't ready.

During the sessions that followed, Andrea shifted gears, helping me to feel safe and cared for. She played calming music while we talked. She wrapped me in soft blankets, she coaxed me to envision angels hovering over me and feeling their wings curled around me. She guided me in meditations, leading me to myself as a child but cuddled safe, and loved. She reminded me that whatever it was I needed to remember was over. Past. It could no longer harm me. Only good could come now from looking at it. She reminded me of how I'd learned the healing truth through my previous sessions with Neville. She also assured me that nothing needed to happen until I was ready.

Ironically, something from my childhood teachings returned to comfort me. I clung to it. It was the line from the 23rd Psalms, in the Bible. *"Yea, though I walk through the valley of the shadow of death, I will fear no evil, for thou are with me"*

Finally, after two more calming sessions with Andrea, I convinced myself I was ready. At that point, I wanted to get it over with.

CHAPTER 19

Removing the Blocks in the Dream

My session with Neville was set up for the following Friday afternoon at four o'clock. I managed to get off work early. I purposely arranged the appointment before the weekend so I could be sure Aaron would be there to stay with me afterwards. I was deeply frightened about what I might learn. I needed the comfort of knowing Aaron would be waiting for me before I committed to do this. "Promise you will be there when I get home," I implored. He promised he would be.

A couple of days before my appointment, a very odd thing happened while Aaron and I played tennis together. We were a few minutes into the first set when running and jumping became a laborious effort for me. It was almost impossible to move my legs because a burning tingling was piercing through my pubic bone. As I scrambled to come to the net, a pain in my pelvic bone exploded like a million pins stabbing me. It rushed in, built to a climax, then subsided and was gone. It felt almost like new energy coming alive in me. Something in me was awakening.

I told Aaron what was happening, but I minimized what I felt, saying it was a sensation similar to when you hit your elbow and the blow strikes your funny bone. But this was much more intense. And it was not funny.

Aaron insisted we didn't have to continue. After I experienced more of the same sensations, we packed up and left the court.

When the day came, part of me felt good to see Neville again. We spent a few moments getting reacquainted. I trusted him. His presence brought back the confidence I'd developed with him in my first session. And then, there I was on that couch again.

Before we started, Neville asked me to briefly explain what I recalled about my childhood visions of before and after my birth. In spite of my commitment, I suddenly felt very resistant. I just skimmed over the details.

I mentioned seeing myself up over the earth before I was born. Descending above the southeastern region of the United States, I spied a large, oblong stone that I later came to associate with a monolith. Just after that, I knew something had happened that I could not remember. An instant later I was lying next to my mother in a warm bed, very grateful to be there but not knowing why. Then I told Neville of the sad, recurring image of me as a toddler in a baby carriage, staring out and deciding whether to live or die.

He then began a visualization process similar to the one he'd guided me through during our first session. With my eyes closed, I tried to picture what he was suggesting…leading me down many stairways, going through several doors, each time describing a more protected and safe space than the previous steps. But my mind kept darting away from his voice. The steps were more frightening than I remembered. Then he took me back from my age of forty-nine years to remembering and seeing myself in my thirties, my twenties, my teen years, my early childhood…suddenly, I had no protection or safety. I was afraid. Impulsively, I rolled onto my side and pulled up into a fetal position.

Neville assured me that was okay. "Let the feelings come," he urged.

And then the dam started to break. Tears poured out and I opened my eyes. My throat ached. Something harmful was building up, struggling to come out of my mouth.

Neville reassured me I was safe and we could take all the time we needed. He asked me to close my eyes, slowly count to ten, and when I finished I would remember myself somewhere in the first two years of my life.

I did as he instructed, but I went farther back. Like flash points of light, my childhood vision from infancy invaded, demanding to be known.

Not yet born, I hovered somewhere above the earth. In a flash, a new image appeared. On earth now, I was an infant inside a giant steel box, lying atop wet garbage and damp newspapers, and surrounded by cans and bottles. It was dark. I was cold. I was weak. I couldn't move.

Then light appeared in the box. A lid above me was lifted away. I was picked up and carried into a house. I was in my father's hands. He had come to get me from a garbage can in the alley where I had been discarded.

Suddenly, I knew the ugly, heartless truth. I knew—I knew—my mother had tossed me into that garbage can after my birth. My voice relating all this to Neville trailed off. I just wanted to go to sleep. I wanted to forget what I had just seen and learned.

"Then what happened, Grace?" Neville urged me on.

I made a supreme effort to refocus, to see through the fog of what must be protective denial. In came that next familiar scene, the one in which I was in a warm bed beside my mother. It made sense now why in my childhood vision I had been so relieved to be there. My traumatized mind had only allowed me to remember this part, the relief.

I knew I was born in an apartment over a grocery store in Morristown, Tennessee. The part of the pre-birth vision where I was suspended above the earth in the southeastern part of the country took on new meaning. I had known in that moment that what I was being born into would be difficult.

My mother had always complained dramatically that my birth was extremely difficult for her, but she would never give any details, only that she'd had no anesthetic and just the help of the woman next door. She mentioned it on many occasions, leaving me to wonder about the rest, refusing to tell me more, even when I begged her. She repeated the same few details over and over, like she wanted to go on but something always stopped her. Then she grew stubborn and refused to answer my questions. I was left to wonder what had happened that was so awful she couldn't talk about it with me. Then I remembered that Mama and Daddy would not have been married back then and to make matters worse, Daddy had another family he'd abandoned.

I was her first child. I was illegitimate and Mama had thrown me away!

Now I was forty-nine years old, curled up on a couch in Neville's office. I cried. I cried like a baby. Her baby.

Huge, heaving sobs came gushing in as the toxic sorrow of abandonment overwhelmed me. My stomach hurt. I pushed on my stomach with my hands as though I could stop the ache. But sadness wrenched my belly, claiming its long-awaited right to be expressed.

From a distance, I heard Neville's voice gently assuring me that the return of this memory was good; it was all emerging so it could no longer control me.

After a few moments, continuing the process of regression, he said, "Now, let us leave that room and go even deeper down into another room. We are closing the door behind us. This new room is a sacred chamber, the most secluded sanctuary of all. Angels guard the door, keeping you completely and totally safe. Nothing can harm you. Tell me, Grace, what is in this room?"

At his mere suggestion my crying subsided. As if suddenly sucked into a time warp, I could see myself standing up in my crib. I was not yet two years old. I was frozen in stark terror. It was the middle of the night. I had been abruptly awakened when, out of the darkness, my mother let out a loud, piercing scream. I could see her body writhing and jerking; she was foaming at the mouth. Frozen in shock, I watched motionless as my father came into the room with some rope. He began tying her down in the bed to make her stop, or perhaps to keep her from falling to the floor. But he couldn't.

I watched my Mama's body wrenching, writhing, helplessly out of control. I was so afraid and wanted her to hold me. I wanted my mother to take care of me. But she couldn't help me, she couldn't even hear me. I gripped the railing and started to shake it. I saw myself screaming and jumping up and down in my crib. Finally, my father's attention turned toward me. He came over to me and I reached my arms out to be picked up.

But Daddy didn't pick me up. He dropped the side of the crib and shoved me down on the mattress. He took off my diaper. He yanked me toward him. Then, all I could see was a pillow, covered with a pink pillow case, coming at my face. Daddy pushed it down over me. I stopped screaming. Sharp stabbing pains were piercing me where my diaper used to be. Everything went black.

My father was raping me.

I couldn't cry anymore. The tears would not come. I just lay there, motionless, a dead weight on Neville's couch. How could any human being do such a thing? How could my own father?

Neville's calm voice was comforting me. He was telling me how very brave I was to face this. Now, he told me, this wretched memory would no longer be lodged in the recesses of my mind, hauntingly dragging me down, holding me in powerlessness.

I opened my eyes and stared blankly at Neville's ceiling. Then once again, I was now in the unhappy body of that little toddler, lying lifelessly in a buggy, looking out at this world, wondering if it was worth staying.

It took supreme effort to concentrate as I drove home. I regretted that I hadn't asked Aaron to drive me to Neville's office. I stayed in the slow lane, my eyes fixed on the white line. I couldn't cry. I couldn't feel. I just wanted to go home. Finally, I pulled into my carport.

I wanted to be held by Aaron. I knew that I didn't want to talk. I was still clinging to deep rage inside me, but I didn't dare let it come out. It might consume me. I might never remember Grace again.

I walked down the sidewalk that curved to my door. It was dusk. But there were no lights on inside my condo. Oh, no! Aaron hadn't arrived yet. I opened the door to the dim emptiness of my living room. I nearly collapsed. After what I had seen, what I had remembered, I couldn't bear to be alone. This world, this nightmare called life, was now darker than I had ever dreamt it could be.

I threw my purse on the bed and snapped on the lamp. I groped for the phone, knocking it onto the floor. Picking it up, I dialed Aaron's number. He was there! He was still at his apartment.

"Why aren't you here?" I shouted without a greeting.

Somewhere in my head I heard him talking, but I couldn't believe his words. He groggily explained that he decided to participate in a day-long seminar that had been previously recommended by Andrea, and the leader's instructions had been to go home and be quiet, light candles, take a bath and go to bed early. So that's what he was doing!

"I was going to call you," he offered.

"What? What!" I screamed at him. "You're doing what? Don't you know what today is? Don't you remember our agreement? We talked about this! You promised me you would be here for me!"

He knew how long I had been preparing for this day. How I dreaded confronting whatever was making me so fearful. How scared I was.

"Yes, I know," he said. "But I need to rest. I'm really tired."

"Tired? Tired? You goddamn son of a bitch! You have no idea what tired is! How can you be so fucking selfish? Just when I need you the most! You bastard! You fucking bastard!"

Now the rage was coming. In primal shrieks I continued to shout and scream hateful things. I didn't recognize the sound of my own voice. I could tell it was ugly. By then, the rage was in control…the door had been opened.

Somewhere in all of that I heard his raised voice saying, "Calm down, calm down. I'm sorry. I didn't know it meant that much to you. I'll be there in twenty minutes. Just calm down." I continued to scream at him. Then I slammed the phone down.

I paced aimlessly through every room, hands over my face, screaming profanities at Aaron, at my father, at the world. I had never felt so deserted in all of my life. I was in a vast, empty hallway between life and death. It was cold. It was heartless.

I heard Aaron's key turn in the door. Hysterically, I flung myself at him, pounding on his chest. "How could you? How could you?"

He grasped my arms and led me to the bed. He sat down beside me, profusely apologizing for not being there. "How could you not be here?" Ignoring his words, I ranted and spewed at his insensitivity, his selfishness, his stupidity—I held nothing back. My voice was guttural as I growled the words out like the lion in the mirror. I was roaring out of control and I knew it.

I was losing control, and I was gaining control. A power inside me was rising up. It would be heard no matter what! "Do you have any idea what I have been through? Do you have any idea what has happened to me? No, you can't possibly know! You can't possibly understand!

"Do you even want to know? Do you even care?"

"Of course, I care," he said, trying to hold me. But I couldn't stop. I paced, screaming more profanity and gesturing wildly.

All of a sudden Aaron grabbed me. He threw me down on the bed. He began to kiss me passionately, the way I liked him to do—but not now! I couldn't believe this was happening. I couldn't believe this was his solution to my panic. His body weight pinned me down. He was removing my clothes.

And then, just like when I was a child, crying hopelessly in my bed after my father's beatings, I was suddenly up above me, looking down. I saw my body submit to Aaron's. He was having sex with me. In his mind, sex was his ultimate consolation. But in my mind I was, again, being raped.

Finally, I cried.

Aaron sat up, bringing me along with him. Swirls of nausea reminded me I was back in my body. My rage had turned into deep waves of sorrow. Sorrow for myself. Sorrow for the cavernous gap between Aaron and me. Sorrow for this sad, senseless world.

Then I focused on what Aaron was saying. He was offering words of consolation as he dressed and then picked up his coat. He was ready to leave! He thought he had succeeded in doing his job to calm me. He picked up his keys. He was going home.

He didn't ask me what had happened with Neville. He wasn't going to stay with me. He wasn't going to hold me.

I was dumbfounded.

I didn't confront him. I didn't say anything. I didn't do anything. I just sat numbly on the bed and I watched him walk away.

I heard his key turn as he locked the door behind him.

Then...I screamed.

I screamed and cried and paced and cursed and threw things. I screamed at Aaron and soon after I was screaming at my dead father.

As part of me observed it all, I heard my screams become roars. I bellowed and cursed my father. I growled and snarled at his inhuman, sadistic, cruel wickedness. I howled at the emptiness of his soul. I vomited the putrid brine that had lined the cellar of my mind.

How could a grown man—a father—molest his own child? A baby! My father! Me! I'd always known while growing up that I was different—sad, serious. I pretended to be normal. But I never was!

My body, my psyche, had been imprisoned by a monstrous secret. A grotesque assault. Why couldn't I be normal? Why couldn't my father love me?

It seemed like hours passed before I finally collapsed, falling back flat on the bed. My storm had subsided. At least for the moment.

My gaze traveled slowly, wearily around my bedroom. In utter exhaustion, I surrendered. I surrendered the fight. The fight to suppress anything, the fight to change anything, the fight to figure it all out. I was simply there.

And then something happened. In that drained state of submission, another door opened. A unique form of gentleness from somewhere deep within my being embraced me for the first time. It was a soft and calm feeling of tender, warm love and respect for myself that radiated from my heart and claimed my body. It was solely in honor of the Grace that now lay there.

How strong and brave I had been to carry on with my life! To even care about being a good person.

A new passageway in my heart was opening. A place I'd never known or felt. It held fresh, pure love. I started to cry again. This time, I wept softly for the little girl whose innocence had been so violently stolen from her. The little girl who had done nothing wrong, who only wanted to be loved. Just like tonight, all I'd wanted was to be loved. To be held and heard; told that I was valuable, that I mattered.

In the silence of the room, I heard a voice intone...you can have love, Grace. You deserve love. Love is free. It's always here. Love yourself. Give love to you. You don't need anyone to give it to you. Love is eternally here. Love the innocence you that you always were.

I awoke to the rays of the noonday sun streaming through my bedroom window. I heard the squealing laughter of children playing in a Saturday afternoon romp in the pool nearby. I didn't even turn over in bed to look at the clock. I didn't care about the time. I would sleep for as long as I wanted. I had at some point unplugged the phone. I didn't want to hear from anyone, least of all Aaron. I pulled the covers up over my head and succumbed to a numbing darkness.

The next time I opened my eyes the light from the window was fading. It was evening. My mouth felt like cotton. I was dehydrated. Dazed, I made my way to the kitchen and poured a large glass of orange juice. I didn't bother to turn on any lights. I sank down onto the sofa. I stared blankly out my sliding glass door. The pool was empty now. Probably everyone had gone out to dinner or started their weekend barbecues.

How frivolous the thought of barbecues seemed after what I'd experienced. I hadn't eaten since noon yesterday. I didn't care.

Inevitability, the memory of my session with Neville returned. Once again, I felt dirty, I felt violated. And as if that weren't enough, I felt that Aaron had violated me too.

Impulsively, I stripped off yesterday's clothes and pulled on my bathing suit. I fastened a crystal necklace around my neck that Elizabeth had given me when we first started the screaming sessions, grabbed a towel, and walked barefoot out to the pool. I'd never used the sauna in the three and a half years I had lived in this condo, but suddenly I wanted to boil every pore and cell in my body. I wanted to purge the poisonous memories and events of yesterday, and all of the past, out of me.

I sat in that little room only slightly bigger than an outhouse, and let the sweat roll off my body. I was glad no one was there. I talked to myself. I talked to my father. I talked to God. All I could think about was the heartless betrayal by my father. Coherently, incoherently, I mumbled anything that moved through my mind. It wasn't enough. I still had memories of beatings, flashbacks of being hit, nights I was afraid to go to sleep, my father kissing me in the hallway as a teenager, his accusations I was a sinner. I was a sinner? Look at him! Look at him! Look at what he had done!

When my body was dripping with perspiration, I opened the door and stepped out. Instantly, a blast of cool spring night air assaulted me. Although I was someone who was always cold, I moved swiftly into the night toward the pool, not allowing the chill to touch me. I stood at the edge. I was not a trained swimmer and actually my association with a pool was more from a lawn chair.

Then it came to me. I would declare this night my initiation. Tonight was my time of transformation. I had been brave to persevere through life as I had. This night would be in honor of *My Self.*

The warrioress part of me who'd persisted through lifetimes would now be re-birthed from the ashes of truth. Truth that I'd bravely uncovered for myself in my relentless journey. I was once again a native of an Indian village, but I no longer fled from fearful pursuit. A sisterhood had bonded me to Lynn in the *Medicine Woman* book. She, the medicine woman's apprentice, had pushed through her fear in spite of the evil Red Dog, until she had found her power and claimed the marriage of herself.

Then I remembered Agnes had told Lynn that by possessing what she feared, she had merged into a whole being and had become able to possess the marriage basket. It was a symbol of the union within her own being—a merging of the raw bravery of her inner male, and the pure heart of her female. The union of herself.

No wonder I'd been so riveted to that book. Now I had managed to come face to face with my own, deeply submerged, unconscious fears. I had stayed on the path. I had not ignored the signs, the symbols. I had continued on, confronting the darkest secrets of my mind with the courageous heart of a lion. They were poisonous secrets ladened with fear that had held me down, that had drained my power.

I had faced them. I had faced my fears. The little traumatized child I carried within had been bastardized, crippled, reduced to speechlessness... all in terror. Terror from that one horrible night.

She would be given new life. She would be re-born.

I sucked in a deep breath, bent over, and dived head first into the pool. The shock of the cold water was empowering. It was a baptism. I was being born again.

Charging through any fear I'd ever held about water, I swam swiftly to the other side of the pool and back again, pushing myself with superhuman energy. I breached from the water and headed for the sauna. Even though under ordinary circumstances I would barely perspire, I lingered until once again I was slippery with sweat. With miraculous energy, I dove headfirst into the pool again, this time swimming the length several times, and then returning once again to the sauna. All the while, mumbling and releasing every angry, outraged thought that passed through my head. I don't remember how many times I repeated this cleansing ritual. After what could have been hours, I was finally calm enough to float aimlessly on the water.

With newfound bravery, I was determined to release any remaining fear I had of the water, of my past. In one last gesture of strength, I dared myself. Floating on my back, I opened my body in a full-on, spread-eagle position, arms wide, legs apart. I would be afraid of nothing. This time my legs opened without the rigidity that had held them locked together my entire life. I proclaimed my own innocent, God-given right to my own body. I surrendered completely to the buoyancy of my body. My new power had become an awakened love of my body's sensations. I became one with the water, the night, and myself.

I looked to the starry sky as I floated on water. There was a bright, nearly full moon rising. I could hear frogs croaking from the creek nearby. At last, real peace was beginning to come.

I stared at the glowing moon, drinking in its healing light. Like Lynn, I too was facing my fears alone. I did not need Aaron or any other man to be whole. Real love, sweet, pure, and eternal love for my truly innocent self was mine, merely by my choosing it. I had united with myself. I had mated the warrior and the warrioress within me. I had claimed *my own smoke spirit*. I could feel my strength, my power, my bravery, and my gentleness...the gentleness of smoke rising from a cleansing fire. I found what I had been missing. I found love for me.

I had followed my intuition, trusting that to solve a problem I had to reach beyond the level of the problem. The symbols I'd found had guided me to higher levels of knowing, guided me to trust the *inner voice* that called me toward the cause of my turmoil. By possessing, facing, moving forward to what I had feared, I no longer felt fragmented. Hidden in the darkness of my childhood had been the source of my anxiety, and the source of my healing. It held the source of love—the source of self-love. I was merging into a whole being. It was the marriage of *My Self.*

From a nearby yard came the smell of barbecued hamburgers. I could hear the sounds of people talking and laughing over the strains of an old, familiar tune. A stereo played out the blended voices of Simon and Garfunkel singing *Bridge Over Troubled Water.*

A bridge! *The* bridge. I had crossed the bridge symbolized in the scrolls I had brought from Maryland! The ones still hanging on the wall in my bedroom. Now I knew why the silent message in my head had urged me not to leave them behind when I moved to California. That symbol of a bridge had hung there for three and a half years, all the while crying to me of something deeply important. I had crossed the bridge to my Self.

Suddenly, I was hungry. Lifting myself out of the water, I wrapped my towel around me and hurried back to my condo. After showering, I put on a warm pink flannel nightgown. I went to the kitchen and made oatmeal, toast and cocoa, just like Mama had made for me when I was sick.

I was emotionally spent. I decided to get into bed and simply allow my mind to absorb the last twenty-four hours. I went to the bathroom to brush my teeth, and there she was. The lovely Indian maiden with her flute. At last there was peace when I looked at her.

The *smoke spirit* suspended above her head now became like the *light bulb* of the painting I had done in college. I had been disconnected from the part of me that was my spirit. My father had robbed me of it years before I ever knew what it was. But more importantly, he'd taken away my sexuality before I knew what *that* was. My husband, Jack, rebuked me that night after we were first married for trying to discover my own natural sexuality. But this was about more than sexuality. It was about my need to feel the joy of my own feminine spirit. I had never been allowed to love freely. Even in my past life as an Indian maiden, I'd been put to death for following my heart.

Now, it was over. I knew I had no reason to feel fear from any more of my past. When I looked into the bathroom mirror, I no longer felt the uncontrolled rage of the tiger desperate to be in the world of the controlled, powerful lion. That had been resolved. I realized that, as *A Course in Miracles* says, the loveliness that I looked upon was simply my own.

I climbed into bed and propped myself up to look at the scrolls on the wall. I had crossed that bridge in a journey over repressed, emotionally troubled water. The bridge represented having the trust to go to my darkest side, and it was trust that had led me out into the light. The trust to know that I could be truly healed. That I could find peace.

A Course in Miracles says that all healing is letting go of the past. I reached for it on the bedside table. In order to wake up from the dream, which it refers to as *the process of healing,* it says that we must let go of what seems to be the past. And that the past can appear to be from another lifetime, or from a present lifetime.

The time had come. My mind was ready to be healed. I had been guided, even urged, by an inner knowing, that inner voice, that became activated by symbols—the painting of the Indian maiden, the lion/tiger, the scissors, and the perpetual image of the bridge.

I found the section in the *Course* that identifies *everything* in our dream world as a *symbol.* It said that heaven waits silently while your creations hold out their hands to help you cross... *"across the bridge is your completion, for you will be wholly in God, desiring only to be like Him."*

I knew now that the symbolic path was leading me on a bridge towards complete wholeness. The conflict inside me was diffusing. My spirit was surrendering to the innocence of me—a simple, blameless child of God. I knew, at least for that night, I would be able to rest my head without the haunting images of my father and my childhood. Those images of hallucinatory dreams that now seemed only to be my past.

I slept well.

CHAPTER 20

The Passing of A Dream

It was the morning after. I had performed my own baptism, cleansing and purging my rage, my hurt, and, yes, my shame. The strength, to which I had given birth, remained a profound and conscious part of me.

But in the harsh light of day, I had to face that I was also part of something shameful and ugly. I fought an irrational urge to laugh and cry at the same time, elevated by the potency of my newly awakened Self, and conversely in shock over the sheer humiliation of what my father had done to me. It was filthy! Dirty. Nothing could ever be the same. The life I knew—the person I thought myself to be—no longer existed. How could I ever feel normal again?

As the week went by, I found myself drifting into a graying melancholy, a downheartedness accompanied with a sense of déjà vu. I'd felt this disquieting mood before. I couldn't identify it. Maybe there was more to be remembered.

In my next session with Neville, we agreed that our intent was to determine if I had been further violated by my father.

Under hypnosis, I learned I had in fact been molested by my father throughout my childhood. I was able to recall him coming into my bed. I couldn't remember how often or for how long the abuse continued in my youth, or even when it finally stopped. It just played out over and over again in my head.

It was during this session that I came to understand several events in my childhood that had been mysteries to me. Four peculiar situations I'd experienced as a child began to make sense.

First, I remembered that I had feared and strongly resisted going to bed at night. Once in bed I'd lay there motionless, afraid to even breathe, fearful that I might draw attention to myself, as if something, or someone, menacing lurked in the darkness of the room. I remember trying to calm myself and wondering why I was so afraid. Once asleep, I slept heavily but walked in my sleep, waking up in other rooms of our house. Also, I always thought something was wrong with me because I wet the bed until I was nine years old.

Then, even though I remembered very little of my childhood, one memory had stood out. Now it began to make sense. I was a pre-teen, lying on the ground on a bed of leaves under one of the large eucalyptus trees in the grove next door to our house. As I had looked up into the clouds, my heart had ached for my life to be different. I knew my life had been different from my friends, but I couldn't account for the depths of my despair. I now realized that that sadness was the same downheartedness I'd felt before the last hypnosis session with Neville. This was the same numbing malaise I'd had on those mornings after my father had molested me.

Finally, remembering when I was in elementary school, there had been mornings when confusion resulting in disorientation overwhelmed me. And I didn't know why. When that happened, I couldn't do any work in class. All I could do was doodle on a blank piece of paper. One time the teacher even called my parents to take me home because I was unable to talk, walk, or communicate. In fact, I hadn't spoken a complete sentence until I was four. I could remember my parents' surprise when riding in the backseat of the car, I said, "See the tees [trees] blow."

Also discovered in that last session with Neville was a repressed memory of times in the evening when my father would ask me to sit on his lap, and make me tell him, "I am Daddy's little girl." Then his hand would slide up between my legs.

I don't know why I hadn't recalled all of this before, but Neville told me it was not unusual. I was only a baby when I was first molested by my father. That deep trauma was so severe that my emotional block was nearly total, except for the recurring childhood vision of before I was born. No wonder my memory of myself as a baby in a carriage carried the weight of a life or death decision. Neville said my brain's protective reflex was to totally block the original molestation, and when similar events occurred later, I immediately fell back into the same protective repression.

I began to understand that those horrible memories remained lodged in my subconscious until that time in my life when I subconsciously sensed it safe enough to confront them. I'd developed more self confidence after leaving my marriage, and with the help of my inner guidance and supportive counseling, I was developing trust in the process of healing. I had come to understand that facing my fears, rather than resisting them, could actually help me to release them.

Then the relief came.

As the month of May approached, the shadowy marine layer, a warm mass of air suddenly cooled by the effects of the ocean water that invades the coast on spring mornings, hung over my condo like a blanket, then dissipated as noon approached as if staging the process in my mind. Here it was, 1988, and I had lived forty-nine years without remembering the horrible things that had happened to me in my childhood. I struggled to order my thoughts and to integrate the bizarre events of the last few months.

As I looked across time, when I'd finally reached out for help to get to the bottom of my unexplained panic and disorientation, I saw how I had buried my fear of remembering so much so that I had strong resistance to seeing Neville, because I wasn't ready. I had needed time to face the truth.

Now, I could appreciate Elizabeth, and the support she provided by helping me to tap into my emotions through screaming and crying; coaxing me to the doorstep of my rage and reuniting me with the image of the lion, my symbol for courage that kindled a flame to go deeper. This revived heroic image, locked in the back of my mind since before going into the mental hospital in 1960, was unlocked twenty-eight years later as it roared awake my numbed subconscious amidst the agony of my own sounds. Getting in touch with my submerged anger and my submerged strength helped me be brave enough to confront my demons. I had persevered.

Then, Susan's *symbol* of the scissors, like a match to kerosene, set off a fire in the buried debris of my psyche. From then on there

was no turning back. I had reached the point where my disorientation and anxiety were greater than my resistance. Only then was I
willing to face what lurked in the basement of my mind. Still, only
after Andrea had helped to prepare me could I cope with the harsh
realities of my infancy and childhood by working with Neville.

However, I still could not accept what Aaron had done,
abruptly abandoning me after having sex. He continued to call but I
didn't answer. I was devastated and bewildered by his behavior.

To my surprise, he had started sessions with Andrea on a
regular basis. Andrea told me because he wanted me to know. She
said my enraged reaction that night and continued rejection had
been a wake-up call for him. His own behavior had shocked him
into admitting his need to seek help. Andrea said he also recognized
that some of his own pain and emotional distance was connected
to ending his marriage. In many of the sessions he was brought to
tears. I wished him well, but I wasn't willing to take on his issues.
Still, I had to admit regardless of our differences and the on-again,
off-again challenges with intimacy, I felt a unique emotional connection to him. Possibly it was related to my memory of our past lives,
and because until that last night together, he had actually been quite
supportive of me.

Right after my final session with Neville where I remembered
more details of the incest by my father as I grew up, Andrea encouraged me to continue to work with her. She graciously offered to see
me on a "pay as I could basis," and she stressed the importance of
continuing until I could resolve the traumatic effects of my memories. I knew she was right. I needed to find a way back to normal,
wherever that was, because I was growing steadily more distant from
all that was familiar. This dark, shameful secret lay heavily on my
heart, and I could find no place to fit into the life of the *new Grace* I
had encountered.

As part of the process of healing, and prodded by Andrea's
questions about my relationship with Aaron, we agreed to take a
closer look at the dynamic that had existed been between Aaron
and me.

Looking back at us, I had to admit that for the most part our mutual respect and shared humor, along with our close companionship and the fun of frequent dining and travel, had opened the door to a new lifestyle for me. I had been led into uncharted waters, a new level of camaraderie and comfort. I had begun to think perhaps this was what a normal relationship was like. I trusted and respected him.

I realized that in trusting Aaron and experiencing his kindness, my defenses against the hideous memories of my childhood had begun to weaken. With Aaron, I had started to let my guard down and my imprisoned pain was free to escape. But all the while there was a door tightly closed and barricaded inside of me.

I also had to ask myself why it was that even before I recalled being sexually abused, I had recoiled at an image of open scissors which suggested vulnerability. It's true, I was not afraid to have sex, to open my legs and to be vulnerable with Aaron *before* I remembered the abuse.

But, of course! With Andrea's help, I realized it was because giving into sex had been what I was *used* to doing. Wasn't that what normal couples did? It was expected. It was habit. I had blocked everything else out. I learned from my father and Jack that my role was to submit, yet I'd also learned to achieve some pleasure from it. I had built walls within me compartmentalizing my feelings, protecting myself while I responded the way I was expected to.

In contrast, for the first time in my life, with Aaron I did not feel continually obligated. Aaron made none of the sexual demands that I expected. My own pattern of submission had been interrupted. It left me hanging… nothing was expected of me! The walls inside of me had started to crumble. Suddenly, I wondered what *did* I, Grace, really want?

Without the protection of my emotional barricade, my long-repressed feelings began to bleed through, to be authentic. To experience native sexual feelings, such as when I rode Rusty. While riding Rusty there were no demands, no threats. There were no reasons to be fearful. I was allowed to *feel*. To have an honest, innocent response to my own body. His safe rhythmic movement invited my genitals to awaken and gave me permission to relax into them and to be embraced by my own life-giving energy—to claim my right to them—to me!

To live life authentically had always been a hunger in my life—perhaps in all of my lifetimes. The stage had been set for my silenced subconscious to give voice to horrified, outrage-filled memories. The lid had come off the pot containing my putrid past.

Aaron's issue with intimacy didn't have anything to do with my hidden past waiting to be remembered. We were each on our own path. The healing for both of us came when the need for our individual personal growth created a *situation* that dramatized and subsequently became a catharsis for what we both needed to see in ourselves.

It was a setup of a divine nature. I could not have coped with my hidden darkness before that point in time. In fact, that night in the condo after the session with Neville when I remembered being raped by my father, I was still not able to get to my real fury until Aaron walked out the door. His leaving me was a horrible re-staging of that rape. Aaron had unwittingly reenacted my father's act of rape, and then abandoned me—just as my father had done. Not only had my father raped me—but he had abdicated his responsibility to me to be a loving, protective parent.

In that moment, Aaron became my father. This opened a floodgate of sorrow and fear-packed rage I'd held at bay my entire life. I could never have reached so deeply inside myself without that reenactment. That catharsis.

Aaron and I had returned together in this lifetime. Whether intentional or not, this man who resembled my father had played a role enabling me to come to my own truth in this lifetime. The moment I realized this, I felt deep gratitude. My anger at Aaron shifted to compassion, and I hoped our relationship had given Aaron greater knowledge of himself. Still, I wasn't interested in getting back together.

Leaving Andrea's, I spied my copy of *A Course in Miracles* in the car which I had brought to read at lunchtime. Something I remembered now made perfect sense. Not only did the *Course* assure that there are no accidents, but it emphasized that any relationship in our lives is always part of an on-going *curriculum* of planned learning experiences.

The *Course* says our inner guide begins to look for those who can teach us as soon as we are ready. The particular form of the universal curriculum, in which we teach *each other,* is best for each of us in view of our level of current understanding. I couldn't help but wonder exactly where my current understanding had brought me to.

I remembered that day on the beach in the harbor when I'd first opened *A Course in Miracles* and read the introduction. The words had bewildered me. Then, it said the aim of the Course was "to help us remove the blocks to the awareness of love's presence." I'd certainly been carrying around an enormous block!

As for love, more than ever I yearned to feel its presence. For so long now I'd allowed symbols to lead and guide me. I'd always come to a better place, feeling lighter, freer and happier. So I had expected the disturbing emotions churning inside prior to the last hypnosis session to be resolved. I had expected that, once again, relief would come, a truth would unfold, and I would be brought to a happier state of being.

When I remembered my mistakes in Atlantis, I'd found peace by letting them go and learning to love myself. The trauma of my past Indian life had been healed as I forced myself to watch the Indian pageant. My heart had lightened by being able to release those events from my past. But now, my world had lost its luster. Things seemed to be going downhill. If I'd had the courage to remember the worst, shouldn't uncovering those horrifying events heal me? Where was the promised relief?

The questions swirled. Would I ever shed these monstrous, ugly memories of rape by my own father? What could I do to make them go away? Instead of relief, after the onset of my childhood memories I felt humiliated and disgraced. I was ashamed. When would I experience the joy of more love?

Love. It seemed crazy, but every time I reached out for love I came back to that cherished vision...the euphoric kaleidoscopic light from decades earlier. Love *did* live inside of me. I believed it. For a few precious moments back then, I'd been bathed in undeniable and all-embracing, unsoiled love—a state of innocence.

Suddenly, I really wanted to recapture the childhood *innocence* that I had lost—that had been stolen by my father. My own father! The man who'd pretended self-righteously to the world to be a high and mighty, God-fearing husband, respectful business and fam-ily man. A man who read the Bible daily. He'd piously preached to me about *my* sins and *my* guilt. He'd threatened the wrath of God's judgment as if he himself could call God down to strike me. He was beyond evil!

I felt debased, used, and discarded. How would I ever find the innocence I'd never had a chance to know? I turned back to the *Course* for a passage about the purpose of relationships. "Relationships" in the *Course* refer to everyone we encounter in our lifetimes. But why in this lifetime had I experienced this relationship with my father? Why me?

The *Course* said the ultimate goal is always the same in *all* relationships; to make it a holy relationship in which both can look upon each other, and everyone else, as sinless. How could that pos-sibly be? I loathed my sinful father.

Sinless? All relationships? My father? How could I view my father as sinless? How could I forgive my father? After what I knew about him! After what he'd done to me! Forgive him? Dear God, why on this earth would I ever want do that?

Three weeks after my last session with Neville, I was still in emotional overwhelm. I flipped in and out of defensiveness, snapping at others. I went directly home after work, withdrawn. I turned down social invitations. My self-esteem deserted me. I was always on the brink of tears. I was embarrassed, tarnished, different from anyone I knew. I had a sordid dark secret.

I knew that what had happened hadn't been my fault. I had been an innocent child. But no matter how I thought about it, I still felt dirty. I'd removed the block, but where was the love I'd known other times, and that the *Course* talked about?

When I told Andrea about my conflicted emotions, she urged me to take part in a group recently formed by well-known author and talk show host, Susan Forward. A nationally respected psychothera-pist, she'd organized a group known as V.O.I.C.E.S. Victims of Incest Can Emerge Survivors.

Incest! The very word made my skin crawl. I didn't want to even be associated with that label, but I knew I needed to act some-how in order to gain control over my roller-coaster emotions.

It took every ounce of courage I possessed to get into the car that following Thursday and head to the Tustin area where the V.O.I.C.E.S. group met. Going there would make me part of that world.

I don't know what I expected, but I certainly didn't expect what I walked into. The group of ten turned out to be mostly teenage girls. I was forty-nine. I felt ill at ease. I knew from their furtive glances and lowered eyes that they regarded me as a mother figure. In this group organized to look at incest and abuse, I suspected that was not a good thing.

Norma, the group leader and the only woman near my age, held a master's degree in social work. She welcomed me and we all sat down in a circle. We identified ourselves on a first name basis only. Her introduction was short. She told us this was a safe place, a place to bring our stories of abuse out into the open in complete confidentiality. She encouraged us to talk about whatever we were comfortable with, and assured us it was all right to express any emotions that might emerge. She emphasized how much it would help us to share our stories and to realize we were not alone. She suggested that, through this process, we could offer support to each other.

Norma and the founders believed that, by helping each other to heal, we would be able to see parts of ourselves in each other. I felt a flicker of hope. This principle was repeated over and over in the *Course:* We heal ourselves by helping others to heal; we learn in order to teach, and we teach in order to learn.

The purpose of that first evening of the ten-week program was for each one to tell about her abusive experience. This would be the first time I'd ever talked about my father raping me with anyone other than Neville or Andrea. I was next to last as we moved around the circle. By the time I'd heard the girls' stories, I felt certain they wouldn't be able to relate to me. For most of them, their abuse was a recent occurrence, often by someone they lived with or were close to. One fifteen-year-old told about being raped by her date. When my turn came, I took a deep breath and decided here goes. What would be the sense in coming if I didn't tell the truth?

I didn't tell about my childhood vision, I just described a few details of the overt facts which boiled down to: I had gone through hypnosis and remembered being raped by my father when I was eighteen months old while my mother was having an epileptic seizure. As I grew up, I'd added, my father had continued to rape me at night.

The girls, squirming from side to side, some with legs crossed some swinging their feet, some chewing gum, sat up in their chairs and began to really look at me. I felt relieved to sense their concern, and I'm sure it was visible. I became more animated. I decided to risk telling them about my childhood vision that returned and prompted me to know more.

Most of them responded sympathetically upon hearing I had been thrown in the trash by my own mother. For the very first time, I felt aware of being angry with my mother. Before that, all of my hate had been directed towards my father. Now I found myself talking about my anger towards both my parents.

My first betrayer had been my mother. I wondered aloud to the girls, whether she had suspected that my father came into my room at night. Didn't she notice? I knew she couldn't have known about my being raped the first time by him, because she'd been out of control in an epileptic seizure. But what about the other times?

One of the girls asked me what epilepsy was. As I was explaining it was a disorder of the central nervous system, I suddenly stopped mid-sentence. A flashback of something in college I'd never understood was now making sense.

I told the girls about that day in psych class when the professor announced our next session would be on the physical disorder of epilepsy. Upon hearing the word "epilepsy" I'd frozen in my seat, and dropped all of my books trying to leave. I'd met with the professor, hoping to skip the class. I forced myself to tell him about my mother. About how terrified I'd always been of her seizures. But, at his urging, I made myself attend. I told them how, as he talked, I'd fought the urge to cup my hands over my ears and stared at a crack in the blackboard instead... not remembering one word he had said. I was beginning to see the connection—why just hearing the word "epilepsy" had created panic in me.

After my sharing, Norma spoke up immediately, summarizing to help me clearly get it: I had been discarded by my mother at birth, then less than two years later I was raped by my father while my mother was writhing out of control and not protecting me. In addition to the trauma of the rape, she emphasized, this was a drastic and premature separation from the protective bond as a baby that I'd shared with my mother.

Norma concluded that for some time I had most likely been struggling with repressed and extreme separation anxiety, adding that from those early traumatic events onward, I had been living with an imprisoning fear of abandonment. And I hadn't had the opportunity to develop my own sense of healthy independence, which normally occurs around two years old. Each time Mama had a seizure it reenacted and magnified the unresolved anxiety in me.

As Norma spoke, I shivered visibly. But this time, instead of wanting to retreat from any thoughts about my mother's epilepsy, I realized this was another piece of the puzzle coming together!

Norma had been right on. As she described what had taken place, I felt deep sadness and tears began to well. I talked and wept, while the girls asked questions which helped me to see that during Mama's seizures I too, was overcome with a paralyzing anxiety that forced me emotionally to re-experience the helplessness of being raped.

It became clear that I was learning to cope with three issues: wanting to understand why my mother had thrown me into the trash can after my birth; accepting that I had been raped by my father when I was a toddler; and a lingering emotional trauma caused by my mother's epilepsy.

During that group session and the next one, I was able to get in touch with the realization that I'd harbored deep feelings of abandonment and disappointment regarding my mother. Even though throughout my life she had been brusque, strict, and distant, I knew she loved me in her own way. Yet that wasn't enough. She was weak, afraid of Daddy. She hadn't loved me enough to protect me from my father!

Growing up, I hadn't known where to address my rage at her shortcomings. Mama's mother had died when she was twelve, at which time her father left her to be raised by two aunts. She'd lost her twin brother to an illness at age sixteen. She never dared to stand up to my father for fear of losing the only security she knew. My sisters and I saw this and tried to be understanding. But, much of the time, we mothered her.

The girls in the group, most of them who lived at home with their mothers, were compassionate. Through their concerned sharing, I began to rebuild a perspective of a more normal way of viewing the young woman I had been. Norma praised me for not abandoning myself. "Grace, you have always had the courage to go within. If we go within, we will never go without," she said. "Our subconscious minds don't know that anything is impossible. We can tap into that."

Hearing the girl's share their tales of horror and watching them confront their own ordeals also, gave me strength. Their stories enabled me to capture and then release the pain of my own teenage years. In the process, I connected with the scared little child who had lingered unattended inside me.

Then a bizarre coincidence happened. That week Mother had a stroke. It was her third one, and we had to admit her into an assisted-care facility. She refused to eat. I could see she no longer had the will to live. She was wheelchair bound and spoke only in broken phrases.

When I went to visit her she didn't greet me. Instead she pulled me close and rambled about my birth, how horrible it had been. She would end with, "if you only knew." Then her words trailed off as she went into a blank stare. I pleaded with her to talk to me, but she only stared at me with abject pain in her eyes.

I was sure she was remembering when she'd thrown me into the trash can after I was born. She wanted to talk about it, but her guilt was too great. I felt so sorry for her. I gently put my arms around her. It was the last time I ever talked to her.

I forgave her. I love her. I miss her.

One Friday evening after work, during the fifth week of the V.O.I.C.E.S. sessions, I walked from the carport to my door. There stood Aaron in the doorway, holding a bouquet of roses. I felt sure he had grown them and cut them from the yard at his house. He held them tightly at his waist, like a little boy with a gift for his mother.

"I know you don't want to see me, but please at least just give me a chance to talk to you. Here, these are for you." He leaned forward, anxiously offering the bouquet to me. "I've cut off all the thorns—I don't want you to have any more thorns."

I said nothing. I didn't know what I wanted to do.

"I had that dream again, Gracie, about the fire on the hill. It always calls me to you...like I'm supposed to help you, or do something...put it out? I don't know."

Reluctantly, I opened the door. He followed me inside.

Rather mechanically, I went to the kitchen to get a vase for the roses. When I returned, Aaron had seated himself on the sectional. He implored me to sit down beside him for just a minute. I sat down, putting some distance between us. With his hands folded in his lap, he leaned forward to look into my eyes as he began to talk.

"Grace, I want to apologize from the bottom of my heart for the ways I acted. For deserting you in every way the last time we were together. There isn't any excuse for it. I know that now. I can only ask you to listen to where my mind was then, and try to understand. Even if we don't get back together, I want you to know how I feel."

Part of me wanted to ask him to leave. Another part of me felt relieved at the chance to talk about it. I simply closed my eyes for a moment, and then I nodded.

With a humility I had not seen in him before, Aaron began to tell me about his frustrations and challenges on that day I had gone to Neville for my hypnosis session.

"About that day—I have to admit I was caught up in myself and my own confusion," he began. He had been to a lengthy seminar that focused on getting in touch with one's own feelings. He had spent the day writing, sharing with a small group, and grieving over his failed marriage, his concerns for his two children and their broken home. He realized he was carrying a lot of guilt, magnified by the strict religious principles of his past. He was working on getting rid of the conviction that he had betrayed and abandoned his family, even though his estranged wife also desired the divorce.

As he continued to talk, he reached out for my hands and tears filled his eyes. I said nothing, I just listened.

"Grace, I can't believe I was so stupid! That I thought having sex with you was what you really wanted that night. I rationalized to myself I was doing the right thing. I'm ashamed to admit it, but I don't think I really wanted to know more. I was so caught up in my own problems." He went on, "That very next morning I was shocked at myself when I realized I hadn't even asked you about your session. When you wouldn't answer the phone or see me, I had to face how out of touch I was. It was then I knew that I needed help. I immediately called Andrea. She is helping me to understand my own feelings. Now, I realize how heartless and insensitive my actions were. I am so deeply sorry. I hope you can find a way to forgive me—if not now, then someday."

When he finished, he touched my shoulder. "Grace, please tell me about your session with Neville that day. I really want to know."

Seeing Aaron in tears, I couldn't deny his earnestness. A part of me just wanted to be heard in the presence of his compassion. But another part of me was suddenly glad for the chance to vent my anger towards him.

"Do you have any idea what I went through?" I blurted out pent-up rage.

"How scared I was even just driving to Neville's office?" Then my fury washed over me in waves of a thousand mixed emotions. A flood of tears overcame me.

"It had been a struggle just to go on, instead of wanting to die!"

I collapsed, sobbing, as I told Aaron the memories and details of the session. I told him how that session had revealed horrible events regarding the mystery my childhood vision, the remembrances of my father raping me, and of being in a stroller feeling unsure I wanted to live. This was finally my chance to tell it all to Aaron, to get it off my chest the way I had wanted to do that ghastly night.

Aaron gently placed his arm around me while I cried my heart out. At times, he actually cried with me. "I am so sorry these unthinkable things have happened to you." Then, he softly whispered, "I am truly sorry for not being there for you. I would have never reacted the way I did if I had made an effort to hear you."

When I was able to, I told him I did understand what he had been going through. But it still didn't justify his actions. Then I told him what had come to me in the weeks that followed: that I could see and appreciate how each of our lives had played out for both of us to come to our own truths. My rejection had made him aware of his need to look inside himself, and his unintentional rape that night had ignited the release of my deeply buried fear and rage.

After my tears subsided, Aaron picked up the book, *The Little Prince*. He had given it to me on our first date. He loved to read, and I was reminded that he liked to use quotes as a way to help him express what he wanted to say. He found the page he was looking for about "baobab trees." Aaron showed me the passage in which the little prince said that on all planets there are good plants and bad plants. The consequences were good seeds from good plants and bad seeds from bad plants. The little prince warned, "Children, watch out for the baobabs!"

"The baobab trees are from bad seeds," Aaron related. He asked me to see ourselves in this way. "You and I are cutting down all the baobab trees right now and clearing out all of what was not good in our lives. We can plant good seeds. We can help each other to start over learning from what has happened in our pasts."

He went on, "Remember, the little prince also tells of his devoted love for one special rose while he ventures from planet to planet." Aaron withdrew a single rose from the bouquet he'd brought and handed it to me. "You and I, we can plant new seeds. We can plant roses—roses without thorns." His voice became intense with excitement.

I couldn't bring myself to answer, but I knew it felt right to be with Aaron again. I nodded silently. I was deeply touched by this simple, innocent analogy.

We talked and cried and laughed at ourselves for hours until we realized we were both starved. Aaron volunteered to pick up some dinner. I was glad for his company. I had not socialized with anyone since we were last together. I set the coffee table with placemats, plates, silverware, and wine glasses. Aaron returned with our favorite meal from the harbor—calamari steaks, coleslaw, sweet potato fries, and beer.

I laughed, popped the tops, and poured the beer into the wine glasses. We sat on the floor, enjoying our first meal together in a long time. I felt especially glad that we were being informal, and it was just the two of us.

Toasting, Aaron quoted again from *The Little Prince:* "It is only with the heart that one can see rightly."

That night, Aaron stayed.

We spent most of the next morning in bed. Sex with Aaron that night had been both passionate and sweet. I'd found myself reacting to him with a new empowered lightheartedness. I was exceptionally gay as we talked for several hours.

We talked about what I'd discovered in the V.O.I.C.E. meetings as well as about Aaron's challenges in letting go of his marriage and how to re-think the parts of his life that now conflicted with his upbringing. I was glad we were finally talking about the guilt he carried. I knew my feedback, enriched by perspectives I had developed through counseling, was helpful to him.

My lightheartedness continued to expand. It wasn't just the opportunity to talk about our issues. It was something deeper. Te nature of our relationship still was hard for me to define, as it had always been. Rather than a powerful romantic attraction so common in new relationships, what seemed to be most prominent between us now was even more of a childlike playfulness, a deeply rooted, shared presence without judgment. It was a sharing of our innocence.

While Aaron went out to get pastries and coffee from Starbuck's, in a bit of a daze, I lingered in bed trying to take in all that had just happened. Last night was the first time I'd experienced sex since that night after returning from Neville's. The first time since the memorable night I'd purged my emotions and my body over and over in the sauna and pool in order to release the horrifying memory of my father raping me. I remembered the exhilarating sensation of floating on my back in the water under a full moon. I had dared to open my legs as wide as they would stretch, completely unrestricted, declaring in an entirely new way my own inner strength, love, and appreciation for myself, and my courage to confront it all.

I had faced my fears alone. I didn't need Aaron, or any other man, to love me in order to be whole. Like the beautiful flute player in my bathroom picture, I had mated with myself.

Just then, I recalled an incredible moment when I was with Aaron the previous night. When I opened my legs to him, a brilliant flashback of a picture from Susan's slide presentation of scissors had come rushing in. It was the last one, the one that was completely different in tone from all the other images. The one with the fully opened scissors with the rose placed between the blades. I realized that, at the time, the scissors had seemed to me like a merciless destiny positioned to annihilate the delicate rose. But I'd found the hidden beauty and power of that rose in myself that night in the pool!

Now, like Aaron's gift of roses to me, the thorns of a dark past had been removed. Suddenly, that image of the rose between the scissors reflected to me what I had learned through my courageous, lion-hearted journey determined to know the illusive invulnerability of wholeness. My true spirit could no longer be violated because I had released the ghosts of my painful past and discovered my own innocence. I had learned to love myself. I'm not broken. I'm whole.

The rose symbolized the truth of my wholeness and strength no matter what the future held. The *rose* represented my own *smoke spirit*...the everlasting love I had found for myself.

And now, sex was different with Aaron. I was different. It was like it had been on Rusty, the gentle horse I rode that had first awakened nature's fire in my loins. Awakened passion that penetrated me when his rhythmic movement first stirred my genitals to authentically feel my own surge of life. That's what was different. I experienced the sensations of my own innate feminine nature, of willfully receiving and containing love. I did not give away my power or lose myself in forced passion. I mindfully surrendered to wholeness as my own flesh united with my own spirit.

As well as an expression of our love and caring for each other, the emotional and physical connection between Aaron and myself during sex had taken on a new dimension for me. I could now know it as the fulfillment of a natural womanly desire. I savored the touching, the cuddling, and the satisfaction of my body's needs. I welcomed Aaron's love, his warmth, his affection. It was as if we were each giving the gift of new life to the other.

And I realized that intimacy held another unique gift for us. By not forcing things through our intellect and logic, we opened ourselves to hear the wisdom of the soft voices within.

This had been a hunger in my life. To know every aspect of that part of me that is my true spirit, my *smoke spirit. That* part of me that knows I am enough. I could see that in the deepest part of me I had changed. *I was enough,* no matter what happened between Aaron and me, or with any other man.

I lingered for awhile, savoring the fullness of that moment. Aaron had brought me the symbol—roses...roses without thorns. He had been the messenger of the voice of my own spirit. The roses had symbolically affirmed my own worth as a woman capable of love and forgiveness, for me and for him. I knew Aaron was committed to protecting me from the thorns. He wanted to provide the love and nurturing space for me to be myself without fear or expectations. Without thorns. And it was my natural womanly desire to support him in the same way.

As he found his way out of his past, and I mine, our progress by the very nature of our relationship seemed to reinforce each other's growth. We had each other's backs just like in my Leroy Neiman print of the tennis doubles players.

I swung myself around to the side of the bed preparing to start my day. I headed towards the bathroom to shower, still basking in the warm glow of the previous night. I smiled to myself as I thought of Aaron's toast at dinner... "It is only with the heart that one sees rightly." I was grateful that he was willing to let his heart lead the way.

All at once I caught sight of my own image in the mirror. Reality hit me. I still had to face the fact that my father was another relationship in my life. I was the child of my father. What was I to do about the profound disgust and resentment that persistently ached deep inside me?

CHAPTER 21

The Unifying Force in the Dream

The following week, every evening after work, I walked the path around the harbor and crossed the bridge to the channel to watch the sailboats gracefully motoring in. Then I returned home and got into bed to read the *Course.* I was still searching for rational ways to understand why a parent, or anyone, would molest a little baby. How could anything have justified that abuse? I could find no logic. It was insanity!

That had been my view of the world ever since the day I'd left the mental hospital so many years ago. My visions in the hospital had brought me beauty and joy. It was the world outside the hospital that was crazy! Harsh and pointless, endless striving, death…a race to nowhere.

Searching through the *Course* for answers, one theme kept appearing…*forgiveness!* It was made to sound so easy. It wasn't! Every chapter extolled the virtues of forgiveness, advising not to even try to judge painful events or explain them, but to give them over to Christ and He will send His angels to answer. I was so weary, going in circles thinking about it. I would have gratefully welcomed the voice of just one angel.

I longed for peace. At the end of the week, instead of walking, I drove along the road in the harbor below the hillside. Now, I experienced no voices, no feeling of anxiety or doom, and no visions of an

Indian maiden being chased. All was calm. I followed the road to its end where I always did and parked facing the ocean.

Here at the road's end, I felt I was coming to the end of a long emotional journey of my own having released and forgiven myself for wrongdoings in Atlantis; having let go of the paralyzing fear carried from my Indian lifetime; and having recalled childhood visions, igniting a process finally leading me to the harshest remembrance of being raped by my father. I had been able to find peace after the previous traumas. But, I couldn't see how that could happen regarding my father.

I sighed heavily and slumped down in the seat. A steel band of resentment gripped my chest. My stomach churned with revulsion at every thought of my father. I couldn't go on like this. The *Course* promised that anyone who calls on God's name will be heard. Could I place my aching heart in His hands?

Through the steps I'd already taken, I'd overcome many fears. I'd let go of my belief in the wrathful God that my father had taught me about. Maybe I could call upon this God I was learning to know. Why not?

"Oh, God, dear Holy Spirit," I pleaded, my voice breaking. "Please help me. Help me to let go of these horrible memories, the shame that haunts me, and the burden of hatred!"

In the dead silence I glared at the ocean. The sky was gloomy and gray. A thick marine layer completely blocked any view of the setting sun. The tide was at its lowest, exposing an obelisk-shaped boulder offshore directly in front of me. It was a good twenty feet high, protruding like a wrecked ship on a reef. It reminded me of the monolith I had seen in my very first childhood vision—that of the moment before my birth.

Monolith was a word I had looked up before the last session with Neville when trying to make sense of what I had seen. A monolith was described as symbolizing something that is whole and organized, a unified power. What could that symbol mean to me?

Symbols. Oh, God, another symbol. They never stop! I knew I should be grateful, but I was so weary of them. Over a year ago I had begun searching the *Course* for the meaning of my symbols. The *Course* said that Holy Spirit uses all symbols for *one* meaning, but I never understood exactly what that meaning was.

I reached over to the passenger seat for the *Course* that had become my companion in recent weeks, and opened it to a book-marked page containing a heavily underlined section that read that while Holy Spirit uses all symbols, "...creation has one meaning and a single source which unifies all things."

Unification. It seemed that was what I was supposed to see in the monolith. But what is the *single source?* What is that *unifying power?*

I read on...symbols all share the name of God, and every-thing, and everyone, and every event within life's dream is a symbol. I had already found this to be true. However, that also meant my father had to be included as part of God. Who could believe he was a piece of God?

I groaned to myself in exasperation. So what the heck was the significance of the monolithic symbol? It must be important; it was my very first perception in this lifetime. How could I stop racking my brain to find its lesson? What is the single source that the *Course* says *unifies* all things?

I closed the book and dropped it on the seat beside me. It fell open to the Introduction—that first, very confusing page I'd read on the beach nearly two years ago. My eyes caught the same last few lines I'd puzzled over before: "It [the *Course*] does aim...at removing the blocks to the awareness of love's presence, which is your natural inheritance. Herein lies the peace of God."

Love is our natural inheritance? It's a part of not only me, but *everyone?*

In a nanosecond, like a seismic shift had cracked in my brain, I got the message! Love is the natural state of creation—of being. It's not just who I really am, it's the essence of *all* of humanity. It's the unifying force that connects *everyone!*

Yes, that was how in the pool that night I'd accepted love for myself. It was just for the taking. I'd realized I didn't need anyone to give it to me. I could just choose it because *I am* love already! I could accept the pure, innocence of myself because it already abides in me. It abides in everyone.

I suddenly knew why, during my first reading of that intro-duction I'd felt something come alive way down inside me, even though I couldn't comprehend its meaning at the time. Now, reading it again, I was infused with warm, eternal, comforting love. I was finally touching the love that embraced me two decades ago while wrapped in the ethereal realm of kaleidoscopic light during those amazing few days before going in the mental hospital where I felt so aligned with goodness. I was so elated that I'd been overwhelmed with joyous laughter. That experience throughout my struggles had been my reference point for the possibility of life's highest expression. At last I was returning to it.

The *Course* says that love *is* life's highest expression. Love is life's goal. There it was!

But there was another perspective. It meant that literally everything that is *not* love is but a block to love—fear, hate, judgment, indifference, lying, betrayal…and rape.

The *Course's* remedy? All blocks are removed by *forgiveness*!

I couldn't deny the obvious message. The message of the *monolith* and of the *Course*. *Love* is the single *unifying* force, and *forgiveness* is the single unifying *power.* Choosing the power of forgiveness must bring the peace of God.

I shook my head to clear away a fog of stubborn denial. During the preceding three years I'd come to trust the *Course*. If I wanted to be happy, if I wanted to live in a natural state of love, I would need to reconsider how I viewed the story of my life, of all my lives.

I picked up the *Course* again, leafing briskly through the many sections I had underlined. Words and phrases jumped out at me and I began to see them in a different way. Within the curriculum of life there is *one* fundamental central theme. All relationships serve a holy purpose, *all* relationships serve to help us to love our *real* selves and the *real* self of others. When that happens, the *Course* refers to it as a holy relationship.

But my father? I was still hung up on my relationship with him. He'd abandoned me, betrayed me, and defiled me! The rape had caused me to separate from part of myself as I'd grown up. My terrified child dwelt all of my life in the deeper regions of my mind. Until recently, she'd believed she was not enough, not whole. Pieces were missing from her, denying her a sense of completeness.

Lines from the song *Summertime* that I'd sung in LifeSong came back to me…"Oh, your daddy's rich and your ma is good-lookin' / So hush little baby, Don't you cry." I had been drawn to that song for a reason. The lyrics reflected my deepest longing to be the child of loving, protective parents.

Then, at last an opening to my separated self emerged with Aaron when he encouraged me to speak my truths and I was heard by him. I had found one missing part of me that night in the pool when I'd realized I did not need a man, or anyone else to be complete. I'd called it the marriage of myself. But even after finding my missing piece that night, there remained a rotting resentment in my belly from a hidden hate and place of angry judgment for my father. Hence, a block to the presence of love and peace in my heart. Without love and peace, I would never be whole.

I knew that block was a lack of forgiveness on my part.

I would never be able to justify or explain what my father had done to me. It was beyond anyone's understanding, especially mine. There was nothing left to do except look for God's light within him.

I had to see him as a Son of God as he was originally created.

I began to reconsider. If my life had been different, I wouldn't possess the strength I do. I wouldn't have developed the courage I've learned in the face of adversity. I wouldn't have realized all that I was now. My father's self-righteous way of living, centered on judgment, guilt and sin never emphasized forgiveness, kindness, or genuine love. But, if I had not lived with the bigotry of my father, I might never have found my guiding voice within, or discovered that I was not a sinful girl "who was asking for it" by wearing a shorter skirt or lipstick, or moving joyfully during sex. I had been compelled to find the love within myself.

Like a caterpillar that needs the confining walls of the chrysalis to push against in order to transform into a butterfly, perhaps my soul required this kind of resistance for my transformation. I'd been forced to find my own strength. I'd been led through so many life-changing challenges that taught me to trust the inner voice of the Holy Spirit within me to see the big picture.

Just then a helpful image came to me. It was like I stood in a stateroom on a ship, looking through a porthole. I could see only one view. But the Holy Spirit was outside the ship, seeing everything, and knowing my destination. I realized that God was my compass and was guiding my ship, leading me, to a place of love and peace.

For so long now I had followed the guidance of that small voice in my head, and the heart-tuned messages spoken through countless symbols. In one form or another, the message so far had always been "forgive and you will see this differently." This was true whether I had realized it or not, and whether I needed to forgive myself or someone else. In the past, my anger toward my father had always felt justified, but the anger kept recreating itself, causing me to feel like a victim. I was sick and tired of being a victim!

Suddenly, I saw that not forgiving him was a form of self abuse! It was as though I wanted to prolong my own suffering by reliving the experiences with him over and over again. Not forgiving someone was the equivalent of taking arsenic and expecting the other person to die.

According to the *Course,* all healing resided in letting go of the past. My father was dead. His body was no longer part of my dream. Now, *I* was the miserable one. My own judgment assaulted me. He'd been dead over fifteen years. Yet, here I was, holding onto my hate as if he still walked the earth. *I* kept the game in play. I needed to give up the hope that the past would ever be different. The past was gone.

Almost amused at myself, I released a faint chuckle and a little tear. I needed air. I left my car and walked the thirty feet or so to the shore's edge. I watched the sun descend over the horizon, glowing brightly then, as the clouds of marine layer had dissipated. It was a perfect example. Like love, the sun had always been there. My view had been blocked by dark clouds, in the same way my resentment and judgment were blocks to letting love into my life.

As tears blurred my vision, I folded my arms around me. I felt myself as part of that eternal love. Who I really am is not a body, I thought. Everything that has happened to me is a journey leading me out of this illusionary dream. My father is not a body. His spirit is part of eternal love. At that level, in that purity, I am unified with my father in love.

In that moment, when I gave myself permission to love, and to release my anger and judgment, relief rushed in and became a soothing balm for my aching heart.

It wasn't enough just to *know* that only love is real and life is a dream or an illusion. I realized there must be the *experience* of surrender; the willingness to *experience* the act of forgiveness, and of letting go.

In that moment of surrender, a tight, heavy, iron chain that had bound my chest, broke. It was a miracle.

A miracle! I'd been studying *A Course in Miracles*! I had read many times that miracles occurred naturally as expressions of love. The miracle—the real miracle—was the love that inspired them. Everything that results from love is a *miracle*! It had all sounded so mysterious before, so beyond my understanding.

Now I understood. I got it because I'd experienced that it worked! Forgiveness happened when I understood that holding the grievance of old emotions and anger would serve no good purpose. When I chose love in my heart, the physical pain was released from my body.

Love. The one constant. Love was real. It existed eternally, even in this fear-filled dream of life. By choosing forgiveness, no matter what, a veil lifted to reveal everyone as creations of God evolving at their own pace. Love was present in everyone, no matter how deeply repressed it might be.

This was the reality. Forgiveness brought *me* back to myself. Forgiveness not only brought peace into the outrageous story of my life, but into my body, and most of all, it calmed my racing mind.

My heart fluttered. I wanted to touch the sky. Reviving my body I reached my arms up and out as far as I could and stretched open my legs. At that moment, I was instantly reminded of the victorious position my body had assumed that night in the pool. In the water, I had fully opened myself, taking in the healing surge of emotional transformation. The moment when I'd learned to love myself as I spiritually mated the male and female parts of me.

With that thought, I extended my limbs out even further, positioned now in the form of one giant X...an X...the same form as the fully-opened scissors that now held no threat for me. They symbolized a condition of protection through love. With a new sense of freedom and well being, I planted my feet firmly onto the earth and stabilized myself against the strong ocean wind. An electrifying wave of wholeness washed over me.

This time, I wasn't just loving and mating with myself though. This time, I was choosing to unite my own wholeness with the divine love of God.

It was not simply a marriage of myself. It was a *holy marriage.* A holy marriage that united me with God, and yes, with my own father. And with all of the innocence, purity, and divine nature of humanity. In that moment, I felt no lack, no scarcity. I felt complete.

I don't know how long I lingered on the shore in that state of empowered wonder. Eventually, I made my way back to my car. As I turned the key in the ignition, the moon caught my glance. Two glowing streaks of light as in the shape of an X radiated across the face of the moon! Why had I never noticed it before? I jumped out of the car to see more clearly, but it was gone. I climbed back into the car, suspecting that my imagination had run away with me. But there it was again! Once again, I left my car, but the X had disappeared. The streaks of light forming an X were only visible through my car window, like a filter.

A filter! Wasn't that what I'd done? Filtered out the truth within the dream of life? And as I'd followed that voice within, it expressed truth in many symbols, as now in this lunar image. Now I had been guided to the truth by accepting love and forgiveness.

I realized that the radiant X-shaped beams of light across the moon would, for me, always symbolize my daily quest for the peace and empowerment of forgiveness and my willingness to see the connection with God, myself, and others. This graphic symbol would remind me of love's contentment when I follow my inner voice—the voice for God.

A new morning dawned! My entire perspective on life had changed the evening before. Love was everywhere! Old thought patterns persisted, causing me to want to laugh and cry at the same time. This went on for days, almost like a process of detoxing. I was committed to kicking the habit of blaming and judging others all the time. I had to admit, old thinking dies hard.

In every situation, at work, in a grocery store, the gas station, or with Aaron, I was inspired by the ever-present option to love, to see opportunities for little kindnesses where before I might have reacted from a self-absorbed rut. As I repeatedly applied this new perspective, there was a surprising payoff. Love found its home within me;

my mixed emotions were being replaced by an inner calm. I even looked forward to moments when I could be alone, when I could quietly savor just being alive.

God's angels *did* answer my desperate prayer for peace that evening in the harbor. It came when I was finally ready to get quiet and listen. And now I understood the symbolic message of the monolith...love is the single, unifying force. Only love brings peace. How corny. How true.

That Thursday was the eighth of the ten weeks of V.O.I.C.E.S. meetings. I looked forward to sharing the excitement of my revelation of the power of love and forgiveness with the girls, but I wasn't sure how to explain it. We had already talked briefly about my visions in the mental hospital and my sense of life being like a dream. Realizing the idea was pretty extreme, I had never attempted to elaborate.

Once in the meeting, I took a deep breath and began by saying that God made everyone, even my wicked father. But there had to be a part of him that was good because there is a light in everyone. And even though he'd abused me in countless ways, I was hurting *myself* by carrying around the past. By judging him, I'd blocked myself from the calming experience of forgiveness.

I didn't want to offer the impression that I was forgiving him in a traditional way. I needed to say it. I told them that I hadn't forgiven him because he'd wronged me, but because, in truth, the "wronging" had only occurred in an illusion...a state of mind that is a dream...adding I knew there were reasons for everything that happened in the dream and that only love matters. Choosing love had brought me true peace.

I felt a restless tension in the room, where before there had been a calm interest. Defending my view, I pointed out that this uncommon perception of the world as an illusion was believed by such greats as Carl Jung and Albert Einstein. I immediately regretted saying the words. They sounded smug and defensive.

Suddenly, I realized it was all about the *experience*. After all, I hadn't been able to find any relief until I had come to the end of my rope. Words weren't enough. Each one of us, I saw, must undertake a personal journey. I'd taken my own. The most I could do was share my relief in a spirit of love.

There were mixed reactions in the discussion that followed, but Norma wholeheartedly affirmed my progress. It occurred to me that we were all in various stages of healing. Some were not ready to forgive, and some might never forgive their abusers, at least in this lifetime.

Nevertheless, I knew they sensed my enthusiasm. I was grateful for this dynamic group, V.O.I.C.E.S. The girls and Norma had mirrored my situation as preparation for me to listen to *my own inner voice*. By sharing their situations and stories, they'd swept me back into my own past, sparking more awareness, propelling me forward to healing and inner peace. Norma had coaxed me through any thoughts of turning away.

As the days passed I felt lighter, my spirit freer. I laughed and hugged spontaneously, and there was a skip in my step. When I looked into the mirror, I almost didn't recognize myself when sparkling eyes in a more youthful face returned my gaze. I wanted to sing and dance. I gleefully watched for opportunities to play jokes and plan surprises. I lived in the present! Everything was more vivid, like wearing glasses for the first time and discovering that the leaves on the trees which had formerly appeared as blurry blobs actually had fuzz, and veins, and hundreds of different textures.

As my healing progressed, the blessing of wholeness gently enfolded me. I didn't know it, but I had *always* carried a disquiet that I was different, that I had something to hide. I came to realize I had endured a low-grade depression absolutely all of my life. "You never know you're depressed until you're not," my psychologist friend, Jane, used to say. She was so right! I now embraced a brand new kind of unconditional love, for myself and others, that would always be present if I chose it. Through the gift of love, vague but controlling shadows from my childhood had been erased.

The ultimate truth is that there's no peace in anger. There is no healing in revenge. The only real healing in the long term is finding love through exercising our choice to forgive and forget.

After the last session of V.O.I.C.E.S. I slowly drove home. I didn't feel inclined to pass the car ahead of me. I was content to be just where I was, and who I was.

At home the silence pleasantly hummed in my ears. Singing a little tune, I undressed, made a cup of almond tea, sprinkled it with cinnamon, and snuggled into bed. I leaned back against big, fluffy pillows to savor my hot elixir.

What a rollercoaster ride the last three and a half years had been since I'd returned to California! Sinking into the pillows, I mused, this period of my life had been full of great storms—and the unfolding of my peace of mind. From the moment I'd first glimpsed the start of my life before my first breath, I'd felt fear and trepidation until I'd seen the monolith. I could have turned away at that point. I didn't have to come into this lifetime; but my higher Self urged me on.

The bar was already set for me from the very beginning of this lifetime! Here is my opportunity to learn about loving and forgiving. A childhood devoid of protective love, a marriage built on destructive domination…that was my *curriculum*. I could have remained a victim. Thank God, I'd had the courage to trust. That trust delivered me out of pain and into peace.

I smiled, imagining the souls of all of humanity joined together like broken pieces of colorful crystals that became a brilliant and beautiful kaleidoscope when *united* by the light of *love* with the soul of humanity displaying indescribable beauty. And the symbols—the road signs—all led me closer to the light of innocence in that kaleidoscope. I chuckled at myself. I was sounding like a 1960's hippie! But, I didn't care. I was content.

I could finally access Grace, the child. I could feel her. I remembered her and the symbolic stepping stones that had led me to the bridge of my own innocence. In fact, destiny had named me, Grace. Grace in the *I Ching* meant, "Simple grace, no blame." That's exactly what I was learning to do. I gazed across my bedroom at the scrolls on the wall and remembered the *Course's* words. "Across the bridge is your completion, for you will be wholly in God, desiring only to be like Him."

After all I'd been through, I now saw one solitary perspective of the symbolic word, *God*. God was love. I knew all I really wanted was to become more loving and to receive more love.

By the next Saturday morning, I was exploding with energy. I bought a bouquet of fresh, white daisies and potted, pink chrysanthemums. I cleaned my entire condo. When everything was spotless, I arranged the bouquet of daisies in a vase, and placed it in the center of my dining room table. After a quick lunch, I tackled the dust-covered porch.

Cleaning felt symbolic of my personal journey. My home shined with the same newness I felt within myself. I'd washed away the past and uncovered the beauty of the present. That day was a gorgeous summer afternoon in late July of 1988.

Had it really only been three months since I'd consented to hypnosis that led me to remember my terrifying childhood? It seemed like lifetimes.

I wondered how far I was along on the "road" of my life. Would this intense, personal transformation continue? Was it over? I recalled countless drives to the end of the harbor in great anguish, but the end of the road had been where the dark images and feelings had departed. Was I at the end of my road of digging into the past, and on a road to sustainable inner peace?

As I sat there on my patio, I savored the reward of inner calm that comes by learning the meaning of forgiveness and the love it brings. Drinking in the beauty of the condo's landscape, the bubbling creek, an array of flowering plants, and the tall, majestic evergreen trees, I was cuddled in profound gratitude for my journey.

Like the pageant at the mission, all of life was a pageant. One dream sequence being acted out after the other...waiting for the next pageant to begin...and another dream to be revealed.

Now, I knew that each dream could lead to more love—if that's what I chose. I don't always get the people in my life I want, but I get the people I need to help me, to hurt me, to leave me, to love me, to transform me into the being I am meant to be.

Life was *not* meaningless or crazy, as I'd thought. From the day I'd left the mental hospital I'd harbored an assumption that life was little more than a zoo or a circus—a world of insanity. Forgiveness had opened my mind to the infinite possibilities of a meaningful life inside the delusional, ego-ruled existence called "the world." Now, I could view with insight both the frailties of this world and the reality of this world...this world of love. Through the path of unconditional forgiveness, I no longer tried to change the world. Instead, I was changing my mind *about* the world.

The *Course* says, *"To let illusions walk ahead of truth is madness. But to let illusion sink behind the truth and let the truth stand forth as what it is, is merely sanity."*

My symbols are leading me to sanity. My inner voice is leading me to know love.

I'd seen no real purpose in life until my first visions occurred, twenty-eight years ago. Then my automatic painting of a lightbulb sensitized me to symbols and to my own intuition. On the resulting journey, I had unblocked so much by learning from this lifetime and past lifetimes. Whether now, or during past lives, a dream ends and another one begins in a different, hopefully more enlightened state. I giggled. I should scratch the word "death" from my vocabulary and call it "graduation."

For over five years, journaling had aided me in understanding the gifts of the trials I'd faced. I'd rejected the nagging notion that I should write a book to share my uncommon story of how life's lessons had been revealed to me. It seemed like a daunting task. I'd never aspired to be a writer, and I'd definitely looked forward to a more carefree lifestyle. Conversely, my thought that perhaps I could help someone persisted. I couldn't be the only person who'd had visions and heard an inner voice. I gave myself permission to at least consider it.

As I looked back upon my life, I was most grateful for my children. I looked forward to David's phone calls, although I knew he was busy settling in after moving to Florida to work at remodeling homes. Jennifer had enrolled in a school nearby further pursuing her goal to become a travel agent. The humorous little notes she left on my refrigerator after crashing on my couch while I was at work made my heart sing. I loved that we were all communicating.

As for my former life in Maryland, I tried to remember only the good parts. My emotions regarding Jack fluctuated. Whenever I had a rush of anxiety about the way he'd demeaned and abused me, I poured my feelings into my journal until calmness came. The hardest part to let go of was the wall he'd tried to build between me and my children, just as he had done with me and his mother. But I had my children in my life and, although the wall was still present, things were improving between us.

One painful memory that persisted was of Jack's domination at our dinner table discussions when I encouraged David and Jennifer to express their opinions about everything, including religion and politics. I loved it when we engaged in spirited, yet respectful, debates. But as soon as rapport was building between me and the children, Jack would slam his fist on the table and always say, "Now don't you talk to your mother like that." They had said nothing disrespectful. I realized now that he knew we were having fun and bonding, which he couldn't tolerate. I had objected to his irrational comments at the time, but they'd already had an impact. The children always grew silent.

But, that was Jack…and another time. I'd found the strength to leave him, and now I needed to find the strength to forgive him. I continued to try.

The afternoon breeze had subsided and it was getting hotter. The garden hose, already unfurled on the sidewalk, encouraged me to water the azaleas bordering the patio. When the ground was sufficiently saturated, I remembered my potted geranium by the front door. Tugging the hose along beside me, I caught sight of my condo address by the door…52.

That number had been the symbolic vision coming to me when I first arrived in Dana Point. Upon first seeing it, I felt sure it meant I would be married when I was fifty-two years of age. I would only be 50 in September.

Then, I subsequently remembered my vision of a hillside bearing *pink houses* with Spanish tiled roofs along the Pacific Coast

Highway by the nearby Ritz Carlton Hotel. But when I'd driven by the location and glanced at the hillside, it was bare.

Thinking of that hillside also reminded me of the most prominent vision I'd seen in the hospital almost thirty years earlier. It was of a *mountain,* and at the foot of it, a multi-lane highway with an enormous completely white and blank road sign straddled over it. An empty sign? These visions had not manifested!

But I knew more would be revealed to me. As I looked to the future, I felt excited about the potential beauty of life awaiting me in the revelations from these symbols. And maybe sharing those revelations with others. Though for now I realized that starting any book would have to wait.

CHAPTER 22

The Gift in the Dream

A s the days rolled by I still felt drawn to the harbor, but now for a
different reason. I drove there more often just to feel its calming inspiration. One Saturday morning a few months after
my last V.O.I.C.E.S. meeting, I stopped on the way home to browse in a
bookstore on the Pacific Coast Highway. As I chatted with the owner,
I caught sight of a small display of business cards from a masseuse. A
massage would be great, I thought. With my new, optimistic outlook
on life, I wanted to take every opportunity to enjoy myself.

Deanna was not just a board-certified, advanced-level massage therapist specializing in spinal decompression, but according
to the bookstore owner, she had also studied with spiritual mentors
around the world. She said Deanna offered classes on the intercon-
nectedness of the body and emotions, and the emerging feminine
spirit in everyone.

A week later, Deanna Eck, a tall, blond-haired woman near
my age, greeted me with a beautiful smile and lively brown eyes. I
asked about the purpose of her classes and the connection between
body and emotions. We developed an immediate rapport and were
soon laughing heartily. She explained that emotional pain can lie
dormant until certain situations or relationships trigger it, particularly if they resonate with a part of your past. I mused at how much I
already knew about this phenomenon.

Deanna elaborated, explaining that we are frequently in denial of our thoughts and attitudes, and if the feminine part of ourselves—our feelings—haven't found peace, this can cause unconscious turmoil to manifest as neurosis, imaginary illnesses, or deep depression.

"Giving ourselves permission to allow suppressed emotions to enter our conscious minds and finding ways to release them is a form of loving ourselves, and is expressed from our nurturing, feminine side," she said. "Many cultures call this our goddess energy." I felt warmed by her reference to the goddess, since it was the feminine part of me that I'd finally learned to cherish.

I assured her I understood the dynamic she described. Thinking of my most recent emotional release, I told her I had just experienced something similar. "In fact, this massage is a treat for me in celebration of that event and now it will be for my goddess energy as well!"

The massage room in Deanna's home was lightly scented by one large candle. A CD played soothing music, a gentle voice in the background offering occasional words like, "relax—let go—breathe." Deanna began rather unconventionally by cupping my feet in her hands with her head bowed. She went to work swiftly, her hands incredibly strong and her strokes deep and purposeful. Any resistance I may have possessed gave way to her silent authority.

After a while, even my mind gave way to the tempo of her pressure. I don't know exactly when time seemed to stop. Then out of nowhere, to my great alarm, distress and righteous rage exhumed itself. But instead of expected release, my emotions were building. "What is it, Grace?" Deanna whispered.

"I don't know...something." I made choking sounds as her hands rotated rhythmically over my shoulders and around the back of my neck. In the next moment, I realized this tall woman had climbed up on my back. Yet she was not heavy—more like a light-footed cat rotating from side to side. Suddenly, I was no longer in the room. The images were overpowering.

"It's Jack. He's choking me!" I groaned helplessly. Deanna's feet kneaded my back until I wailed. Anger from my heart and my throat emerged as I wept and spewed out my fury. I gasped for air, which turned into fits of coughing. In that moment, I realized how close I'd come to dying at Jack's hands that day, long ago, in Maryland. I broke into uncontrollable sobs.

Deanna's touch turned gentle, lightly stroking the length of my body. "That's enough for today," she whispered. "This trauma has been held in your body. Now you are ready for it to be transmuted. You've brought the light of your consciousness into the pain. We let go in layers. We can't release all of our traumas at once. You'll need to rest this evening, and don't forget to drink lots of water. "

I could barely roll over to face her. Totally regressed in surrender to my anger of the moment, I blurted, "I can't believe I ever married someone like him."

Deanna said, "I know, dear, but maybe it helps to understand that we're constantly finding the person we need to grow with. Relationships, especially romantic ones, can trigger psychic wounds, but they can also become a path to consciousness. In our imperfect relationships, we are able to strengthen each other where it's needed. Whatever stirs emotion or anger in us is all about the lesson we're learning."

And there it was in a nutshell. Oh, how I'd learned this. But, I didn't want to hear it just then.

Finally, gathering enough strength to leave Deanna's that afternoon, I tried to calm myself by breathing deeply as I headed south to my home along the beautiful coastal highway that wound its way through Dana Point. All at once, in a spectacular flash of déjà vu I realized this was the very same segment of highway I'd driven upon as I entered Dana Point that first day when I was out sightseeing. It was the exact place in which I'd heard the voice asking, "Where are the houses?"

Instinctively, I looked to my left … *and there they were!*

The pink houses with Spanish tiled roofs set atop the embankment beside the highway, just as I'd envisioned them five years earlier in 1984—before they'd ever been built.

Oh, my God. Another symbol.

I was astonished, but at the same time, I'd known it would come.

By then, I'd learned that the symbols signaled it was time for me to give up my expectations—whatever it was I thought I knew— and surrender into the wisdom of where I was being led.

Arriving home, I collapsed on my living room sofa, emotionally exhausted from all that had occurred. It was dark when I awoke, so I undressed and climbed into bed.

The next morning, I still felt a little groggy, but the fog had begun to clear. I instinctively knew what was required of me now. The bitter emotional memory lodged in my body had come into my consciousness for one reason, and one reason only.

It was time to forgive.

I'd tried to forgive Jack before, but only in my thoughts and journaling. Now, with Deanna's help, I'd reached into the core of my rage as I had when the horrendous emotions of my childhood led me to forgive my father. I couldn't hold anything back and still be truly forgiving. Only the present mattered now. The *Course* says that all healing comes from letting go of the past.

But this moment was easier than when I'd forgiven my father because I didn't fight it. I prepared a light breakfast and took it out to the patio. The summer sun gleamed brilliantly. I replenished my body, and then sat back with my coffee. My chair faced east toward Maryland. I wondered what Jack was doing.

My forgiveness must be without judgment or reservation, I thought. I didn't have any need to revisit our past or dredge up details of his abuse. I had done that in my journals. I did not want to wallow in the darkness any longer. I closed my eyes and pictured Jack's face in my mind. I remembered what I had learned that evening in the harbor, in that *holy instant,* as I had braced my feet and raised my arms to the heavens, inviting myself, my father, and all of creation into oneness.

I drew into my lungs all of my remaining anger and resentment for Jack. Then, with a cleansing, audible outward breath, I released it. Finally, inhaling deeply, calmly, I summoned his image once more and I saw only that innocent part of him that was also me. The part of us that is joined with the divine love that is God. That part of both of us that brought two beautiful children into this world.

I was relieved to find I could finally, genuinely, hope he was happy.

CHAPTER 23

Revelations in the Dream

It was late in August and summer was in full swing. As a teacher, I'd appreciated the freedom to enjoy the season. Now, I was working year-round as an office manager in a mortgage brokerage. On a day that I felt particularly cooped up, it was a relief when my employer asked me to drive to San Diego to deliver time-sensitive information to a customer. This meant I could enjoy a scenic drive along Interstate 5, bordering the ocean.

After I dropped off the documents and lunched in Old Town, in San Diego, I entered the freeway, savoring the sun-splashed Pacific on my return. It was a pristine day, not a cloud in the sky. The stately queen palms along the shore swayed gently in the ocean breeze while sailboats leisurely drifted along the coast. Catalina looked close enough to reach out and touch. It was an image right out of a travel magazine. My heart hummed with contentment to co-exist with such beauty and to live in California.

My spirit felt freer, my heart lighter. I was more. I had expanded, and more than ever before, I could fully enjoy the exhilaration of that beautiful day.

Since I was returning to the office, I had to drive past the exit to my condo, continuing north on Interstate 5. Just as I neared the exit to Dana Point, I was astounded! There it was! An old image that had been burned into my mind now loomed ahead of me. I gasped out loud because I couldn't believe my eyes.

The mountain! There was the mountain—the one from my visions in the mental hospital.

The same sphinx-like mountain rising to a flat top and protruding out to the edge of the freeway. And at its foot, a huge, *blank,* white sign straddled over the southbound lanes of the multilane freeway!

That sign was the *reverse* side of *my* exit sign, which I had never seen. I had seen only the sign I drove by each day as I returned from work in Newport Beach, which bore the names of my freeway exit—Beach Cities—*and* the road leading to the mountain-Las Ramblas.

My condominium sat directly below those exits—that sign—that mountain!

"Oh, my God!" I laughed out loud. I had lived at the foot of that mountain for over four years without realizing it! This was the mountain I'd seen almost twenty-nine years earlier in my visions at West Virginia State Mental Hospital—a time during which I'd never been to, or heard of, Dana Point.

I was in awe of life and the mystical way life was unfolding to me. Then, the shock really hit me. Cold shivers rippled through my upper body. I broke into sobs of gratitude. This mountain had, decades earlier, been in my vision. It had marked the place where I would live, and where I had now undergone amazing years of personal transition and understanding. I was on the road below my mountain. The road I'd traveled each day. This mountain had steadfastly hovered above me all the while. My sobs turned into grateful, light-hearted laughter.

As the weeks unfolded, a physical reaction developed every time I drove onto the freeway. As I passed by the foot of my mountain, cold shivers overtook me. I made a conscious effort to ignore those sensations, telling myself it was all in my mind. The best I could do was deny them, I couldn't stop them. Eventually, I couldn't even put them off. I didn't have a lot of emotion with them, and when they were gone, they were gone. It felt a little bit like an energy charge. I realized the mountain itself held some significance. I knew its image embodied something monumental. Wonder and anticipation were building in me. Once again, I stood on the threshold of something new, something more. Like a student in a classroom, I joyfully awaited what I would soon learn.

But, one thing puzzled me. Why had I not seen the now familiar side of the mountain that I'd traveled by regularly in my early visions? Why had I seen the mountain in *reverse?*

Later that fall at a talk at the Helix Center—where I'd discovered the book *Medicine Woman,* I'd listened to a noted American Indian medicine man who spoke about his culture's view of the evolution of the ages. At a reception following his presentation, I met Esteonahda, an American Indian woman who lectured about the life of American Indians of south Orange County.

Our conversation flowed easily. I told her I was part Cherokee, that I lived in Dana Point, and I shared with her verbal sketches of my vivid images of a previous life as an Indian maiden. Interested in what I had to say, she invited me to lunch.

We met at a hotel in Newport Beach where she was scheduled to speak later that afternoon. Esteonahda told me that the major Indian population in Orange County was Shoshonean. In the late 1700's, the Spaniards invaded California's harbors to colonize the west coast of the new world and Spanish missionaries followed immediately thereafter to convert the native peoples. Mission San Juan Capistrano was the first modern building in Orange County, the very mission that had come to mean so much to me.

I told her about the pageant I'd witnessed at the mission, as well as the dream during which I was brutally murdered. I described my memory of being dismembered, carried by the tribal members to a hilltop, and placed on a rawhide bed elevated by stilts, where I'd begged God to take me.

Esteonahda listened intently, perceptive enough to recognize that I had remembered a past life. She seemed fascinated by the coincidence of my dream and the pageant. She wanted to hear more. As we talked, I explained my visions at the mental hospital, my visions of an Indian village in the harbor, as well as the ensuing years in which I'd used symbols as my guides. I even shared my recent discovery that I had been living at the foot of the mountain which I'd first seen in the mental hospital. As I described the mountainous hill just above my Dana Point exit, she straightened in her chair.

"Grace, the land on the top of that mountain is well known to be an Indian burial ground."

I was stunned. Not only had I lived in the shadow of that mountain, but now, here I was being overcome with chills while simply driving by the foot of this mountain—a reaction I couldn't explain; a reaction of a similar magnitude as had happened to me in the harbor. Eventually I had come to understand there was a connection between my feelings in the harbor and my Indian past life where I was dismembered and carried to a hilltop to die. This mountain was within walking distance of the harbor! And it was the mountain I had seen in my visions. I was sure I'd returned to the place where I had once died a tragic death. I'd returned to relive and release the horror of the past. And I had!

With this piece of the puzzle, I thought all would be resolved. Surely when I passed the mountain, the cold shivers in my upper body would no longer occur.

But, they did.

To keep us on the right track, Aaron and I were still seeing Andrea for counseling sessions. Our relationship, as well as our intimacy, continued to improve. Aaron was less preoccupied, and my outlook on life had changed for the better. Laughter filled our days and nights, and we traveled together more frequently on his business trips.

I had developed a sixth sense about many things. One day, on the way to work when a song came on the radio, I was so overcome by it I had to pull off the road. It was the duet, *Endless Love* by Aaron Neville and Linda Ronstadt. I didn't just love the song, it was more than that. It seemed familiar, even though I had never heard it before. The words expressed what I wanted in a relationship. Was it a longing? Or a premonition? I couldn't get it out of my mind. I felt compelled to buy the CD.

I loved surprises, and Aaron still enjoyed surprising me. But, I was not prepared for what he presented to me one Sunday afternoon in November.

He drove us to an elevated scenic overlook at the end of a street in Dana Point. As we got out and walked towards a park bench, I realized we were actually standing on the crest of the hillside overlooking the harbor and the road on which I'd driven so many times. The same road where my visions and memories had erupted inside me.

When I acknowledged that I recognized our location, Aaron said, "Yes, I know."

I never held back from talking about my experiences with him, but he had always refrained from forming or expressing any strong opinions one way or another. So bringing me here was especially meaningful. He took me by the hand, seating me on the bench. He carried a large canvas bag under his arm and I knew he was up to something.

While we looked out over the harbor, Aaron began by gently reminiscing about some of the hard times I had to bear in my childhood and in my marriage. He spoke with tenderness and compassion for what I had been through.

"But now," he turned to me and said, "that's all over and it's time for Gracie to break lose!"

He whisked away the bag and withdrew a large, white photo album with my picture set into a slot on the cover. I took it, a puzzled look on my face. On the first page he had artfully sketched the words, Gracie Goes Out. I felt strangely vulnerable, and I hesitated. He urged, "Go on. Turn the page." Staring into his eyes as I turned the page, I finally looked down. There I was…picture after picture, page after page. An entire collection of snapshots he had taken of just me—some as I sat at my dressing table putting on the finishing touches to get ready to go out, others getting out of a car, off of a train, in the airport, coming out of restaurants. Warm tears fell as I began to crumble. I blotted my face with Aaron's handkerchief, turning each page. Aaron cradled me in his arms.

No one had ever cared for me so much to take the time and effort that had gone into this precious book. As I turned the last page, I rested my head on Aaron's shoulder, my own shoulders shaking as I cried away old defenses and embraced a new kind of love. This was a day I would never forget.

About a month later, after Aaron's very special gift to me, I was helping him sort through boxes that had been mailed to him from his mother in Ohio. They contained various possessions belonging to his father, who'd passed away years earlier. There were things like a chess set his father had made, his Timex watch, a handmade belt. From the bottom of the carton, Aaron pulled out a small, silver-filigreed, black jewelry box. I watched as he opened it.

I gasped. Aaron did too.

It was a gold-plated ring with a hematite seal. In the center of the raised seal was carved the image of the head of a *centurion*.

We looked at each other in a moment of disbelief. Of all things, the symbol of a centurion. Aaron knew early in our relationship about my past life in Atlantis, my role as a priestess and my trustworthy and faithful centurion. Why had his father owned a centurion ring?

"Did he wear it?" I asked. Aaron could not remember ever seeing his dad wear the ring, but he had a clear childhood memory of the day his father had taken him along to purchase it. He even remembered the store.

"Try it on," I prompted. Slightly reluctant, he shrugged and slipped it on. He held up his hand. It fit him perfectly. Without a word, our eyes locked.

Even then, I thought his gaze expressed his uncertainty about my belief in our shared past life. To my surprise he began to wear the ring on occasions, such as if I'd had a hard week at work, or on the anniversary of the day we met, or my birthday. He said he wore it because he believed in me and he wanted to support me. He affectionately called me his "queen."

As for me, the ring was symbolic confirmation of our mutual life purpose. I knew then no matter the issues still to be worked through in counselling, we were meant to be together in this lifetime.

A few weeks before Christmas, I felt restless. Aaron and I had been together for two years. Although things were better than ever between us, I still wondered where the relationship was going. I had all the confirmation I needed to believe we were meant to be together. But did Aaron feel the same way? Was he ready to fully commit to our relationship?

As the weekend approached, Aaron suggested we have a quiet dinner at a local restaurant. He had already made a reservation. I suspected a surprise because something in his manner was different. So I decided to buy myself a new outfit for the occasion.

When Saturday evening arrived, I was dazzling in my new clothes. Aaron was animated and a little edgy as we walked to the car. He drove down toward the ocean, to my old familiar harbor road. When he came to the road's end, he parked, got out, and opened my car door. The ocean roared against the rock sea wall where just beyond lay the obelisk-shaped boulder I'd seen the night I'd forgiven my father. This boulder had reminded me of my first vision of a monolith. Just off to the right was the cove beach where for seven months I had come in discovery of my passion for the *Course*.

Aaron knew I had spent many hours here, remembering, reading, contemplating, and searching for peace of mind. I had told him everything. We walked hand in hand to an asphalt covered knoll. There he reached into his blazer pocket and pulled out a little black box. He opened it, and turned it for my full view.

It was a large, glittering, marquise-cut diamond set in a gold band shaped like a crown. It was exquisite.

"It is my heart's desire, my dear queen, to make all of your dreams comes true, and to give you everything you've ever wanted. Will you marry me?"

In an exhilarating rush, I knew in the deepest part of me this was right for me. I was ready to surrender to that strong, abiding sense that we were meant to be together.

I brushed off a fleeting thought in the back of my mind as to why he'd spoken words of giving to me, rather than telling me of his love. That was the way he wanted to phrase it. He had told me he loved me many times. He felt so much like the centurion from my past life, and his main concern was to care for me.

Misty eyed, I answered, "Yes."

Our evening was gay and joyful—all I ever wanted it to be. His reservations for us were at the same restaurant, the El Adobe, in San Juan Capistrano where we had gone on our first date. We dined, laughed, talked, hugged, and, every few moments, I looked at my beautiful ring, this elegant symbol of our love. Aaron bought a very fine bottle of champagne. We celebrated our life and began to make our plans together.

From that moment on, everything fell into place. Aaron and I seemed to be floating like that dream image he'd used to put me to sleep—the one of the two of us sailing through the stars arm in arm on a magic carpet ride. I remember thinking, here we go! Another dream comes true and I'm entering yet another new dream in this life of dreams.

That spring, as we cruised around different areas looking for a place to live, I impulsively asked Aaron to stop the car. I caught sight of a lovely campus with Spanish style buildings forming a courtyard set off by a water fountain. It was a private school named St. Margaret's.

I asked him to walk the grounds with me. It was Sunday and no one was there. As we stood in the front courtyard by the fountain, I had a deep feeling of connection. I didn't know anything about the school, but I could not ignore what I felt. "Aaron, I will be teaching here one day," I said. Aaron said nothing but he squeezed my hand in support.

Aaron and I found a perfect, brand new, two-bedroom, one-story home under construction in the seaside town of San Clemente with a 180 degree view of the ocean and Catalina Island. When the summer came, desiring once again to work with children, I applied for and was offered a contract by St. Margaret's School to organize and teach in a resource center that offered enriched learning for students who are gifted and for those with learning differences.

In early April of 1989, nearly four months after our engagement, the construction of our house was completed and Aaron and I moved in together while we made plans for our wedding. I had never had a wedding. Like many girls, it had been my dream. Aaron wanted to give me my dream.

And a dream wedding it was. That next spring, on May 12th, 1990, our beautiful ceremony took place in view of one hundred guests in a sunlit sanctuary in a church on a scenic hillside in Rancho San Juan Capistrano. The guests represented many areas of our lives, and it felt like a reunion. Six friends from Maryland came, one of which was my dear friend, Jill, who had helped me through the hard times while I'd waited for a divorce. Another girlfriend from Maryland, a trained vocalist, now living in Northern California, sang *Ave Maria*. She was the friend I'd stayed with the night Jack had locked me out of the house. Bill Wolfe from LifeSong was our pianist, and he also sang the John Lennon song *Imagine*. Aaron's business colleagues came from many states, as did his childhood friend from Ohio. My son walked me down the aisle, and my family and Aaron's children were all part of the ceremony. As we lit candles on the candelabra, Aaron and I sang the duet, *Endless Love*. It was all more wonderful than I'd ever imagined it would be. The best part was my spirit had been freed to take it all in.

The wedding was followed at sunset by a full dinner reception with a five-piece band at our tennis club overlooking the ocean.

Garlands of lavender roses and white daisies, as in my bouquet, were strewn everywhere, and the servers and photographers wore tuxedos. I truly did feel like a queen as we arrived in a white limousine. I wore a full-length bone-white lace gown and my four attendants were dressed in street-length coral and lavender satin. My gown, tailored to my form, had a dropped V-shaped waistline with a scooped neck, and long, lacy-pointed sleeves, and a full train which I was able to remove when the dancing began. After many loving and humorous speeches from family and friends, we danced the night away! The band started the evening with, *My Girl* and *Stand by Me* and ended with *Celebration.* Everyone was having so much fun that we hired the band to stay on an extra hour.

It was a dream come true.

A few weeks later, we received very rare, special permission to have a photo session taken in our wedding regalia in the courtyard of the Mission San Juan Capistrano—the same place where we'd witnessed the pageant. I posed in my wedding gown seated on the decorative wall that surrounds the fountain where the pageant took place, and again in front of the door to the little chapel where I surrendered on my knees that day.

How different it was being there then. All was calm, peaceful, and my anxiety was gone. I heard the birds chirping as they lapped up the water and, for the first time, I noticed roses and bougainvillea vines everywhere, and smelled the fragrance of honeysuckle. Little had I known in Maryland when I'd seen this Capistrano mission on TV, just how important it would become to me.

I would be *52 years old* that year. On September 5, 1990 I celebrated my fifty-second birthday—the number of my condo in Dana Point. It was the age I knew I would be when I was married again. And so it was. I have learned to trust what I know.

Aaron and I spent seven supremely happy days honeymooning in a luxury thatched-roof beach hale on the ocean in Kona Village,

Hawaii. Everything seemed brand new. The welcome freedom from guilt, innocent sense of sweetness, and a free spirit. What I'd first experienced in my journey through the kaleidoscopic light was now becoming more accessible to me in my daily life.

At our home on the hill in San Clemente I considered starting to write the book I'd been thinking about for some time. I was deeply grateful for all the symbols had taught me and the journey that had brought me to know myself, my strength, and my inner peace. I wanted to share my story with the hope it might encourage others on their path to peace.

One thing remained unsettled, though. I traveled every weekday to San Juan Capistrano from San Clemente to teach. When I passed the mountain I'd first seen in my vision thirty years earlier, I still could not pass by without shivering chills rippling through my upper body.

There was still a piece of life's puzzle I was to learn.

CHAPTER 24

The Dream is an Echo

I had found a passion for life. Now I wanted to learn about the philosophies of other non-traditional thinkers. Were their views similar to
mine? How would the *Course* align with other philosophies? Or would
it? Whenever I wasn't teaching, I eagerly read. In the process, I collected
a small library of books. I took part in many spiritually-based events, and
I attended gatherings led by internationally known authorities

Even though I never stopped exploring, for me the *Course*
presented the most radical, yet simple, message. Just as I had found
in my life's journey from those first visions thirty years earlier, the
Course also says we live an insane dream; in the illusion of time
that we call life. It tells that we reach our divine eternal self by loving and forgiving each other, and that in this, or any lifetime, when
we laugh at ourselves and others' mistakes, judgment falls away and
thus, through forgiving, peace comes.

As I became familiar with other beliefs, I found one common
thread. Each system of thought circled back to one thing. Love. The
Course said there were thousands of ways to know God, and they all
lead to God in the end. From my experience, God *is* love. God is not
an eternal body or an ethereal image of man. No *body* is eternal. *God
is,* and, as part of God, *we are.*

I really thought I understood the full message of the *Course.*
At least enough for it to become a daily guide. That is, until March

26th, 1994, when I underwent open-heart surgery at UCLA for a mitral-valve repair. Ironically, it was the same surgery Aaron had undergone when he was thirty-eight.

As I awoke in the cardiac care unit that day, a tune played in my head... "Row, row, row your boat, gently down the stream. Merrily, merrily, merrily, merrily. Life is but a dream!" Again, an expression of what life had become for me. Here I was in a hospital, but this time I didn't wake up to life as a nightmare, as I had after my 1960 stay in a mental hospital. I was waking up to the understanding that life is a series of dreams, and that I continue to awaken from those dreams through love.

This time I wasn't closing down my heart in fear, I was opening my heart, *literally,* confident of my path.

My memory of the ten-day recovery in the hospital was like floating in and out of *the dream.* Finally, the time arrived to go home. Still on moderate pain medication, leaving the hospital had a surreal, almost mystical feel to it. Aaron drove south along Interstate 405 through Los Angeles while my attempts to recognize my surroundings were delayed and slowed. I'd turn my head to take in a sight but then it took a moment for it to come into focus. It was fascinating to be an observer of my own brain's lag time.

After the highway merged into Interstate 5, we approached Dana Point. There it was. That mysterious mountain I had driven by daily for over four years before recognizing it as being from my visions prior to entering the mental hospital.

I focused on the mountain... then re-focused.

In an instant, I knew! I knew the message of the symbolic mountain!

And I knew why I saw it in reverse.

I hadn't recognized the mountain because in my vision I saw the *reverse* side of the mountain. Everything I'd seen in my visions was reversed because everything that seems to be happening to me is already finished. It's already over! In fact, the visions were already over when I saw them!

My mind couldn't have seen in 1960 what was going to happen in 1988 unless it had already happened! I had recalled what had already happened.

For example, in the mental hospital I had *dreamed* of the scene with the evergreen trees. When it actually happened I felt like an observer watching a rerun of my life—a movie. Even my painting of the bare lamp and lightbulb, a symbolic message of my troubling future, was first a vision, or a dream from my own mind, that I saw, and then painted *before* I lived out its message

And while still in the hospital for heart surgery, I had reread about the concept of time in the *Course*. It said something like we undertake a journey that is over yet it seems to have a future unknown to us.

Oh my God, I thought, it's like watching a beautiful star in the night sky. Yet knowing it had burned out millions of years ago! The illusion of the entire universe is being seen and experienced by the one collective mind, and I am a part of that mind. The entire world is a collective mind, dreaming, in which from time to time some of us wake up for a few moments to see the dream isn't the real thing—just as I had seen in the kaleidoscopic light. I was able to see beyond the veil of time.

The dream of life is a state of being in our mind where we are learning something so overwhelming about our beingness that, like Einstein said, we need time to figure it out. This dream of life is not happening *to me,* it's happening *for me!* Our awakening humanity is approaching the doorway to the eternal divine.

That, literally *love is all there really is,* is too much for our mortal being to take in all at once. Our need for time will simply fade away when at last we really get it. And my moments in the kaleidoscopic light showed me there is no need to fear anything. The eternal condition of sublime *allness* has always existed—but "always" is a puzzling concept in a world of time. In that *allness,* only love exists—and God is. And we are learning that we are made in the likeness and image of God.

As a dreamer it would seem in *that* state of mind, that being *simply* love could only happen in paradise. But that is what I am waking up to. The *Course,* like many spiritual beliefs, says that earth shall pass away and it promises a heaven, or an everlasting life, or Nirvana, or an afterlife. Even though it may not seem like it sometimes, I know love is winning. Love works! It is the warrior's and warrioress' dream, and victory is assured.

Driving by that mysterious mountain while coming home from the hospital that day, this transitional state of becoming was an immediate knowing as clear as any vision I'd ever had. I knew it was profound.

And then, I saw an image. It was an image of myself on the mountain and the *Word* of God was being spoken to me from another mountain top far away. But, there is a brief delay as the Word is carried in the *echo* until it reaches me! That precise moment *between* the expression of God's *Word* and my hearing it is the moment that seems like the dream of time! Yet, it is only a millisecond of eternity while we take in the reality of our grand creation. It's as if the divine *Word* of God's love has been spoken from a sublime regency. And in the delay that is the echo, time was born. Time was born so that the *Word* could be heard and digested by the heart and mind of the Son of God, of which I am a part.

Then my mind jumped back to the first time I'd met the Course in the seminar with Dr. Wapnick. I had completely zoned out when he'd said, "You are at home in God, dreaming of exile but perfectly capable of awakening to reality." Then he added, "We think we have separated ourselves from God. Yet we are only in a dream, and like a child, we are gradually awakening." These thoughts were so alien to me then. But now they made sense.

I realized that this is the nature of dreams. Whenever I dream or have a nightmare, I always wake up, and then understand it was all in my mind. I can picture myself as a little girl on a couch having an insane, frightening dream, as this world of form can seem and God, the Father, is sitting beside me comforting me not wanting to scare me by waking me too abruptly. But I begin to hear his gentle *voice* of love in the dream. Eventually, *over time* I release the fearful images, and I awaken. I realize my fear thoughts were craziness. They were illusion. And all the while I'm with God waking up. I have never been separate from him. How comforting. How amazing!

But, what I know is that we learn from our dreams. This dream state is for learning, for growing, for our transformational awakening to our own eternal divine condition. And God's law is that we can take on our power only through our *experience.*

Nature animates this dynamic for us in expressions such as the process of an embryo that becomes a peep that breaks from its shell into an unknown world as a chick, and matures as a hen. And in the metamorphosis of a caterpillar that develops its strength by pushing against the walls of it's cocoon to emerge an elegant butterfly, and in the ugly duckling that nature transforms into a graceful swan. This dream is our shell, our cocoon, our metamorphosis of maturing into that which we were created to be. Love. The dream is about one thing. It's about accepting that love is all there is. And we are created in love's allness. As God *is* love, in his likeness we are becoming. The illusion of time exists only to serve our awakening from the dream. We have never left God.

And now what I had read in the hospital made sense. Time is a trick, but there is a plan behind it. I'm seeing the journey looking back from the point at which it has already ended, yet imagining that I am making the journey once again. Like the burning out of a star or the sound of an echo, that process is already over. What remains is my complete surrender to my own existing immortality, and to my willing and conscious reunion with my creator, the One from whom I've never left. Like the prodigal's son who had to leave his father's home in order to return with the realization that the thing he craved, the love he wanted, was already given him. As I release the dream, I am in the process of returning home.

And that's actually what it's been like for me. Along the way, I've been led and comforted by the gentle voice of God's love through the signs and symbols in the dream. I am in a dream that keeps dreaming death. But there *is no* death. In this lifetime I've had memories of other lifetimes. I may go on to others, unless I choose not to. Unless I decide to wake up from the dream by *always* choosing love instead. I know now that it's up to me. It's my choice.

I remember how in the mental hospital my mind broke away from the world when I surrendered into the kaleidoscopic light and its visions, and the joyous feeling that I was somehow standing outside of time. My visions, and the truth they led me to, opened me to see a different reality. Just as a madman thinks the distorted world he sees is real, he cannot be swayed by questioning within the realm of his insane thoughts. But when he realizes he is crazy, then those thoughts are raised to question, and then the way is opened for truth to come in.

Answers cannot be found by using the logic *of* the dream. In God's eternity, the dream is the problem. As Agnes said in the book *Medicine Woman,* to solve a problem one must reach beyond the level of the problem. Through my experiences that were not of this world, I'd found another way. Inside that embracing kaleidoscopic light where I first sensed love, an awareness of oneness came to me, as well as did the knowing that I am God's innocent child. Along with that loving presence, came visions of events from the dream I was dreaming. I am awakening to see the dream, and thereby have had glimpses into the realm of the divine.

I knew how crazy it would sound to tell anyone—Aaron, my family, my friends—that life is a dream and that it's already over. Yet my journey has led me to trust in what I know. It is a solitary journey. Everyone takes the journey back to the One in their own time, and in their own way

Right then, riding home from the hospital on Interstate 5, I knew I had to go to the top of that mountain. I had to explore the place of my first vision...where it all had begun. I had to find a way to walk on that soil.

CHAPTER 25

The Happy Dream

I began physical therapy after my heart surgery and took daily walks with a determination to become stronger quickly. I had an unstoppable drive to be on that mountain. After ten weeks I knew I was ready. For the first time, instead of going south toward the beach via my old exit below the mountain as I had done for so many years, I went north onto a residential street called Las Ramblas. This time, I experienced no chills. I had heard the message of the mountain.

At the first stop light, I turned left towards the mountain.

Oh, no! I saw huge, yellow bulldozers parked all over the mountain. A portable office had been set up, and the road leading onto the mountain had been gated.

Resolved not to be deterred, I knocked on the door of the office. I was greeted by a hefty young man who looked to be in his thirties.

I swallowed hard and asked him if there was any way I could go out onto the precipice of the mountain just over the highway. "It's kinda special to me."

"Really. How's that?"

I couldn't lie. "Quite honestly, I saw it in a vision when I was twenty-two and lived on the other side of the country. Then, when I moved here, I lived below it for a few years before I recognized it."

The man stepped out of the trailer and introduced himself as Max. "You know, I'm not supposed to let anyone but workers up there, but they're gone for the day, and it just so happens I was gettin' ready to check out the day's progress. You can ride with me in the truck if you like."

"Oh, I would love that."

On the way up the mountain, Max shyly admitted to me he had read a book written by Dan Millman called *The Peaceful Warrior.* I was very familiar with that book by a young man who was Olympic-bound until he suffered an injury. He'd experienced the image of an old man who had appeared to him and had taught him about the remarkable power of the human spirit.

"A lot of things happened to him that I never thought about before, but now I'm beginning to wonder about my own life," Max said as we bumped along a dirt road. I knew he was being generous to me because he had associated the reason for my request with that book. He inquired, and I gave him a quick overview of the mountain's importance to me, including remembering being left to die there in another lifetime.

"Tell you what. I have to go onto the other side of the mountain to see if everything is up to spec. If you want, I can drop you off at the place you mentioned near the highway. I'll come back in about ten minutes or so."

"Oh, thank you. I truly appreciate this." How fortunate to meet this thoughtful construction worker. How many others would be so accepting of my spiritually-based request?

"Jus' watch out for the hawks. They prey on snakes exposed by the cut brush. They swoop down to catch the snakes, fly up high and then drop 'em to kill them before they eat them."

Oh, great! But, it didn't really scare me. I had encountered snakes in dreams, and at the Indian pageant. They no longer held any power over me. This mountain was a safe place for me.

As my feet touched the ground, they practically vibrated. I was here. I was standing on top of my vision! There had been no "me" in my vision in 1960, but now here *I* am. I had come to the mountain. I had entered my own vision. I had come full circle.

I had lived below this mountain. I had died on this mountain—in this spot. And now, I had returned in peace and joy.

A large boulder still remained, providing a perfect place to sit. As I bent my knees to perch on the rock, I scooped up a handful of dirt. It was real. I wasn't dreaming. Then I laughed out loud at my thought. Or *was* I dreaming? Of course, I was! This was what my visions had taught me. The *whole world* was a dream, but the part of me that lives on lifetime through lifetime, the *I* am that I am was real.

What a journey to this place of understanding! For so much of my life I'd thought I was different, even crazy. But now I felt only gratitude for all I'd been through, for all I'd learned. For all that the symbols had taught me.

I was grateful that even from the moment of birth, I had carried a vision of a monolith, a symbol that had returned later in life to lead me through the lessons of forgiveness and love. I'd come into this world helpless and powerless, and I'd remained so at the hands of my mother, my father, and later, Jack. At a time when I was in deep despair and estranged from God, I thought I was going crazy when my mind snapped, taking me to a better place of kaleidoscopic light and visions. I was amazed to find another realm. But experiencing visions and being a victim of abuse had caused me to feel different. It wasn't until after the lightbulb painting that I'd secretly begun to find hope.

In college, for the first time, I'd started to respect my own abilities and to see the dysfunction of my life with Jack. How shocked I'd been when the visions began to occur. And then, how astounded I was when I later realized they were guiding me, and affirming my direction. Each symbol had led to a *light bulb moment*. Moments when I could hear an inner voice.

The vision of the evergreen trees had brought calm during a painful time with Jack's infidelity. Even when the name *Lawless* turned out to be my best friend who'd betrayed me, I was beginning to appreciate the validation of the visionary symbol and that whatever was happening was meant to be.

During the nightmare of the separation, the sighting of the vision of the highway road sign while being chased by Jack, also affirmed my intended destiny. Al-Anon stoked the fire of bravery in me, and the mysterious appearance of the scrolls reassured me of a purposeful path and helped me to fight for myself. When it dawned on me that I'd become estranged from myself, with the help of my therapist, Denise, I'd learned about loving and respecting myself. Gradually, I saw that Jack's abuse wasn't because of something I'd done wrong. I'd been addicted to the minuscule bits of attention he'd shown even though I was deserving of love that didn't hurt.

All along there had been a beacon of light shining in my mind. I was on a treasure hunt to know more about the peaceful calm of the kaleidoscopic light.

I gazed around from my queenly perch on the boulder atop my mountain, in gratitude for the pristine sunny day. I remembered how glad I was when I'd returned to California, thinking that the mysterious part of my life had passed. I was completely overcome as new visions came flooding in, but by then I had an unwavering trust in the guidance I was being given.

It had been such a blessing to find the Psychosynthesis program, and Cliff Ishagaki, who respected my mental hospital experience as simply "a psychic break," and gave me the courage to talk about my secrets. There, I found friends who accepted the part of me I'd always kept hidden. They'd guided me to Neville, where hypnosis offered the release of submerged blocks of fear from my past, starting with an Atlantis past life, enabling me to face the guilt and shame that blinded me and numbed my spirit. This revelation fueled me to continue to explore the alarming visions I'd had in the harbor and my recurring nightmares.

Thank God for my journaling of the history of the many ways in which my visions continued to arise, and the ongoing events affirming my eccentric conviction of life itself as a series of dreams. And my dreams were coming true!

The symbols in my dream brought me such joy when I'd found LifeSong. It was a chance to release old, abusive and binding memories, clear the way to truly open my heart, and sing from the authentic me.

And then there was the day that I'd found *A Course in Miracles*. Not only had I been given a certificate of sanity, it proclaimed the insanity of the world—the insanity I'd recognized the day I'd left the mental hospital. Somehow after that, the dream never fully owned me again. The *Course* teaches openly about my hidden secret that all of life is a *dream,* and that everything in the dream is a *symbol.* I laughed, celebrating confirmation of what I'd already known. And then I learned that *laughing* is the *Course's* answer for releasing the world's insanity as was my first reaction in my experience of the kaleidoscopic light. For that I'd been admitted to an institution.

Oh, how I loved the *Course* as it became my beloved companion in my quest turned to a search for an understanding of the *purpose* of those *"light bulb"* moments. Life revealed to me that they are ah ha's—those awakening flashes of clarity—when I could release fear and see only love. They were *holy instants,* also known in the *Course* as a *miracle.* Wow, it all seemed so simple.

Then when meeting Aaron and recognizing *him* from my Atlantis lifetime, an entirely new dimension of life opened, joining the past with the present. He brought a new kind of love, which we'd celebrated in the hot tub—the one I'd seen in my first visions. But, things took a turn. As I accepted his love offered without thorns, I was met with an inexplicable anxiety.

Through dreams and visions my psyche was again barraged with the haunting emergence of my tragic Indian past life. In stark contrast, riding in the energy of Rusty's timeless loyalty, ignited virgin womanly vibrations. On the back of this gentle creature, I'd felt no fear. Only the rhythm of nature flowing through me.

Instead of finding calm in the uncomplicated love of Aaron, I became nearly dysfunctional as my anxiety heightened. Little did I know that I was harboring a deeply buried, dark secret. Finding Elizabeth, who evoked screams, helped tear down my wall of fear and unleash the lioness within. Susan had offered the gift of healing by transposing her hideous sexual assaults into symbols of scissors that ripped me open. With Andrea's comforting, through hypnosis I'd finally faced the monstrous memory I'd locked away from infancy of having been literally thrown away by my mother and raped by my father. I grew to understand the meaning of the rose between the scissors—an exquisite symbol of the safe, sexually whole, and complete woman that I'd learned to know.

Yes, it was horrifying to remember being raped by my father as a baby. But facing the darkest fear of all brought me the greatest light. After purging in the pool to release that atrocity, my cleansed spirit could finally accept my Self as a whole person. I'd found my own *smoke spirit.*

The greatest trial of all taught me that if I did not forgive my father, my hate would forever bind me to his dark deeds. I would be stuck in the past. Consumed by judgment.

With the help of the V.O.I.C.E.S. group, I forgave my father, and united my re-birthed Self with God; a transformation midwifed by the timeless symbol of the monolith. A transformation of total commitment to life's one *uniting* purpose—to love, instead of hate. Then there was that night at the water's edge when I'd stretched my arms and legs into an X position embodying an affirming symbol of complete surrender. The symbol was immediately christened by my citing of a simple, glowing X overlaid upon the moon. I'd united my whole *Self* with the love of God in a *holy marriage*.

The dream went on as Aaron and I came back together. I saw that relationships are purposely intended, and function as mirrors for each to recognize their own emotional blocks and erroneous thinking. We mirrored what we each needed to learn. Everything, and every relationship, is a lesson that teaches us how to find love. With Aaron I found the truth that love does not limit. Real love does not threaten or demand. I daily continue the process of learning to let go of expectations of him, and of myself, and allow love to lead.

The vision of the pink houses upon a hill was my first in California. Fittingly, it was the last image to be revealed. When I met Deanna, and the remaining trauma lodged in my body from Jack's abuse was expelled, I knew it was time for me to apply what I had learned. The actual presence of the pink houses confirmed the lesson that my intuitive voice had led me to understand over the last year; that the quicker I could truly forgive Jack, the happier I would be.

My lessons continue. There will always be challenges. One is to continue to extend love to break barriers placed by Jack between me and my children, and to release any need for judgment of how those barriers were created. And at the same time, to release expectations for my children and accept that they, too, are on their intended paths. The symbols still come in my life, but now in a less dramatic way. Spirit has already gotten my attention.

In the session I spent with Deanna and in several of her workshops following, I also learned to honor the body that houses my spirit. Now I view it as a vessel for Self-love, and for extending love—which always comes back to me in some form. My body is now an ally that alerts me to hidden fears through feelings and emotions. It also notifies me when I have something to release, something to gain, and something that wants to make my life better. There is always a gift in the pain. I know the release has come when I can feel the joy of the oneness in myself, and in my connection to others—when I let go of separateness. Nothing happens by accident. Some part of my higher self, driven by an insatiable longing for more than this dream has to offer, has dictated lifetime after lifetime to bring me back to my real Self, the innocent Self as a child of God.

That insatiable drive is a vague distress that something is missing, a nagging, deep-down knowing that this dream of life is not all there is. It's the innate longing to be at home with God. There's a tendency to mask that longing with all kinds of relationships, looking for others to fill the vacuum, and to avoid looking inside. That missing piece is found when there is an eternal love connection between the whole Self, and Others, and God. Even in the dream, glimpses of love's eternal rapture can be seen in the laughing eyes of a small child, in the unconditional love of a pet, in the beauty of fields of blooming flowers, or in a blazing sunset.

I have to laugh at myself as I look back on the cycle of my learning. My mind works in slow motion—blundering and then grasping...blundering and then grasping—until finally I make my way to love. I can never know why I am the body, or the personality that I am. The answer is not found within the dimension of the dream. But the dream is not meaningless! Just because it's an illusion of form does not mean that something grand isn't taking place. Meaning comes through the *process* of waking up *from* the dream. It's an awakening guided by an eternal Spirit, our One Spirit, that extends beyond this dream. It's guiding me to remember that I, too, am a creator. Created and made in the likeness of the One who made me. Only the journey matters. How simple it is. It's Love's *simplicity* in an insane world of *controversy* that makes it hard to grasp!

I shudder to think what would have happened had I not listened to the messages of the symbols and followed my inner knowing. I would still be miserable as a victim in an abusive marriage, not knowing the strength that lived inside me. I would not have found the joy of hearing my own voice, or the release of past life fear. I would be living under the blanket of depression that comes from holding back the memory of past atrocities, and I might never have come to appreciate the fullness of my womanhood. I might never have found the happiness that comes by learning how to love and to forgive. I would still think I was crazy. I would never have realized that, to find sanity is to understand the insanity of the world.

I am not special. I am not more psychic than anyone else. What I've learned comes from my soul's journey. The most important part of this lifetime for me is that I've learned to listen...to listen to what I know. Many others have had glimpses of the divine. I believe there is a voice to be heard inside of everyone, a voice that guides the willing listener to love, by facing fear, and honoring feelings. Our ultimate function in the dream is to extend love by sharing and caring, living our visions of oneness. It has been my story, my play, my dream, to remember past lives, though I realize many don't. That's alright too. We're all in the same school, but each in our own classroom, and we will all eventually graduate. Ultimately the path is all the same...listening to the voice within that survives sorrows, tragedies, assaults, abuses. That small, loving voice can be heard in the midst of the fiercest emotions and deepest despair. Every problem holds its own solution, a gift waiting to be received. It's all a journey to sanity. By trusting an inner knowing that leads to the light, darkness cannot hide. Everyone can hear the call of truth through their own unique symbols. In any form, they will serve as guides to that missing piece, the all-encompassing love we all hunger for. By learning to trust the inner voice, it gets easier and easier. To postpone the lesson is to postpone love.

In the end, the dream brings us home to ourselves, and to God, as we follow the eternal light of sanity that glows softly in the illusion of insanity. As we realize it was always there within waiting for its welcome. This is a dream to find the love that can transform our nightmares into a happy dream of life.

I am glad I am free of the imprisoning threat of God's wrath as dictated by my father to keep me in line with his fears. In the happy dream, fear is but a clown that would distract us from remembering who we are. We always laugh at clowns, because we know they are not real. Fear is not real unless we *make* it real. In the happy dream, we remember to laugh. We laugh at ourselves, our judgments, and we laugh with each other. Judgment and love are opposites, and laughing releases judgment. If we choose joy, we choose peace, then, we choose the happy dream. And the beautiful caveat is, all the while, as we journey from insanity to sanity, we are safe at home with God learning as we listen to the echo of our oneness. For me, that understanding takes the "clout" out of fear!

And now, the final lesson of the mountain was to show me that even though the dream of life seems to go on, it's really over. As I reflect on my past, it doesn't exist. All time exists now. 1960 is now. In 1960, it was 1994...and it was the tenth century, and the 1800's. Time is but a burned out star that represents a brief interval, an echo, containing a lesson that we aren't really separate from anyone, or from the mind of God. I know how radical it is to suggest that this thing known as life is already over. Call me crazy, but in my heart I have no doubt.

In advance of a blazing sunset, sitting contentedly alone on my mountain, I noticed three big black crows feasting on the bounty of the freshly-turned earth and my thoughts returned to the mountain under me.

The physical expression of all of my original visions had now taken place. In coming full circle, I had come home. *This* was my homecoming. I remember how desperately I'd wanted a homecoming when I was being driven to the mental hospital. I'd wanted to be a queen because I'd wanted to be loved. Then the visions in the kaleidoscopic light started me on a journey to an all-encompassing love. Now I had come home. I had come home to myself.

I drew in a refreshing breath of sea air. I heard the faint drone of traffic from below. I savored the spectacular panorama of coastline and endless ocean that lay beyond. In about two hours the May sun would set on the marine horizon beyond my beloved Dana Point.

I knew that soon to become visible within the misty molecules and atoms of this illusory world would be in the starry night of the dream, a symbol. I will always recognize the two glowing streaks of light forming an X across the moon as a wordless message broadcasting its heavenly bid to reclaim God's extension of love and empowerment to me. This symbol graciously lures me to remember that the opportunity for harmony in my life, and in all my relationships, is always present. It reminds me that all relationships can become holy relationships through the miracle of forgiveness.

As forbidden lovers in an Indian lifetime, both Aaron and I had gone to our dream of death...a death that had taken place for me right here on this mountain. But there is no death. Death is not an end or an escape. It's only the illusion of an end but still a part of the dream, the end of one act in a grand play. Here I am, again! And these are only the past lives I happen to remember. There could have been thousands. I may have murdered Aaron, or I could have been his sister. I may have abused Jack or ruled an empire with him. I could have been married to my mother or my father. I could have been a man. I could have been homeless, a slave, an empress. Who knows? It doesn't matter. Each possibility is a stepping stone. Parts in a play, dreams within the dream.

I looked down and realized I was still clutching the soil I had scooped up. I let the dirt slowly fall through my fingers as my memory with Aaron in our Indian past life began to fade. The *Course* says the holiest place on earth is where an ancient hatred becomes a present love. For me, this was hallowed ground. It had served its purpose.

My first vision of the kaleidoscopic light was through a vaginal-like opening when my mind was whisked out of the womb of limited consciousness into an expansive world of brilliance and unlimited ecstasy. When I look at the exact intersection of the moon's rays, it takes me back to that moment when I was sucked up into the heart of a prism, when the lens and mirrors of a kaleidoscope whisked me into a visionary world of innocence.

Now, within that kaleidoscope, I see the many pieces of my Self, and Others, in lifetime after lifetime that are being reformed. And with each turn to love, these pieces are exotically transposed into an infinite oneness of exquisite colors, shapes, and patterns—as infinite as the stars. The *Course* urges us to look up and see our radiance in the stars.

There on the mountain, the sun a little lower now, I started to giggle...then laughed like I had never before known how to. I jumped up, spreading my arms and legs wide and turning my face up to the sky, I roared like the lioness I am, "Thank God I'm Crazy!"

"All things are echoes of the voice for God."
—A Course in Miracles, Lesson 151

Acknowledgments

W hen I finally made the commitment to put my journey into a book, I had no idea how to do so, but I had learned that if it is to be, the way will be shown. There are so many amazing people I've been guided by. To each one I extend my heartfelt, eternal gratitude.

The hardest part was in the beginning when I had no choice but to burrow through the pain of the past to mine the miracles. Deeply intuitive, Jane Lemos flowed into my life, enabling me to untangle the obvious. Thank you, dear one. When the day came to tell my story to the public for the first time, I was sure the stage would open and swallow me—but two beloved people held me up. I love you, dear Ron and Susan Vail Hoffman.

My gratitude also goes to the eagle-eye editing of award-winning author, editor, Laura Taylor, the first to see my finished manuscript. And dear, dear Gary Ducharich, my friend, my Minch, and whose loyal support urged me on to share my secrets, then used his photographic mind to comb through the book for one more edit, and his legal skills to advise me. You steered me to the finish line, Gary, and you are indeed one of my life's greatest blessings.

Also, this book would never be as it is without the professional advice and encouragement of my unerring ally, published theologian, Dr. Jim Van Cleave. With objective vision, he gifted me with his expert advice and editing of my dreaded proposal. Thank you for believing in me. And I hold heartfelt gratitude to friend, author, and psychotherapist, Leonard Szymczak for his informed counsel in the world of books, and his ever-present, lighthearted support.

I have been embraced by so many loved ones too numerous to name, but I know that you know who you are. My everlasting love for you who have believed in me and my purpose, have urged me onward, and were there when I needed to pour out my heart, and to play, when my battery was low. Also, to those devoted friends who gave of their precious time to read my developing manuscript, I thank you. To the beloved members of my A Course in Miracles classes, my heart overflows with God's unconditional love as you are my greatest mirrors, and you continue to teach me how to love.

To my dear and blessed first teachers, Kenneth Wapnick and Beverly Hutchinson, you have completely changed my lens on life. Thank you both for your selfless and dedicated service, which continues to lead us to our own light.

What a blessed day it was when Marianne Williamson, meeting me for the first time, not only agreed to read my manuscript, but shared the vision I had penned, and then blessed this book with a prayer that lives forever in my heart. We have grown to know each other as kindred spirits. She continues to be a miracle and an amazing inspiration in my life.

When Gary Renard and I met in 2003, there was an immediate meeting of the minds. Although he read my manuscript before endorsing it, he told me after first hearing my story that he would do so. I have so much love for you Gary, and your beautiful wife, Cindy.

To beautiful and gracious Lynn Andrews who is my medicine woman—and the catharsis for my awakening to life's freedom—my undying love. Your visionary wisdom opened the door to myself. When we finally met it seemed we had been together for lifetimes. Our sisterhood lives on in my grateful heart. And to Bill and Linda Wolfe, whose loving, unique vision awakened the song in my heart—bravo!

And what can I say about Kyle Cease? When I first heard his outrageous and spiritually inspired approach to finding sanity by laughing at life's craziness, I thought I would explode with joy. My friendship with you, Kyle, your gifted team Kari, Dan, Heather, and particularly Chris Taylor, media artist, who artfully rendered the book's picture-symbols, have all so earnestly and lovingly nurtured me to continue to Evolve Out Loud.

At last, my visionary path has come into book form through the brilliant tutelage of author, agent, publisher, and producer of documentary films, Bill Gladstone. Marianne's recommendation of Bill was all I needed. Upon meeting him and his lovely wife, Gayle, at Waterside, the only agency I approached, I knew Bill was the one to build the bridge from my heart to others, and that our journey together was meant to be. I extend my heartfelt gratitude to all of you, and most specifically to your kind friend, and my publishing editor, Kenneth Kales.

And the book's cover...Neight Adamson, of FIND Art Media, cheerfully brought me into the world of cyberspace, holding my hand as he effortlessly created my website, designed the cover art and layout of this book. Neight, your patience and talent are rare and your visions have brought my own to life. Immense thanks to my friend, and photographer, Angenieta Van Lyndt Wuerth, who has a unique talent for reaching from the beauty inside her to awaken the beauty in others. And my endless gratitude to Michael Vasquez, computer technician, who is there any hour of the day.

And finally, this book truly would never have been at all without the loving support and persevering optimism of my husband, Ron. My heart lives in gratefulness for the countless times he asked me, "How's it going?" and really wanted to hear the answer, and for unfailingly reminding me that, "slow and steady wins the race." I've never known what it was like to have the kind of consideration that he has offered me in every aspect of my life. He has delighted in giving me everything I ever wanted. Thank you, dear Ron, from the depths of my heart.

Most of all, I hold a deep, abiding love, eternal thankfulness, and awesome wonder for the voice of the One that speaks within us all, and relentlessly guides us to love and laughter.

About the Author

Grace Avalon, a business woman and educator for thirty years, is an honors graduate of Hood College in Frederick, Maryland, and served as master teacher for Hood's student-teacher program. Invited to present her original workshop, called Learning Differences, to county board members, PTA, and faculties, she later adapted it for placement in the county library for classroom use. In addition to six years as a kindergarten teacher, director, in private schools, she taught classes for addiction-recovering teens, and established the first resource center for gifted and special needs children in a large parochial school.

For nearly three decades, she has been a student and teacher of A Course in Miracles and has taught an ACIM class for nine years. As a facilitator of a Global Alliance peace circle, she lobbied in Washington D.C. and publicly spoke for the congressional bill proposing "A Department of Peace." She was also a spokesperson for Laura's House, established in memory of Nicole Brown Simpson, to raise awareness about domestic violence.

Having trained in psychology and Psychosynthesis as well, Grace currently counsels individuals and holds workshops nationally to inspire others to know their own inner voice and personal symbols. Her career and personal journey have taught her to "see only love for that is what you are." She resides in San Clemente, California where she delights in playful time with friends, in addition to enjoying reading, singing, walking at sunset, chocolate, and dogs.

www.graceavalon.com
www.facebook.com/Grace-Avalon
grace@graceavalon.com

CPSIA information can be obtained
at www.ICGtesting.com
Printed in the USA
LVHW021518230222
711837LV00009B/717

Service Quality